Student Edition

Bring Science Alive!
Exploring Science Practices

Chief Executive Officer
Bert Bower

Chief Operating Officer
Amy Larson

Director of Product Development
Maria Favata

Strategic Product Manager
Nathan Wellborne

Senior Science Content Developer
Ariel Stein

Curriculum Consultants
Kim Merlino
Joan Westley

Program Editors
David Fraker
Mikaila Garfinkel
Edward Helderop
Rebecca Ou
Ginger Wu

Editorial Consultant
Glenda Stewart

Production Manager
Jodi Forrest

Operations & Software Manager
Marsha Ifurung

Designer
Sarah Osentowski

Art Direction
Julia Foug

Teachers' Curriculum Institute
PO Box 1327
Rancho Cordova, CA 95741

Customer Service: 800-497-6138
www.teachtci.com

ISBN 978-1-58371-978-7
2 3 4 5 6 7 8 9 10 -WC- 20 19 18 17 16 15

Manufactured by Webcrafters, Inc., Madison, WI
United States of America, May 2015, Job # 121652

SUSTAINABLE FORESTRY INITIATIVE

Certified Sourcing

www.sfiprogram.org
SFI-00617

About the Next Generation Science Standards

What Teachers and Families Need to Know

The Next Generation Science Standards (NGSS) describe the science skills and knowledge all students need to know to succeed in college, careers, and citizenship. The standards were developed by a panel that collaborated with representatives from 26 lead states. They are based on *A Framework for K–12 Science Education*, which was written by a team of scientists, engineers, and science educators, and published by the National Research Council in 2012.

The NGSS were released in Spring 2013, and TCI's science instructional program, *Bring Science Alive!*, was developed to meet them.

Each performance expectation has three dimensions: disciplinary core ideas, scientific and engineering practices, and crosscutting concepts. Together, these describe what students should understand and be able to accomplish at each grade level.

What are performance expectations, and how does *Bring Science Alive!* prepare students to demonstrate mastery?

Performance expectation 4-LS1-1. has students construct an argument that internal and external structures function to support the survival, behavior, reproduction, and growth of plants and animals.

Performance expectations describe what all students should be able to do at the completion of a unit of study. They guide assessment and are supported by the details in the disciplinary core ideas, practices, and crosscutting concepts. Many performance expectations are followed by clarification statements and assessment boundaries. Clarification statements provide examples and details, and assessment boundaries limit what students should be tested on.

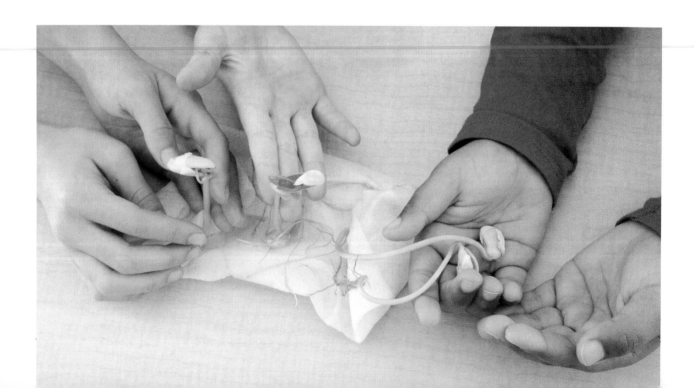

Bring Science Alive! prepares students to meet the performance expectations. Performance expectations are identified in the Student Text at the beginning of each unit and each lesson. They are also incorporated into the investigations in the online Presentations for students to practice.

How are the Next Generation Science Standards related to Common Core standards?

The NGSS are aligned to the Common Core State Standards for English Language Arts & Literacy in History/Social Studies, Science, and Technical Subjects and Common Core State Standards for Mathematics.

Similarly, *Bring Science Alive!* is aligned to Common Core English and Mathematics. For example, all Reading Furthers in the Student Text align with the Reading Standards for Informational Text K–5. Interactive Tutorials address Common Core reading and writing standards. Lesson content and investigations are aligned with Common Core Mathematics, such as when students learn about measurement units and tools and graphing.

One part of the disciplinary core idea PS2.A: Forces and Motion focuses on observing and measuring the patterns of an object's motion in different situations so that the object's motion can be predicted in future situations.

What are Disciplinary Core Ideas, and how does *Bring Science Alive!* meet them?

Disciplinary core ideas focus instruction on the foundational knowledge students need for success in each grade. Core ideas build from year to year, from Kindergarten to Grade 12, in learning progressions that revisit each topic several times, each time with greater depth and sophistication. Therefore, students are expected to understand the core ideas that were taught in previous grades.

For these reasons, teachers and parents may find fewer topics taught in each grade than they have seen previously. Additionally, many topics are taught in different grades than they were under previous standards. By limiting the content at each grade, students are able to learn with deeper understanding.

Bring Science Alive! guides students through these core ideas as they read their Student Text, complete Interactive Tutorials, carry out hands-on and online investigations, and write, draw, diagram, and calculate in their Interactive Student Notebooks.

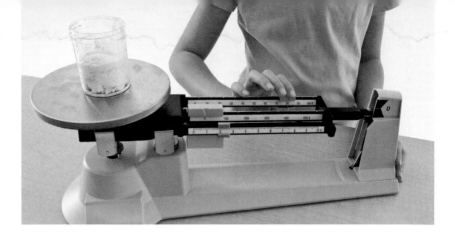

What are Science and Engineering Practices, and how does *Bring Science Alive!* meet them?

Science and engineering practices describe the abilities students should develop to engage in science and engineering. Students use these eight practices to master the principles described in the core ideas. The practices also help students understand how professional scientists and engineers answer questions and solve problems.

- **?** Asking questions and defining problems
- Developing and using models
- **Q** Planning and carrying out investigations
- Analyzing and interpreting data
- Using mathematics and computational thinking
- Constructing explanations and designing solutions
- **?!** Engaging in argument from evidence
- Obtaining, evaluating, and communicating information

The science and engineering practice Engaging in Argument from Evidence asks students to use data, evidence, and models to support an argument they make.

Every lesson in *Bring Science Alive!* develops several science and engineering practices in the online lesson Presentation. Practices are used explicitly and help teach the lesson's core ideas. Each of the eight practices is taught at every grade level with increasing sophistication from grade to grade.

What are Crosscutting Concepts, and how does *Bring Science Alive!* meet them?

The crosscutting concepts are used to organize students' understanding of science and engineering in the same way that scientists and engineers do. They give students specific ideas to consider when learning about a new topic. These ideas are intended to help students understand the topics at a deeper level.

In addition to supporting core ideas, the seven crosscutting concepts support one another. They are listed below with descriptions of their importance for all upper elementary students.

Patterns Recognizing patterns helps students sort and classify objects, describe rates of change and cycles, and make predictions.

Cause and Effect In their investigations, students observe patterns and then identify and test how two events may or may not be related.

Scale, Proportion, and Quantity Students recognize that objects and systems vary greatly in size and learn to measure using standard units.

Systems and System Models Describing and modeling systems helps students understand complex phenomena in terms of parts and their interactions.

Energy and Matter Students learn that matter is made of particles, that energy is transferred between objects, and that matter is neither lost nor gained when it changes.

Structure and Function Students explore identifying the smaller structures within larger ones and the functions of these structures.

Stability and Change Recognizing that change occurs at different rates helps students understand systems.

Each lesson is carefully developed to explain and integrate the crosscutting concept with core ideas.

While learning about the crosscutting concept Systems and System Models, students will discover how to describe a system using its components and interactions.

Connections to Engineering, Technology, and Applications of Science

The Next Generation Science Standards address engineering design as a process similar to, and just as important as, scientific inquiry. Engineering design is divided into three broad steps, each of which encompasses several of the science and engineering practices.

The steps are described by the grades 3–5 engineering design performance expectations, listed below.

- *3-5-ETS1-1. Define a simple design problem reflecting a need or want that includes specified criteria for success and constraints on materials, time, or cost.*

- *3-5-ETS1-2. Generate and compare multiple possible solutions to a problem based on how well each is likely to meet the criteria and constraints of the problem.*

- *3-5-ETS1-3. Plan and carry out fair tests in which variables are controlled and failure points are considered to identify aspects of a model or prototype that can be improved.*

Bring Science Alive! provides many opportunities for students to understand the work of engineers and use the engineering design process to solve problems relevant to the scientific knowledge they are simultaneously developing.

Engineering, Technology, and Applications of Science in the Investigations

Engineers often work as a team. When students carry out engineering-related investigations, they learn that teamwork is helpful in solving real-world problems.

Engineering, Technology, and Applications of Science in the Student Text

Interactions of Science, Technology, Society and the Environment in the Student Text

While studying how energy is stored and used, students learn how engineers solve real-world problems. The engineer in this photo is designing a park ranger station.

Connections to the Nature of Science

The science and engineering practices describe how to engage in scientific inquiry. The disciplinary core ideas describe existing scientific knowledge. The crosscutting concepts provide a framework for connecting scientific knowledge. Students integrate these dimensions of learning when they learn what kinds of knowledge are scientific, how scientists develop that knowledge, and about the wide spectrum of people who engage in science.

Nature of Science in the Student Text

One of the basic understandings about the nature of science described in NGSS is that investigations use different tools, procedures, and techniques.

Nature of Science in the Investigations

How to Use This Program

1 The teacher begins each lesson with a **Presentation** that facilitates the lesson and the investigation.

2 In the Presentations, students participate in a hands-on **investigation** that blends the core ideas, science practices, and crosscutting concepts of NGSS.

3a In the online **Student Subscription**, students expand their knowledge through reading the Student Text, completing an Interactive Tutorial, and processing what they've learned in the **Interactive Student Notebook**.

3b Alternatively, students can read from the **Student Edition** and complete a consumable Interactive Student Notebook.

4 The lesson ends with students demonstrating their knowledge of each core idea, science practice, and crosscutting concept through a variety of paper and online **assessments**.

Literacy in Science

The Next Generation Science Standards were developed to work in tandem with the Common Core State Standards to ensure that students develop literacy skills through learning science. *Bring Science Alive!* builds on this synergy by emphasizing reading, writing, speaking and listening, and language skills while guiding students in developing their science knowledge.

Key Points from the ELA Common Core	*Bring Science Alive!*
Reading	
Informational and literary texts are balanced with at least 50% of reading time devoted to expository texts.	CCSS changes the emphasis in reading from being based primarily on literary texts to being balanced between literary and informational texts. *Bring Science Alive!* reflects this balance in its text. Each lesson has several sections of purely informational text that explains the content of that lesson. Each lesson is followed by a Reading Further, which blends literary and informational style text to engage students with the content even further.
Establishes a "staircase" of increasing complexity in what students must be able to read as they move throughout the grades.	*Bring Science Alive!* is written with close attention paid to the text complexity to make sure it fits into the "staircase" of increasingly sophisticated text that students should read as they progress through the grades. However, within each grade's text, there is variation in the complexity to ensure that there is challenging text for all students.
Emphasizes the close reading of text to determine main ideas, supporting details, and evidence.	The digital Interactive Tutorials encourage close reading of the text. They require students to answer questions using evidence from the text. Answering the questions requires a clear understanding of the main ideas and other details provided in the section.
Writing	
Three types of writing are emphasized from the earliest grades—writing to persuade, writing to inform/explain, and writing to convey experience.	NGSS and *Bring Science Alive!* require students to use all three types of writing emphasized by CCSS. In the investigations, students are often asked to construct written arguments to persuade their classmates of their explanation of a scientific concept. They also write accounts of their experiences in these activities and investigations, describing details of the experiment or design process. In the Interactive Student Notebook, students write explanations to demonstrate their understanding of the scientific concepts described in the text.
Effective use of evidence is central throughout the writing standards.	In all three types of writing, students are expected to use evidence appropriately to support their claims. They are given support in identifying key details which will serve most effectively as evidence. They also reflect on their use of evidence in various contexts to build an explicit understanding of the role evidence plays in science and argument in general.
Routine production of writing appropriate for a range of tasks, purposes, and audiences is emphasized.	Students routinely write in all of *Bring Science Alive!*'s curricula. The program emphasizes the flexibility and usefulness of writing to accomplish a variety of assignments. It also gives students exposure to the different expectations in writing for different purposes and audiences.

Key Points from the ELA Common Core	*Bring Science Alive!*

Speaking and Listening

Participation in rich, structured academic conversations in one-on-one, small-group, and whole class situations is emphasized in the standards.	Classrooms using *Bring Science Alive!* will regularly have structured science talks in which students reflect on their experiences and understanding of the investigations. They will also have regular discussions in smaller groups, ranging from discussions with a partner to groups of four or five students. These discussions are designed to build clear communication skills that are critical to success in science and all other fields of study.
Contributing accurate, relevant information; responding to and building on what others have said; and making comparisons and contrasts are important skills for productive conversations.	In all discussions, students are given support to help them learn to contribute relevant and accurate details and evidence. The cooperative tolerant classroom conventions emphasized throughout all of TCI's curricula encourage students to respond to and build on ideas and arguments presented by other students. *Bring Science Alive!* uses NGSS's crosscutting concepts to help students to compare and contrast relevant experiences across domains of science in discussions.

Language

Demonstrate command of the conventions of English when writing and speaking.	Throughout all the components of *Bring Science Alive!* students are expected to demonstrate command of the conventions of written and spoken English.
Acquire and use general academic and domain-specific words.	*Bring Science Alive!* has a progression of increasingly sophisticated vocabulary built into it with complexity suggested by the language used in NGSS. It is designed to emphasize key words used throughout a lesson or unit of study without overwhelming students with too many unfamiliar words. Every component of *Bring Science Alive!* makes use of the vocabulary and includes activities to help solidify comprehension.
Focus on developing skills to determine or clarify the meaning of unknown words or phrases.	Other science-related words which may be unfamiliar to students, but do not play a key role in the overall understanding of a concept, are put in italics and defined in context. This gives students ample opportunity and support in determining and clarifying the meaning of unfamiliar words using clues from the text.

Considerate Text

Sample Graphic Organizer

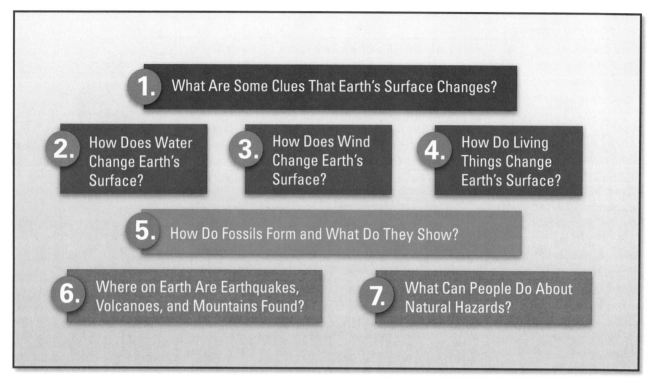

You are about to discover that *Bring Science Alive!* is both interesting and easy to understand. That's because our authors wrote it as a "considerate text," which is another way of saying that it makes readers want to read it. Here are some ways this book is considerate for all levels of readers:

- Each unit is carefully mapped out so that one lesson builds on the next. So, you will find a clear graphic organizer, like the one above, in each unit opener. The graphic organizer shows how all the lessons in the unit relate to one another. A **purple** lesson is the main idea, **blue** stands for lessons that support the main idea, and **green** and **red** lessons take those ideas even further.

- Short lessons make it easier for you to understand and remember what each one is about.

- Each section has a subtitle that provides an outline for your reading and is written with a clear focus. Information is presented in easy-to-manage chunks for better understanding.

- Important new words are in bold type. These words are defined in the glossary in the back of the book.

- Photos, illustrations, and diagrams provide additional information about the topic on the page.

How To Read the Table of Contents

The **lesson title** is also the lesson's Essential Question.

Each lesson has a **crosscutting concept** or 'theme' associated with it.

The **unit name** tells you the overall topic of the unit.

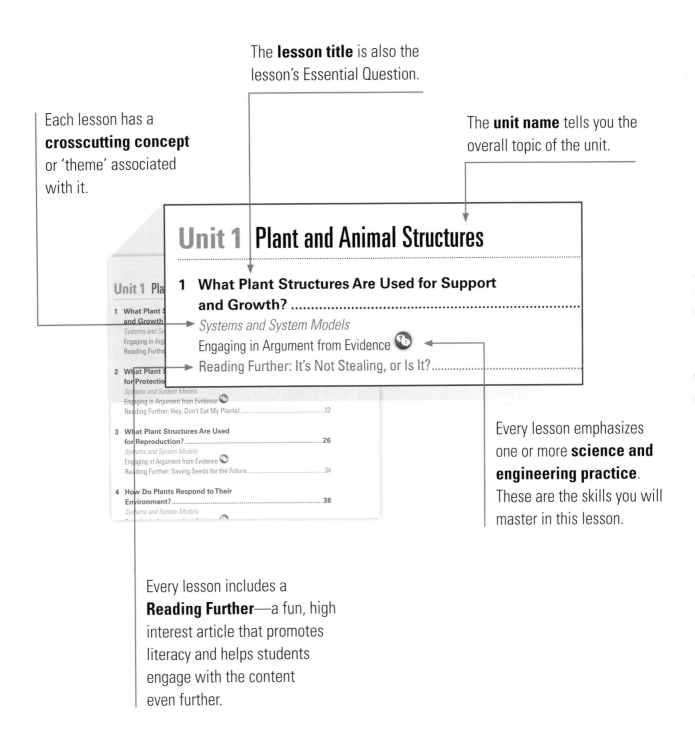

Unit 1 | Plant and Animal Structures

1 What Plant Structures Are Used for Support and Growth? ....

Systems and System Models

Engaging in Argument from Evidence

Reading Further: It's Not Stealing, or Is It? ....

Every lesson emphasizes one or more **science and engineering practice**. These are the skills you will master in this lesson.

Every lesson includes a **Reading Further**—a fun, high interest article that promotes literacy and helps students engage with the content even further.

Contents

Unit 1 Plant and Animal Structures

Unit 2 Energy

Unit 3 Earth's Changing Surface

Unit 4 Waves and Information

Plant and Animal Structures

Next time you see a flower, pay close attention to its different parts. You might see brightly colored petals and pollen on the flower head. These structures help a plant reproduce. Animals also have many structures that help them live. In this unit, you will discover how different structures help plants and animals live and grow.

Unit Contents

Unit 1 Overview

Graphic Organizer: This unit is structured to establish a framework for understanding the functions of **plant** and **animal** structures.

Growth	Support	Protection	Reproduction	Sensing
1. What Plant Structures Are Used for Support and Growth?		**2.** What Plant Structures Are Used for Protection?	**3.** What Plant Structures Are Used for Reproduction?	**4.** How Do Plants Respond to Their Environment?
5. What Animal Structures Are Used for Digestion and Circulation?	**6.** What Animal Stuctures Are Used for Support, Movement, and Protection?		**7.** What Animal Structures Are Used for Reproduction?	**8.** What Animal Structures Are Used for Sensing the Environment?
				9. How Do Animals Respond to Their Environment?

NGSS Next Generation Science Standards

Performance Expectations

4-PS4-2. Develop a model to describe that light reflecting from objects and entering the eye allows objects to be seen.

4-LS1-1. Construct an argument that plants and animals have internal and external structures that function to support survival, growth, behavior, and reproduction.

4-LS1-2. Use a model to describe that animals receive different types of information through their senses, process the information in their brain, and respond to the information in different ways.

Disciplinary Core Ideas

PS4.B: Electromagnetic Radiation

• An object can be seen when light reflected from its surface enters the eyes.

LS1.A: Structure and Function

• Plants and animals have both internal and external structures that serve various functions in growth, survival, behavior, and reproduction.

LS1.D: Information Processing

• Different sense receptors are specialized for particular kinds of information, which may be then processed by the animal's brain. Animals are able to use their perceptions and memories to guide their actions.

Crosscutting Concepts

Cause and Effect

• Cause and effect relationships are routinely identified.

Systems and System Models

• A system can be described in terms of its components and their interactions.

 **Developing and Using Models**

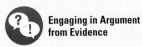 **Engaging in Argument from Evidence**

Have you ever wondered...

When you look at plants and animals, you can observe their different structures. This unit will help you answer these questions and many others you may ask.

Why do plants grow toward the sun?

Why do some plants have thick roots and some have thin roots?

How does a dog learn to fetch a ball?

What Plant Structures Are Used for Support and Growth?

Science Vocabulary

chlorophyll

leaf

photosynthesis

root

stem

vascular system

When you look at a plant, you may notice different structures such as stems, leaves, and roots. But plants also have structures inside that you cannot see. Plants have many structures that help them survive and grow. They have structures that help them get sunlight, air, water, and nutrients. They also have structures that support them and help them make food. These structures interact to form a system that helps plants survive and grow.

NGSS **4-LS1-1.** Construct an argument that plants and animals have internal and external structures that function to support survival, growth, behavior, and reproduction.

LS1.A. Plants and animals have both internal and external structures that serve various functions in growth, survival, behavior, and reproduction.

Systems and System Models A system can be described in terms of its components and their interactions.

 Engaging in Argument from Evidence

1. Plants Need Sunlight, Air, Water, and Nutrients

The next time you visit a park, look around you. You probably will notice many plants, such as trees, bushes, grass, and flowers. What do these plants need in order to grow?

Plants require four main things to stay alive and healthy. They need sunlight, air, water, and nutrients. They use sunlight, air, and water to make their own food. Like all organisms, plants need food to provide energy, which helps them grow and develop. That is why you see trees growing outside. They are exposed to sunlight during the day, and air is always around them. They get water that they need from underground.

Plants also need *nutrients* to grow and develop. Nutrients are similar to food, but they do not provide energy. Instead, nutrients keep a plant healthy. Plants get most nutrients they need from the soil they grow in.

To get enough water, sunlight, air, and nutrients, plants need space to grow. Large plants, such as maple trees or pine trees, need a lot of space. Their branches and leaves spread out in sunlight, and their roots spread out to find water and nutrients. Small plants like pansies or daisies do not need as much space. Lots of pansies can grow in the space that one tree needs.

Large plants like maple trees need a lot of space to spread out their branches and roots. Small plants like pansies need less space.

2. Roots Take in Water and Provide Support

Think of a few kinds of plants you know. Where are their roots located? In most plants, their roots are underground.

A **root** is a plant structure that usually grows into soil or water. Roots help support the plant so that it does not fall over. A plant must grow upright so that its stems and leaves can collect sunlight. Roots also anchor a plant in soil so that it is not washed away or blown away by wind.

Roots have another function. They take in water and nutrients from the soil. The tips of roots have very tiny hair-like structures, called *root hairs*. Water and nutrients enter the root through these root hairs.

There are two different kinds of root systems. Some plants have spread-out roots that are all similar in size. These roots are called *fibrous roots*, and they take in water that is close to the surface of the soil. Plants that grow in dry places often have fibrous roots because these roots can quickly collect water and nutrients when it rains. Other plants have one main root that grows straight down into the soil. This kind of root is called a *taproot*. A taproot has smaller roots growing from it that reach water deep in the soil.

Fibrous roots collect water and nutrients near the soil's surface. Taproots collect water and nutrients deep in the soil.

Fibrous roots

Taproot

This maple tree has a thick, woody stem. Tree trunks support the branches and leaves of trees.

3. Stems Support Plants

When you munch on a piece of celery, you are eating a plant stem. Stems serve many functions for a plant. What do you think some of them are?

A **stem** is a plant structure that connects the roots with the leaves, which grow above ground. One of its functions is usually to support the plant and hold up the leaves so they can absorb sunlight. A tree *trunk* is a thick, woody stem that supports the branches of the tree. Because a trunk is strong and sturdy, the tree can grow tall. Other stems are small and flexible. Corn stems, for example, can blow in the wind and bend over. They will not break unless the wind is very strong.

Some stems also store water or food for the plant. Cactus plants have thick, fleshy stems that hold water that the plant can use when there is not enough rain. Other stems grow underground and can store food. For example, potatoes grow underground, but they are actually big stems that store extra food. The potato plant can use this food at night, or during the winter, when the sun is not shining as much.

Cactus plants have thick stems that store water for the plant. The cactus plants can use this water when it does not rain for a very long time.

4. Leaves Make Food

Think of the different kinds of plants that you know. Now think about their leaves. Are their leaves all the same size, shape, and color? Although most leaves are green, they are usually differently sized and shaped.

Leaves

A **leaf** is a plant structure where food is usually made. Grasses, rose bushes, and maple trees all have differently shaped leaves, but they are all green.

Many plants, such oak and maple trees, have leaves that are wide and flat. The leaves of lettuce and spinach plants are also wide and flat. Having wide and flat leaves allows a plant to receive more sunlight than smaller or skinnier leaves would.

Other leaves are thick and fleshy. Many plants that live in hot and dry places, such as the desert, grow this type of leaf. These leaves store water for the plant to use when there is very little rainfall and the soil is dry. If these leaves break open, drops of water would leak out—some desert animals get some of their water from these drops!

Conifers, such as pine and spruce trees, have thin needle-shaped leaves. A needle shape helps plants conserve water. Needles, and other types of leaves, are covered in wax. Wax prevents water loss from the plant.

This agave plant has thick leaves. Many desert plants have leaves like these to store water in dry environments.

The leaves of a pine tree are sharp and needle-like. They are covered in wax to prevent water loss.

All of these leaves have different shapes and sizes, but they also have some things in common. What do you think are some of their similarities?

Chlorophyll

One similarity shared by many leaves is that they are green. They are green because they contain **chlorophyll,** a green substance that captures the energy in sunlight. Maple leaves are green because they are full of chlorophyll. Grass blades are green for the same reason. Some plants have other structures, such as stems, that are green and contain chlorophyll as well.

Plants use three things from their environment to make sugar. They need energy from the sun, water from the soil, and carbon dioxide from the air.

Photosynthesis

The process in which plants use energy from light to make food is called **photosynthesis**. Most photosynthesis takes place within the leaves. In this process, many plant structures interact to make sugar. Sugar is used as food for the plant. To make sugar, plants need energy from the sun, which they capture with chlorophyll. Second, plants need *carbon dioxide*, which is a gas found in the air. Third, plants need water, which they get from the soil they grow in. The plant combines energy from the sun, carbon dioxide, and water, to make sugar, which it uses as food. That is why you do not see most plants eating—they make their own food. Photosynthesis in plants also makes oxygen. This oxygen goes into the air from the plant's leaves.

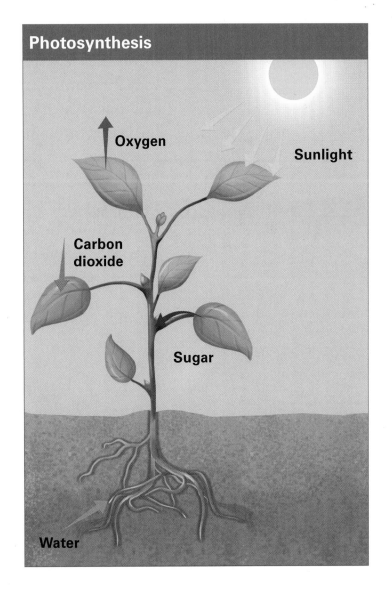

Photosynthesis

Oxygen

Sunlight

Carbon dioxide

Sugar

Water

5. The Vascular System

On land, a system of roads and highways helps move people and things around the country. Roads move materials from where they are made or grown to where they will be used. One of the most important jobs of a stem is similar to that of roads and highways.

Stems help move materials throughout a plant. A plant's **vascular system** is a system of tubes inside the plant that connect the leaves, stems, and roots. The tubes carry food, water, and nutrients to all parts of the plant. For instance, the vascular system of a tall oak tree carries water all the way from its roots underground to the highest leaf on the tree. The vascular system also brings food all the way from those leaves down to its roots.

If you examine a piece of celery, you can see the tubes inside the stem. Like the one-way lanes of a highway, each kind of tube carries materials in only one direction at a time. Water and nutrients move up from the roots to the leaves through one kind of tube. Food that is made in leaves moves down from the leaves to all parts of the plant through another kind of tube. In a potato plant, for example, food from the leaves is moved by the vascular system down to the potato underground. The food is stored there until the plant needs it. Then the vascular system transports it to the part of the plant that needs it.

Many plants have vascular systems throughout their stems. If you cut open a piece of celery, you can see little tubes that are part of the plant's vascular system.

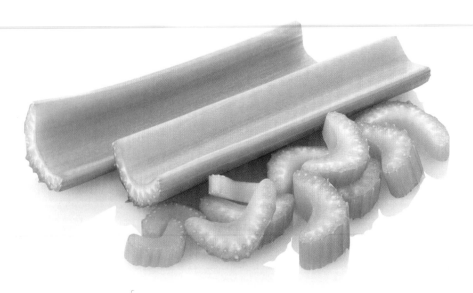

What Plant Structures Are Used for Support and Growth?

1. Plants Need Sunlight, Air, Water, and Nutrients   Plants need sunlight, air, water, and nutrients. They use sunlight, air, and water to make food. The food provides energy to grow and survive. Nutrients do not provide energy for the plants, but they help keep a plant healthy.

2. Roots Take in Water and Provide Support   Most plants have roots that grow underground. The roots help a plant stand upright, so it can face the sun. Roots also gather water and nutrients from the soil for the plant. Different plants have different types of roots to help the plants meet their needs.

3. Stems Support Plants   Stems serve many functions in plants. They help support a plant so it will not fall over when it is windy. Stems also can store food and water for a plant. Some stems are hard and woody, like a tree trunk. Other plants have stems that are flexible and bendy.

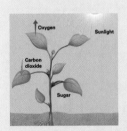

4. Leaves Make Food   Different plants have different types of leaves, but almost all are green. They are green because they contain chlorophyll. Chlorophyll allows them to absorb energy from the sun and produce their own food in a process called photosynthesis.

5. The Vascular System   Many plants have a system of tubes running inside of their stems, leaves, and roots. These tubes move materials through the plant to where they need to go. They move water up from the roots to the leaves, and they move food from the leaves down to the rest of the plant.

It's Not Stealing, or Is It?

For most plants, leaves are the structures that produce the food they need by soaking up sunlight. But plant parasites get their food in a different way. You cannot see most of a *Rafflesia* plant because it is inside another plant. What is it doing there? It's having dinner!

Even though every plant needs food for energy, a *Rafflesia* does not make food using sunlight the way other plants do. Instead, it gets everything it needs from another plant. Taking food, water, and nutrients from another plant is how this plant and others like it survive. They are plant parasites. The plants that they live on are their hosts.

Plant parasites live all over the world. You may have seen some plant parasites in your neighborhood. Look carefully around you. Plant parasites sometimes grow on small plants or trees in the park.

The *Rafflesia*, also called the corpse flower, is a type of plant parasite. This plant only grows in parts of Southeast Asia. A *Rafflesia* lives inside the vines of another plant. The only part of the parasite that you can see are its bright red flowers, which come out of the vine. The rest of the parasite is inside the host! It gets what it needs to survive from the vine, its host plant.

A *Rafflesia* is a type of plant parasite because it depends on other plants for food. It does not contain any leaves or structures to make food through photosynthesis.

What's Yours Is Mine

Plant parasites have vascular systems, just like many other plants do. However, the roots of plant parasites are not like the roots of these other plants. Instead of growing into the soil, the roots of plant parasites attach to the host plant. The root forms a bridge between the parasite's vascular system and that of the host. Water and nutrients then travel from the host's vascular system into the parasite's system by way of the bridge.

Some parasites attach themselves to their host's roots. They create a bridge to the roots to draw out water and nutrients from the host.

Other plant parasites attach themselves to their host's stem or its branches. Corpse flowers get water, food, and nutrients this way. Most of the plant lives inside of the long stems, or vines, of its host, where it can easily get what it needs.

Many plant parasites do not carry out photosynthesis at all. They do not need to. They can get all that they need from the host. A few plant parasites have green leaves that perform photosynthesis. But most of what they need comes from the host.

A *Rafflesia* depends on its host for water, food, and nutrients. The roots of a *Rafflesia* grow into the host's vascular system and steal what they need.

Mistletoe is a plant parasite that grows on tree branches. Birds spread the mistletoe seeds when they eat the berries.

More Than One Way to Eat

For some people, it is a tradition to hang mistletoe above a doorway during the winter holiday season. But trees may not enjoy mistletoe as much. This is because mistletoe is another plant parasite. It lives on tree branches, which are parts of the stems of the tree. The mistletoe's roots act as a bridge between the two plants.

Mistletoe is an example of a plant parasite that has green leaves. So, it can make its own food by photosynthesis. However, it gets most of its water and nutrients from the host tree.

Mistletoe forms small white berries. The berries are poisonous to people, but birds can eat them. Seeds inside the berries pass through the bird's digestive system and are deposited in the bird's droppings. If the seeds happen to fall onto a tree branch, they can sprout. New mistletoe plants grow, develop roots, and connect to the tree stem.

So, if you see mistletoe hanging from the branches of a tree, you will know what it's up to. It is a plant parasite getting what it needs to survive from a host tree's vascular system.

Stealing from the Thief

Another plant parasite that lives on trees is dodder. Dodder often surrounds a tree completely so you cannot see the tree! It is yellow and stringy and looks a bit like spaghetti. It has very tiny leaves, and it usually does not perform any photosynthesis. Instead, dodder depends on its host for food, water, and nutrients. After dodder seeds sprout, the developing stems wave around in the air. They move around in the air like tentacles until they reach a host. Then they attach to the host to get what they need. Dodder can grow until it takes over and destroys many kinds of plants, including crop plants such as potatoes.

Dodder may be bad for useful crop plants, but plant parasites are not all bad. In fact, many of them can make a tasty dish! People in China and the southwestern United States use the seeds of dodder as a food supplement, a source of nutrients you might not get enough of in your normal diet. In China, the plant parasite broomrape is grown for food and medicine. *Rafflesias* in Malaysia are used in energy drinks. Now who is stealing nutrients?

Broomrape is a plant parasite that is grown for food. In this picture, you can see the flowers growing above ground.

Dodder is a plant parasite. It can grow until it completely surrounds its host.

What Plant Structures Are Used for Protection?

Science Vocabulary

bark

spine

thorn

Different plant structures form a system that can be used for protection. Some plants have waxy leaves that protect them from insects and water loss. Other plants have sharp parts that can hurt animals that try to eat them. Plants may have a thick covering that animals cannot bite through, and some even produce bad-tasting or poisonous substances so insects and other animals will not eat them.

 NGSS **4-LS1-1.** Construct an argument that plants and animals have internal and external structures that function to support survival, growth, behavior, and reproduction.

LS1.A. Plants and animals have both internal and external structures that serve various functions in growth, survival, behavior, and reproduction.

Systems and System Models A system can be described in terms of its components and their interactions.

 **Engaging in Argument from Evidence**

1. Protection Against Drying

You have learned that all organisms, including plants, need water to survive. You have also learned that most plants get water from their roots. How do they keep enough water to survive?

Plants that live in dry places have structures to slow the loss of water. Desert plants often have fewer or smaller leaves to save water. The leaves of some other kinds of plants are covered with hairs. Hairy leaves do not lose water as quickly as smooth leaves, because the hairs trap water that is leaving the plant. Many kinds of plants have leaves that are covered with a thin layer of wax. Waxy leaves are structures that prevent water loss. For example, conifer needles and oak leaves have a waxy coating.

Cactus plants have structures that hold extra water until it is needed. Their swollen stems can store water. They have a kind of leaf that is thin and sharp. These leaves have no holes and a small surface, so they lose little water.

Certain behaviors can save water. Plants can open or close the holes in their leaves. This behavior saves water if the holes are closed during the hottest part of the day. Mimosa trees have leaves that fold up during dry, hot days. Folding leaves are structures that prevent the tree from losing water through the tiny holes.

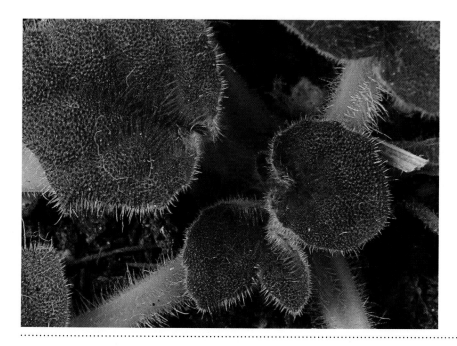

These are the leaves and stems of an African violet. They are covered in small hairs that help them keep their water when it is sunny and hot.

2. Spines and Thorns

Plants cannot hide or run away from animals that want to eat them. They need ways to protect themselves so that they can survive. Many plants have special structures for protection against animals.

You have learned that cactus plants have unusual leaves. These leaves are called *spines*. A **spine** is a kind of leaf that is stiff, thin, and very sharp. In addition to reducing water loss, spines protect a plant from animals that would use it for food or as a source of water.

Another sharp structure that some plants have is *thorns*. A **thorn** is a sharp, pointy structure that is a kind of branch or stem. Thorns have the same function as spines. Like spines, thorns keep animals from eating these plants. An animal that tries to eat a plant with spines or thorns may get hurt and will not try again. For example, acacia trees have many thorns growing out of their branches. Animals might choose to eat a different plant and leave the acacia alone.

A third structure that is similar to thorns and spines is *prickles*. Prickles grow out of the outer covering of a plant stem. They are hard, sharp, and pointy. Rose bushes and raspberry plants have prickles, although some people mistake them for thorns.

These are the thorns on an acacia tree. Look how long and sharp they are! An animal trying to eat the leaves has to get past the thorns first.

These are cork oak tree branches. Their bark is the light gray part surrounding the inner brown wood. The thick bark protects the plant.

3. Plant Coverings

A thick coat or even a heavy sweater can protect you from cold weather. It can also protect you from harm if you fall down or bump into something. Plants, too, have coverings for protection.

Some plants, like trees and bushes, are covered with bark. **Bark** is the tough outer covering of the stems of most trees and many bushes. It protects a plant from insects and other animals that try to eat the softer inner parts of the plant. Bark also helps to protect a plant from being killed by fire.

Different kinds of trees have different kinds of bark. A cork oak tree has very thick bark. Thick bark protects the tree against fire, water loss, insects, and disease. A white birch tree has thin white bark. White bark keeps the tree cooler in the sun.

Seeds, too, are protected by hard coverings. For example, coconuts made by some palm trees have such hard coverings that many animals cannot eat them. Another seed, called a nickernut, grows inside a spiky ball.

You already learned that some plants have waxy leaves to save water. But the wax that covers leaves is also very slippery. Slippery leaves are hard to eat, so caterpillars avoid them. Holly plants have leaves covered in wax. The wax covering makes it so the plant does not lose very much water and is hard for insects to eat.

This is pine tree resin. It is very sticky, so if an insect touches it, it becomes trapped and will die. The resin protects the plant from insects that want to eat it.

4. Poisons and Bad-Tasting Substances

What happens when you eat bad-tasting food? Do you want to take another bite? No. You and other animals try to avoid food that tastes bad.

Many plants make substances that are poisonous or taste bad. For example, foxglove plants have poisonous substances in their leaves, flowers, and seeds. Some animals that try to eat these parts can get sick or die. Other kinds of plants have fruits that taste bad to some animals but not to others. For example, the Jerusalem cherry is poisonous to humans and some types of birds. So, some birds avoid the fruits while others eat them and spread the seeds for the plant.

Many conifers produce a sticky liquid in their stems and leaves called *resin*. When an insect bites into these plant parts, it gets trapped in the resin. Since the insect cannot move, it dies.

Plants need to protect themselves from other plants, too. Sometimes, if plants grow too close together, they cannot get enough sunlight, water, or nutrients. That is why some plants, such as black walnut trees, produce poisonous substances in their roots that prevent other plants from growing nearby. Many plants get sick and die if they are growing near black walnut trees.

What Plant Structures Are Used for Protection?

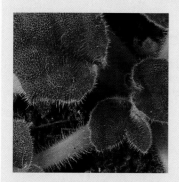

1. Protection Against Drying   All organisms, including plants, need water to survive. Some plant structures help to protect plants from losing water. Those structures include waxy or hairy leaves, stems that store water, and tiny holes in leaves that close at night.

2. Spines and Thorns   Plants cannot run away or hide from animals that want to eat them. Plants need ways to protect themselves so they can survive. Many plants have thorns, spines, or prickles that are very sharp. These make the plant difficult to eat for many animals.

3. Plant Coverings   Many plants have thick coverings to protect them from the sun or from animals that want to eat them. Some trees have thick bark to protect them from animals, and others have thin bark to protect them from the sun. Even some seeds have thick coverings so that animals cannot eat them.

4. Poisons and Bad-Tasting Substances   Some plants have structures that make poisonous or bad-tasting substances. They help protect a plant from animals or insects that want to eat it. Some plants even make poisons that hurt other plants, so they can grow in an area alone and get a lot of water, sunlight, and soil nutrients.

Hey, Don't Eat My Plants!

Every day, a gardener checks to see if a tomato in her garden is ripe. Today, she goes to pick it, only to find that a squirrel got to it first! Many plants have structures that defend them from hungry animals. But how can you protect defenseless garden plants?

A gardener tends his garden plot, watering plants and picking vegetables. When he goes to water his peas, he frowns. The pea plants have been shorn down to the ground! Then he spies a rabbit nearby, munching on what is left of his pea plants. Aha, this furry creature must be the culprit!

Many plants have some defenses against the pests that want to eat them. Some plants have spines or thick coverings. Others taste bad. On the other hand, garden plants and the vegetables they produce have few natural defenses. They are meant to be eaten. That is why people raise them.

Many gardeners try to protect their gardens from unwanted visitors, like this rabbit.

If people like to eat certain plants, chances are that other animals like them, too. Squirrels like tomatoes, and rabbits like peas. Birds like many of the fruits and vegetables that people raise. Aphids are small insects that like almost any kind of soft plant.

What can a gardener do to protect a crop? Many gardeners try to copy the natural defenses of plants to keep away pests. If they succeed, they can be sure that they are the only ones enjoying the fruits of their labor!

Keep Out!

A physical barrier is one way to keep pests out of the garden. Gardeners use barriers like fences and nets to keep out animals. This is similar to how a tree's bark protects its soft inner parts. Netting placed over and around a garden can keep out birds and other animals that could climb, jump, or fly over a barrier with an open top. The problem is that they can keep out the gardener, too! The gardener must lift up the netting to reach the plants. Of course, many animals can chew through netting or dig under fences. Using a strong material and burying the bottom of a fence can often keep those problems from happening.

Fences and nets can stop many animals, but what about bears? Bears are large and powerful. They can tear through netting or knock down a fence to get at a delicious fresh-grown meal. How can you keep a bear out of your garden? Some gardeners use flashing lights or loud sounds that are hooked up to motion detectors. The motion detector can tell when an object as large as a bear is near. Flash! Pow! The light and noise scare the bear away. Electric fences also may be used to keep out bears. However, some bears do not mind a little shock. These tough guys will go right through an electric fence!

Netting and fencing are physical barriers. They can protect garden plants from unwanted visitors, like rabbits or bears.

Spraying plants with soapy water, pepper solutions, or insecticides protects the plant. These sprays keep unwanted visitors away.

Try Tasting This!

Another way to keep animals from eating garden plants is to spray the plants with materials that animals do not like. Some sprays imitate a plant's natural defenses by tasting bad. For example, some gardeners spray their plants with soapy water or pepper solutions. These sprays do not hurt the plants. But they can keep rabbits and other unwanted visitors from thinking garden plants are tasty. They also wash off easily, so a gardener does not have to worry about the sprays becoming part of his or her meal. But that is also a problem! A gardener may have to spend a lot of time re-spraying plants again and again to keep them tasting bad throughout the growing season.

Other kinds of plant sprays are insecticides. Insecticides kill the insects that eat plants. Aphids are insects that can ruin a garden. Spraying plants with insecticides can kill the aphids and save the plants. A gardener may not need to reapply an insecticide for a long time. However, insecticides kill good insects, too. Many garden plants cannot produce fruits or seeds without the help of insects such as bees or butterflies. The insecticides may get rid of pests. But they also get rid of a plant's natural helpers!

Win-Win?

Many gardeners worry about using chemical sprays. They think it may cause too much harm to the environment. Instead they use insects to protect their gardens. This can be better than an insecticide. Insecticides kill insects, both good and bad. Using insects can also be better than using a barrier. Fences and nets may not keep out all insects because some are usually small enough to fit through the spaces.

Ladybird beetles, or ladybugs, are insects that can help protect gardens. They love to eat aphids. Releasing a bunch of ladybird beetles into a garden can help protect the garden from aphids without hurting bees or butterflies.

One type of wasp can help protect gardens from a pest called the tomato hornworm. Tomato hornworms are huge caterpillars. They can devour a gardener's tomatoes. Some gardeners plant dill to attract the wasps. The wasps eat the dill and lay their eggs on the tomato hornworm. When the wasp eggs hatch, the wasps eat the hornworms from the inside out. That may sound disgusting, but it is better than letting the hornworms eat your tomatoes from the inside out!

Ladybird beetles are biological pest controls. This orange ladybird beetle eats the small round aphids seen among ants on this plant stem.

Tomato hornworms can devour a gardener's tomatoes. A type of wasp protects gardens from tomato hornworms by laying their white oval-shaped eggs on a tomato hornworm.

What Plant Structures Are Used for Reproduction?

Science Vocabulary

cone

fertilization

ovary

pistil

pollen

reproduction

seed

spore

stamen

All plants need to reproduce, and many plants do it by producing seeds. As with protection and growth, many different structures form a system that allows plants to reproduce. Different structures in flowers and cones help form seeds. And some plants reproduce by making spores instead of seeds. Both seeds and spores are often scattered far from the parent plants. The offspring then grow in a new area.

 NGSS

4-LS1-1. Construct an argument that plants and animals have internal and external structures that function to support survival, growth, behavior, and reproduction.

LS1.A. Plants and animals have both internal and external structures that serve various functions in growth, survival, behavior, and reproduction.

Systems and System Models A system can be described in terms of its components and their interactions.

 **Engaging in Argument from Evidence**

1. Plants Make More Plants

You may have seen a small daisy plant growing in a garden last year. This year, several more daisy plants may have grown. Even more plants may appear next year. Each plant will make more plants of the same kind.

A living thing is called an *organism*. All species make more organisms of the same kind. Daisy plants make more daisy plants. They do not make dandelion plants. Pine trees make more pine trees. Making more of the same kind of organism is called **reproduction**. The new organisms are called *offspring*.

Plants have different groups of structures they use for reproduction. Similar to animals, most kinds of plants have different male and female structures that interact to perform certain functions. When a male structure and a female structure come together and combine, it is called **fertilization**. Fertilization is the first step in reproduction. For example, before a daisy can grow seeds that will sprout into new daisies, it must be fertilized. That means that male and female daisy structures have to come together and combine inside the plant.

Daisy plants, like all kinds of organisms, reproduce. These daisies are offspring of other daisy plants.

2. Some Plants Produce Flowers

How did the plants in the sidewalk crack produce new plants? Daisies, like many other kinds of plants, reproduce by forming flowers.

Most flowers have both male and female structures. The male structure of a flower is called a **stamen**. A flower often has more than one stamen. A stamen makes a powdery material called **pollen**.

The female part of a flower is called a **pistil**. A flower may have several pistils or only one. At the bottom of each pistil is an ovary. An **ovary** is a structure that will develop into a fruit. Seeds are found inside the fruit. Most flowers have stamens and at least one pistil. That means that unlike most animals, many flowers have both male and female structures for reproduction.

Petals surround the male and female parts of flowers. The petals are often colorful and smell sweet. Flower petals attract insects such as butterflies and bees. When an insect lands on a flower, its body rubs on the top of the stamens. Some of the pollen sticks to the insect's body. The pollen is then carried to the pistil of the same flower or to a pistil of another flower that the insect visits later. Now that the pollen is near the pistil, the first step in reproduction, fertilization, can occur.

Most flowers have stamens, pistils, and petals. Pollen is found on top of the stamens, and the ovary is the bottom part of the pistil.

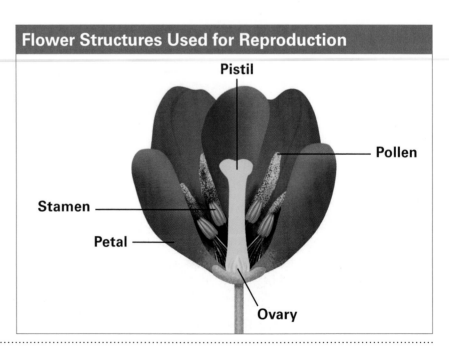

Flower Structures Used for Reproduction

Pistil

Pollen

Stamen

Petal

Ovary

Now that the plant has been fertilized, the next step of reproduction can happen. The second step of reproduction is making *seeds*. A **seed** is a structure that contains a tiny baby plant and a supply of food. It forms in the ovary. The seed is surrounded by a tough coat that protects it. The tiny baby plant inside the seed will get its energy from the food supply inside the seed since it cannot perform photosynthesis yet.

While one or more seeds are forming, a fruit also forms. The fruit surrounds and protects the seed. Many fruits, such as certain kinds of cherries and apples, are sweet and juicy. These fruits taste sweet and juicy so that they can attract animals. Animals eat the seed-containing fruit, and eventually the seed is deposited on the ground in a new place that is far away from the parent plant. The scattering of seeds is important to plants. The new plant that grows from the seed will have more space, water, and nutrients if it is not near the parent plant.

When a seed lands in a place with warm, wet soil, it sprouts. Roots grow out of the seed and hold the seed in the soil. The roots also take in water. A stem grows upward from the seed. Tiny leaves grow from the stem. The new leaves turn green and start to produce their own food by photosynthesis.

This apple is a fruit that grew to surround the apple seeds on the inside. The apple protects the seeds while they develop. It also attracts animals to distribute the seeds.

These are the different stages of growth a plant goes through after a seed sprouts. The seed grows roots down into the soil and a green stem up into the light. As it reaches the light, new leaves unfold at the top of the stem.

A female pine cone has woody scales. When pollen gets to a female cone, fertilization happens.

3. Some Plants Produce Cones

You have never seen flowers on a pine tree. Plants that have needle-like leaves do not form flowers. Instead, they produce cones.

A **cone** is a reproductive structure that has no petals, stamens, pistils, or ovaries. Pine, fir, and spruce trees reproduce using cones. These trees are called conifers. The word *conifer* means "cone forming."

Pine, fir, and spruce trees do not have flowers with pistils and stamens. They reproduce using male cones and female cones. The male cones are small and have soft scales. Like a stamen in a flower, pollen is produced within male cones. Female cones are larger than male cones and have hard scales.

You have read that insects transfer pollen in many flowering plants. In most conifers, however, wind transfers pollen. The wind carries pollen from a male cone to the scales of a female cone. When the pollen gets to a female cone, fertilization happens.

After fertilization, seeds form in the female cone. Unlike the seeds of flowers, pine seeds are not surrounded by fruit. Instead, the seeds are protected by the hard cone, and when they are fully developed the wind or animals carry them away. When a pine seed lands on warm, wet soil, it sprouts. A new plant grows.

This cluster of male cones is releasing a cloud of pollen into the air. Wind will transfer the pollen to the female cones.

4. Seeds Must Be Scattered

Have you ever tried to catch a dandelion "parachute" that is floating in air? Did you notice the attached seed? Many kinds of plants must scatter their seeds far from the parent plant. Many seeds have structures that help them move far away from their parents.

Wind scatters the seeds of many different plants. Maple seeds have structures that look like wings. They help the seed catch the wind and move far away. Dandelion seeds form fluffy parachutes that float in air and are blown around by the wind.

Water scatters seeds that can float. The seeds of water lilies have structures that let them float in the pond where the parent plants live. Eventually, the structures fill with water and the seeds sink to the bottom of the pond where they can sprout. One kind of palm tree produces large seeds called coconuts. There is a large hollow structure in the center of the coconut that lets it float for a very long time.

Many seeds have tiny hooks. These structures grab the fur of animals or the clothing of humans and are carried away from the parent. You have probably seen these seeds stuck to a dog before!

It is important for seeds to move so they can grow in a new area. That new area might have better sunlight, more water, or more nutrients.

Many kinds of seeds have structures that help move them away from the parent plant. Coconuts can float on the ocean for days before finding land and beginning to grow.

Spore capsule

Moss plants produce capsules on stalks. Each capsule is filled with tiny spores. When the capsule breaks open, the spores will drift away in the wind and grow into new moss plants.

5. Plants That Reproduce with Spores

Have you ever seen a small patch of fuzzy, green plants growing on a rock or a tree before? Those plants are called mosses. Mosses do not grow flowers, cones, or seeds. They have another way to reproduce.

Some plants, like ferns and mosses, reproduce by forming spores. A **spore** is a tiny reproductive structure that grows into a new plant. Spores are similar to seeds, but much smaller.

Mosses are small plants that have no vascular system. Each part of the plant must get water and nutrients directly from the environment. With no vascular system, the sugars that mosses make move through the plant slowly.

To reproduce, a moss plant grows a tall stalk with thousands of tiny spores inside a capsule at the top. When the capsule is ripe, it breaks open. The spores shoot into the air and are scattered by wind or water. A spore that lands on damp soil grows into a new moss plant.

Ferns are taller than moss plants. And, unlike mosses, ferns have a vascular system for moving materials. To reproduce, a fern plant forms clusters of spores on the undersides of its leaves. When a cluster dries out, it breaks open. Wind and water carry the spores to new places, where they grow into new fern plants.

These are leaves of a fern plant. Fern plants produce clusters of spores on the undersides of their leaves. When those clusters break open, the spores will be carried away in the wind.

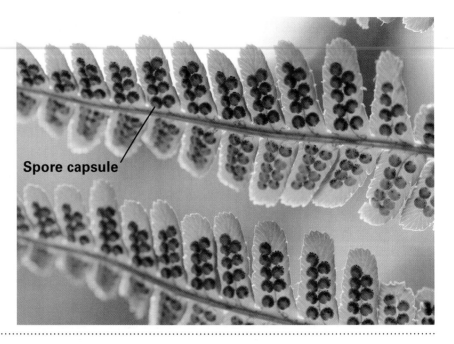

Spore capsule

What Plant Structures Are Used for Reproduction?

1. Plants Make More Plants   All plants make more plants of the same kind. This is called reproduction. The new organisms produced after reproduction are called offspring. Plants have different structures they use for reproduction.

2. Some Plants Produce Flowers   Many kinds of plants produce flowers. Flowers often have male and female structures used for reproduction. When the plant is fertilized it can grow seeds surrounded by fruit. These seeds allow the plant to reproduce.

3. Some Plants Produce Cones   Many kinds of plants that do not produce flowers make cones instead. These plants, such as pine trees, have male and female cones. The male cones produce pollen, which is transported by the wind to the female cones. Seeds develop inside the female cones after fertilization.

4. Seeds Must Be Scattered   Seeds from many kinds of plants have structures that help them move far from the parent plant. Some seeds are blown by the wind. Others can float on water. Some even use animals to move away from their parents.

5. Plants That Reproduce with Spores   Some kinds of plants do not grow cones or flowers. They produce spores instead of seeds. Mosses and ferns are two examples. Their spores are very similar to seeds, but they are usually much smaller. Spores are released into the air, and the wind or water carries them away.

Saving Seeds for the Future

Farmers grow many food crops, like wheat, from seeds. Imagine that a natural disaster, such as a volcanic eruption, wiped out all the crops on Earth. There would be no way to get new seeds. How would the people of Earth get the food that they need without seeds?

It sounds like a science fiction thriller. But in fact, Earth has been gradually losing plants for a long time. For hundreds of years, people have developed crop plants with certain qualities, like larger vegetables or sweeter fruit. As people have developed these new crops, they have also kept alive fewer older crop plants. They just don't see the need to keep growing the less useful crops. The problem is that any change in the environment can wipe out a particular crop.

To protect crops for the future, scientists began to start seed banks. A seed bank is a way to store seeds for future use. The first seed bank was created by Nikolay Vavilov. He was a Russian scientist who lived in the early 1900s. As a boy, he experienced the famine that results when crops fail. He wanted to end famine in Russia and the rest of the world. He knew having many different kinds of plants was important. If one kind of plant died out, there would still be other kinds to feed people. To preserve plant variety, he started collecting seeds from five continents. Thus, he started the first large seed bank.

Large fields of a single kind of plant can feed a lot of people. However, if a plant that people depend on dies out completely, there is no way to get it back.

Why Save Seeds?

Does a seed bank have a large metal vault and security guards like the banks where we keep money? A seed bank is not exactly like that. A seed bank does need to keep seeds safe and secure though. Some seed banks look like an ordinary farm, only the farmer grows crops just for the purpose of collecting and storing their seeds. Heritage Farm in Iowa is an example. At this farm, farmers save seeds from the crops grown there. They store the seeds in refrigerators, freezers, and underground dirt cellars. Keeping the seeds cold prevents them from sprouting or rotting. The farm is a place where other farmers can also store seeds and exchange them with each other.

From large farms to small, many farmers recognize the importance of saving seeds. For example, one farmer has a small farm in Ethiopia. He stores seeds in hollowed-out gourds. He rubs the seeds with ash to keep insects from eating them. He stores seeds for all of the crops he grows. If he ever loses his crops, because of a disaster such as a flood or a drought, he can replant them. His family will not starve, because he has his own personal seed bank.

Farmers harvest and save the seeds that will go in seed banks. These are just a few of the thousands of different kinds of seeds that people grow for food.

It's Like Money in the Bank

Today, there are 1,400 seed banks around the world. How do we know that they have all the important crops covered? And what happens if one of them loses its precious seeds? Not a problem! The Svalbard Global Seed Vault in Norway, one of the biggest seed banks of all, has a backup plan.

This giant seed vault stores seeds that match the kinds of seeds found in all of the other seed banks in the world. Thus, each type of seed there acts as a backup copy in case something happens to the others of its kind at another bank.

This seed vault works like a bank that manages money. Instead of money, it manages seeds from various seed banks. Seed banks deposit their seeds in the vault. Each seed bank owns the seeds it puts into the seed vault. No other bank can take the seeds out of the vault. Only the original seed bank that put them there can.

The seed vault in Norway takes in lots of seeds. In one week, it can take in more than 25,000 seed samples from 17 countries. It currently stores more than 800,000 seeds. It is able to store even more— more than 2 billion seeds. And its vault stores a great variety of seed types. It stores seeds from rice, corn, and many other food crops.

Racks of seeds are stored inside the global seed vault in Norway.

Step Inside the Seed Vault

So, how does the most important seed bank in the world keep seeds from going bad? Keeping them cool is the trick! So, rather than waste energy on refrigeration, the bank uses the planet's natural refrigerator—the Arctic!

The Svalbard Global Seed Vault lies deep inside a mountain on an island halfway between the mainland of Norway and the North Pole. The area is far from civilization. All year round it is freezing cold. The thick rocks and freezing temperatures keep the seeds frozen and preserved even if there is a power outage.

To get to the seeds, you must pass through four locked doors. The first is the steel entrance door. A second door is located 100 m down an entrance tunnel. Next, there are two doors that form an air lock. They keep outside air from entering and mixing with the clean air inside the vault. And finally, the seeds themselves are kept in vacuum-sealed packages inside sealed boxes to keep out even the clean air.

Could all this keep the seeds safe during a natural disaster? The vault is designed to be earthquake-proof and flood-proof. It is even supposed to withstand the impact of a medium-sized asteroid striking Earth. Anything larger and the seeds are on their own!

The Global Seed Vault lies deep inside a mountain in Norway. The low temperature keeps the seeds frozen even if the electricity goes out.

How Do Plants Respond to Their Environment?

Science Vocabulary

gravity

response

stimulus

Plants can respond in different ways to their environments. Most plants change which way they grow based on where the sun is. As some kinds of sunflowers grow, their flower buds turn to face East. Many plants can grow their roots toward water, and some are even able to sense touch. Finally, many plants can sense what season it is based on day length. These responses require many different plant structures to work together to help the plant survive.

 NGSS

4-LS1-1. Construct an argument that plants and animals have internal and external structures that function to support survival, growth, behavior, and reproduction.

LS1.A. Plants and animals have both internal and external structures that serve various functions in growth, survival, behavior, and reproduction.

Systems and System Models A system can be described in terms of its components and their interactions.

 **Engaging in Argument from Evidence**

1. Stems and Leaves Respond to Light

Imagine you put a plant on a sunny windowsill. After a few days, where are the plant's stems and leaves pointing? They probably point toward the sunlight coming in through the window.

Stems and leaves are structures that usually grow upward and toward light. A plant must grow toward the light because it needs light to make food. For example, in a rainforest where there are many tree branches overhead, very little light reaches the forest floor. That means that plants that grow on the ground do not get very much light and cannot make very much food. So, many plants sprout in the soil and then grow long stems called *vines* that cling to the bark of trees. The vines grow up, climbing the tree trunk to reach the light. Once the vines reach the light, they start growing sideways, spreading out their leaves to absorb the light and make as much food as possible.

Light is a stimulus for a plant. A **stimulus** is anything in the environment that makes an organism act in a certain way. Whatever the organism does when it senses the stimulus is called a **response**. Plants respond to light by turning their stems and leaves toward it. This response helps the plant gather the energy it needs to survive, grow, and reproduce.

Vines like the ones on the side of this house grow upward, toward the sun. Many plants have stems that grow toward the sun.

2. Roots Respond to Gravity and Water

Suppose you have a plant growing in a pot of soil. The stem and leaves are growing straight up and the roots are growing straight down. How does a sprouting seed grow its stem up and its roots down?

When a seed sprouts, the new root grows down into the soil in the same direction as gravity pulls. **Gravity** is a force that pulls objects down. In this case, gravity is a stimulus that makes a plant's roots grow downward. This response of the growing roots holds the seed in the soil so it does not wash away.

The stem of a sprouting plant grows upward toward the surface. In this case, the stimulus is still gravity, but the response of the plant's stem is to grow in the *opposite* direction of gravity, unlike the roots. As the stem approaches the soil's surface, it can respond to the stimulus of light as well, growing toward it.

Once a new plant grows roots down into the soil, how do you think it finds water? The presence of water is also a stimulus that plants respond to. Many roots are able to respond to water by growing toward a water source. If a pond or stream is nearby, the roots will grow toward the water. This helps the plant find enough water to grow.

As an acorn sprouts, its roots grow downward, in the direction gravity pulls. Many plants respond to the stimulus of gravity in this way.

These are vine tendrils. They grow until they touch something like a chain-link fence, and then they wrap around it for support.

3. Leaves and Stems Respond to Touch

You have read that vines in a rainforest grow up along tree trunks to reach more light. But how does the vine know where the tree is?

The vine cannot see the tree, but it can feel it. Many plants can respond to the stimulus of touch. When the stem of a vine touches an object such as a tree trunk, a wall, or a fence, it grows and coils around the object. This response supports the vine and helps it climb toward sunlight so it can make more food.

Many climbing plants have structures that help them find and cling to objects. Coil-like structures, called *tendrils*, bend and turn until they touch an object. Then the plant grows toward the object and grows around or along it. For example, you may have seen grape vines that are twisted around a fence.

Some plants respond to touch by trapping insects. For example, Venus flytraps have leaves covered with tiny hairs. When an insect touches those hairs, the leaves close very fast, and the plant can digest the insect to get extra nutrients. That reaction happens very fast, and requires many different structures all working together. As soon as the hairs feel a fly, they cause the leaves to close around the fly. When the leaves close around the fly, they start to produce substances that digest the insect.

A Venus flytrap leaf responds to the touches of an insect by snapping shut. The plant digests the insect to get nutrients.

These are Japanese cherry trees. They grow pink flowers in the spring before they grow any leaves. They grow flowers in response to the amount of daylight in day.

4. Plants Respond to Seasons

How do you know what season it is? You might look at a calendar or check the weather report. But a plant cannot do those things. How do you think a plant senses what season it is?

Plants can respond to the temperature changes from season to season. Winter days have fewer hours of daylight than summer days. So, the ground and air are colder in winter than in summer. When there is more light in spring, the weather is warmer. Many plants grow flowers. It is important for many kinds of plants to produce flowers in spring. Many plants grow their flowers even before they grow new leaves. This means that the flowers are on bare branches, and insects can see them more clearly, making pollination easier.

During fall, many plants respond to the decreasing number of daylight hours. Their response is to stop making chlorophyll in their leaves. When the plants stop making chlorophyll, their leaves change color. Soon, the leaves fall off the plant. Not having leaves in cold weather prevents water loss in a plant. Branches without leaves are also less likely to break when they are covered by heavy snow.

How Do Plants Respond to Their Environment?

1. Stems and Leaves Respond to Light   Nearly all plants are able to sense where the sun is. These plants can grow in the direction of the light, so they are able to absorb more sunlight and make more food. Light is a stimulus for a plant. A plant can respond to this stimulus by turning its stems and leaves toward sunlight.

2. Roots Respond to Gravity and Water   When seeds sprout underground, the roots are able to respond to the stimulus of gravity. They grow down, farther into the soil. Many roots are also able to respond to water, growing toward water sources. These responses help the plant find enough water to meet its needs and grow.

3. Leaves and Stems Respond to Touch   Some plants are able to respond to the stimulus of touch. Many plants, especially vines, are able to grow along a fence or wall. Many climbing plants have structures that help them find and cling to objects. Other plants, like Venus flytraps, can respond to the touch of insects.

4. Plants Respond to Seasons   Many plants can respond to the changing seasons. They respond to changes in both day length and temperature. Each of these is a stimulus that tells plants to grow flowers. During fall, many plants stop producing chlorophyll. These responses help the plant to survive in its changing environment.

Plants That Trap Insects

If a fly buzzes near your face, you might swat at it. What does a plant do when the same pesky fly comes by? Some plants might actually capture and eat it. All plants respond to their environment. However, the response of plants that eat insects can be deadly.

A fly flits about, looking for something to eat. Lured by a sweet smell, it zooms in for a closer look. Uh oh! Now it is stuck to its delicious snack. Instead of enjoying a meal, the fly has become dinner for a sundew plant.

Sundews are a type of carnivorous plant. Carnivorous plants trap insects and eat them to gain the nutrients they need.

Plants usually spend their whole lives rooted to one spot. So, how can carnivorous plants catch an insect that can move around? They have to wait for the insect to come to them. Also, many can respond quickly when the unwary insect comes near. For example, a carnivorous plant like a Venus flytrap quickly shuts its trap when it senses the touch of an insect. The insect becomes trapped inside. Pitcher plants are also carnivorous plants. They do not have moving structures like the flytrap, but they still respond to their trapped prey. When insects fall into their pitchers, the plants release substances that digest the insect to get energy.

Sundews are like the "flypaper" of the plant world. They produce a sweet, sticky substance that attracts insects. When an insect lands on them, it gets stuck.

A Sticky Situation

Like many other carnivorous plants, sundews respond to their prey in order to trap them. Sundews are small plants that grow close to the ground. On many sundews, the leaves form a circle. Each leaf has many hair-like structures called tentacles. Sundews got their name from the droplets that cling to their tentacles. The droplets look like dew but they are actually a very sticky mucus.

How do sundews trap insects? The tentacles on a sundew can sense when something has touched them. Suppose a fly lands on the sundew. As soon as the fly lands, it becomes caught in the sticky stuff. As the fly tries to escape, nearby tentacles sense the fly's movement. The tentacles begin to move and surround the fly. The more the fly tries to escape, the more the tentacles surround it. In a few minutes, the fly is completely trapped.

Next, the tentacles determine if the fly is something good to eat. They give off a substance that tells the sundew if the thing landing is a fly or something else like a grain of sand. Sundews do not want to eat sand! If the thing landing is a fly or other food, then the sundew begins to digest its doomed prey.

Each leaf on a sundew has tiny tentacles that produce sticky mucus. When an insect lands on a sundew, it becomes trapped by the mucus. Then the tentacles move and surround the animal.

Welcome to My Home

Carnivorous plants may seem like the stuff of science fiction, but they are real. So, where could you go to see one? Many live in bogs. A *bog* is a type of wetland. The ground in a bog is squishy and covered in water. The plants that grow there form large mats over the water. The mats on the bog surface look like they are firm. But it is often too soft to support the weight of a person.

Bogs can be sunny places that have tall evergreen trees growing around their edges. Mosses and ferns can blanket the ground. In open places, you might find clusters of carnivorous plants. Venus flytraps, pitcher plants, and sundews thrive in the damp soil.

Even though carnivorous plants eat insects, they do not use them for food energy. They still carry out photosynthesis to get all of their energy. However, other plants normally get nutrients from a rich soil. The soil in a bog is not rich. So, carnivorous plants digest insects to get their nutrients. The reason a bog's soil is poor and squishy is because water does not drain off very well. Thus, the ground is made up of wet, decaying plant matter. This causes the soil to lack nutrients. So, while it cannot support other types of plants, it is the perfect home for many carnivorous plants.

Bogs have wet, squishy soil. Carnivorous plants live well in this environment.

I Would Like Another Insect, Please

Carnivorous plants have captured more than just insects. In the 1800s, their unusual habits captured the interest of a very famous biologist, Charles Darwin. "I was surprised by finding how large a number of insects were caught by the leaves of the common sundew," wrote Darwin. He is most famous for observations he made as a ship's naturalist, studying plant and animal life wherever the ship landed during its explorations. But he also studied sundews.

Darwin did experiments with sundews to study how they caught insects. He observed how the leaves curled around objects, whether he placed insects or bits of paper on them. However, he noticed one important difference. Leaves of the sundews curled faster and stayed curled longer around insects than they did around paper.

Darwin did more experiments with sundews. He fed insects to some sundews but not to others. Sundews he fed insects to were healthier than plants he did not feed. The sundews that were fed insects had more flowers. They also produced more seeds. He concluded that the nutrients from insects helped the plant survive and reproduce. So, the next time a fly buzzes in your face, remember it is not such a pest! It is a healthy snack for a sundew.

A healthy sundew produces flowers when it receives enough nutrients.

What Animal Structures Are Used for Digestion and Circulation?

Science Vocabulary

arteries

blood

circulation

digestion

heart

large intestine

lungs

small intestine

stomach

veins

All animals need food, air, and water to survive. Animals use different structures to find food, take in air, and get water. After finding and eating food, animals have structures that form a system to digest it. This way animals can use the digested food for energy. They also use blood to move digested food throughout their bodies. The digestion and circulation process in animals involves many different structures all working together.

NGSS

4-LS1-1. Construct an argument that plants and animals have internal and external structures that function to support survival, growth, behavior, and reproduction.

LS1.A. Plants and animals have both internal and external structures that serve various functions in growth, survival, behavior, and reproduction.

Systems and System Models A system can be described in terms of its components and their interactions.

Engaging in Argument from Evidence

1. Animals Need Food, Water, and Air to Survive

When you are in a park, you might see birds building nests, squirrels chasing each other around trees, and bees buzzing in the air. These activities require energy.

All animals need energy to move and grow to survive. Animals get energy from the food they eat. Before an animal can use the food it eats, the food must be broken down into smaller pieces. These substances can be used for energy and building materials needed for living and growing.

Animals need water to survive. Water helps them move materials through their bodies. Different kinds of animals need different amounts of water. For example, desert animals can store water in their bodies, so they do not need to drink as much. A few animals do not drink water at all. They get all the water they need from the food they eat.

Animals also need to take in air to survive. Many animals have **lungs,** balloon-like structures that take in air and release waste. Air, as well as food, is needed to provide the energy that the body needs. Some animals, such as earthworms, take in air through their skin. Insects get air through small holes in their bodies. Fish breathe with gills. Gills take in air that is in water.

Like all animals, horses need food, water, and air. Many kinds of animals drink water from rivers, lakes, or ponds.

2. Structures for Getting Food and Water

When you are hungry, you can bite an apple and munch on it. What body structures do you use to eat an apple?

Animals that eat plant material, such as grass and leaves, have teeth with a certain shape. These teeth are large and flat. Because plant material is tough, a plant-eating animal must chew and grind its food for a long time. That is why cows are almost always chewing! Animals that eat meat have long, sharp teeth they use to bite into other animals.

Birds have no teeth. Instead, the structure they use to get food is their beaks. Their beaks are shaped for the kind of food the bird eats. Short, thick beaks crack seeds. Long thin beaks can get insects out of trees.

Each kind of insect also has mouthparts adapted to eating a certain kind of food. Grasshopper mouthparts are shaped like scissors for biting and chewing leaves. Mosquito mouthparts are long and pointed. They cut holes in skin and suck blood. Butterfly mouthparts are shaped like drinking straws for sipping nectar from flowers.

Animals have structures for getting water, too. A bird dips its beak in water to drink. An elephant sucks up water into its trunk. Then it puts the end of its trunk into its mouth and releases the water. Frogs and earthworms take in water through their skin.

Bird beaks are shaped for the type of food they eat. This bird has a strong, pointed beak to grab insects quickly.

3. Structures for Digesting Food

Think about the food you ate for breakfast today. How do the materials in that food help you live, move and grow? First, they must be broken down by your digestive system.

Digestion is the process that breaks down food into smaller substances that the body can use. Food is broken down in digestive structures. Each structure has its own job to do, but they all work together to break down food. Together, these structures make up the *digestive system*. When the structures work together, an animal gets enough energy to grow and stay healthy. It gets enough materials to grow and repair its body parts.

The digestive system breaks down food in two ways. The food is mashed into tiny pieces. The mashed food is also mixed with digestive juices that break down the food into even tinier parts. Digestive systems vary from animal group to group, but some are similar. You have a digestive system with many different structures, including a mouth, esophagus, stomach, small intestine, and large intestine. A mouse has the same structures, and they perform similar functions. Let's look at a mouse's digestive system in more detail.

This mouse is eating a blackberry. The mouse's digestive system will break down the berry into parts that its body can use.

Food starts to break down in the mouth. The mouse's teeth grind and mash the food into small pieces. Its tongue mixes the food with saliva. *Saliva* is a digestive juice that breaks down some of the materials in food.

The mouse swallows the food. It passes through a tube called the esophagus. Next, it moves into the stomach. The **stomach** is a digestive structure lined with muscles that stir the food and mix it with more digestive juices.

The food then moves into a long tube where it mixes with even more digestive juices. This tube, called the **small intestine,** is the digestive structure that absorbs useful parts of the food.

Food is digested as it moves through different digestive structures, starting with the mouth and ending with the large intestine.

The Mouse Digestive System

Mouth

Esophagus

Stomach

Small intestine

Large intestine

The digested food passes through the walls of the small intestine and moves into the blood. Blood carries the useful materials from digested food to all parts of the mouse's body. The digested food will be used to supply energy and raw materials to build and repair its body parts.

Meanwhile, food that was not broken down in the small intestine moves into the large intestine. The **large intestine** completes digestion and removes water from the undigested food. The water moves into the blood. The solid material that is left leaves the mouse's body as waste.

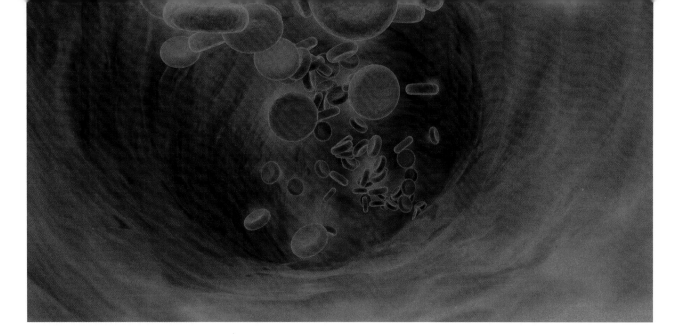

4. Blood Transports Materials

You have read that blood carries digested food and water from the intestines to all parts of the body. But what else can blood carry?

Blood is made up of solid parts floating in liquid. The job of blood is to circulate materials. **Circulation** is the process of moving blood and the materials it carries through the body. Blood carries digested food, water, and gases throughout the body. Animals need some of these gases to get energy. When you breathe in, air enters your lungs. Oxygen moves into your blood and is carried through the body by one of the solid parts of blood. Other parts of the blood help the body fight disease and form blood clots to stop bleeding.

The liquid part of blood is called *plasma*. Plasma is mostly water, but it has two important jobs. Plasma carries digested food to all body parts. It also carries away some of the waste that other body parts make. This gas waste is released back into the air from the lungs.

Many animals have blood to transport needed materials. Even earthworms have blood. But not all blood is red. Squids and octopuses have blue blood. Other animals with no skeletons use green or pink liquids.

In some animals, blood might look like this. You can see the solid parts of the blood floating in the liquid plasma. Blood moves oxygen, digested food, and wastes throughout the body.

5. The Heart Is a Pump

What causes blood to move through the body? It must be pumped, or pushed. This is the job of the heart.

The **heart** is a pump made of muscles. When heart muscles contract, blood is pushed out of the heart. A contracting and relaxing heart causes heartbeats.

Blood moves through blood vessels. There are three kinds of blood vessels. **Arteries** are tubes that carry blood away from the heart. **Veins** carry blood back to the heart. Tiny blood vessels called *capillaries* connect the arteries to the veins throughout the body. Arteries, veins, the heart, capillaries, and blood make up the *circulatory system*.

The blood carries oxygen, waste, and food throughout the body. The heart's pumping is what moves the blood.

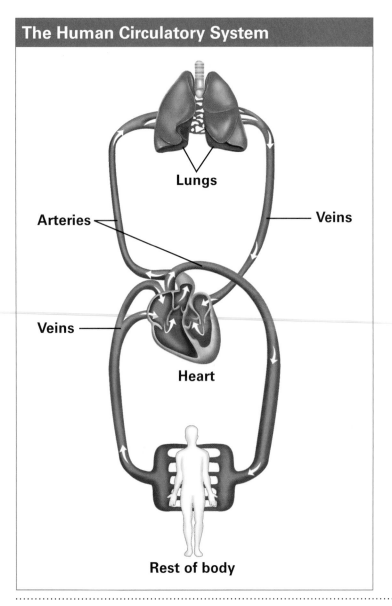

The Human Circulatory System

Lungs

Arteries

Veins

Veins

Heart

Rest of body

Let's follow a drop of blood as it moves through the body. The drop of blood enters the heart and is pumped into the lungs. Here, it picks up oxygen, a needed gas, and drops off the waste gas carbon dioxide. Then the drop of blood that has oxygen returns to the heart. Some of the oxygen might be used by the heart, but the rest needs to go to the rest of the body. The next time the heart beats, the blood drop is pumped to the rest of the body, where it can deliver needed materials like oxygen or food to other parts of the body and where it can pick up waste. It travels to the rest of the body through arteries, capillaries, and veins. The drop of blood then returns to the heart. Each time the heart beats, blood moves through the body.

What Animal Structures Are Used for Digestion and Circulation?

1. Animals Need Food, Water, and Air to Survive   All animals need food, water, and air. Different kinds of animals have different structures to get those things. Some animals breathe air using lungs. Others get air or water through their skin. Some animals eat plants, while some eat other animals.

2. Structures for Getting Food and Water   Animals have many different structures to get food and water. Some animals that eat plants have strong flat teeth that they use to chew. Birds have beaks shaped for the kinds of food they eat.

3. Structures for Digesting Food   After animals eat food, they need to digest it before their bodies can use it. There are many different structures for digesting food, but some of the more common ones include the stomach and the small and large intestines. These structures break down and absorb food so the body can use it.

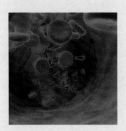

4. Blood Transports Materials   Many kinds of animals have blood. Blood has many structures that all do different things. Some structures carry oxygen. Others carry digested food or waste. Some even fight diseases or help heal wounds.

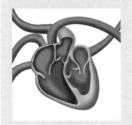

5. The Heart Is a Pump   In most animals, the heart pumps blood throughout the animal's body. The blood travels through arteries and veins, and carries oxygen, digested food, and waste. Together, the heart, blood vessels, and blood make up the circulatory system.

Some of My Best Friends Are Bacteria

The different structures in your digestive system help you break down food so that your body can use the energy and building materials it provides. But you also get help from trillions of creatures that live inside your guts. Wait, who lives inside your guts?

What do this mother and her newborn infant have in common? You can look at the picture and see that their hair color and skin color are similar. What you cannot see is what they have in common inside their digestive systems. Helpful bacteria!

Babies get a lot of things from their mothers. Their looks and their abilities are two things they can get. Hair and skin color are part of a person's looks. Being right-handed and having a good singing voice are examples of abilities. Babies also get substances that help them to fight diseases. A nursing infant gets disease-fighting substances from his or her mother's milk.

Why would a baby have its mother's bacteria? People have bacteria that live inside the gut. These bacteria are called *gut microbes*. Gut microbes are important to a person's health. They are passed from mothers to their babies during birth. The baby also gets microbes from the foods it eats and the environment. As the baby grows, the gut microbes increase in number inside the baby. After a while, the baby has enough of its own gut microbes to remain healthy.

Mothers pass on many things to their infants. They include looks, abilities, and things that are important to health, like gut microbes.

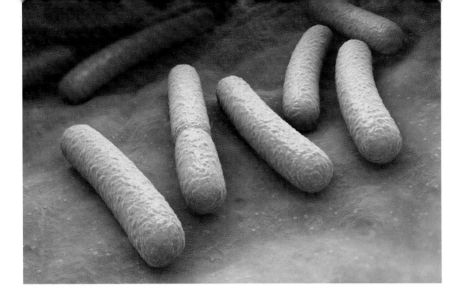

Gut microbes, like certain kinds of *E. coli* bacteria, have important roles in keeping your body healthy.

Microbes to the Rescue

Many types of microbes cause disease. But most of the microbes in our bodies do not. This is a good thing because there are a lot of them in your gut. Scientists estimate that there are 100 trillion microbes living in a person's gut. That is more than 10,000 times the number of people on Earth!

Just what are all these microbes doing? One of their jobs is to help break down the food that you eat, which releases energy. This energy fuels your body's activities. Another job of gut microbes is to make vitamins that you need to stay healthy. They also break down wastes so that it is easier for your body to get rid of them.

So, if gut microbes are so helpful, why do they often get such a bad reputation? You may have heard of *E. coli* outbreaks. They are caused by a kind of *E. coli* microbe that can make you sick. When this kind of *E. coli* gets into food or drinking water, it can make people very sick. This can happen when people fail to wash their hands thoroughly after using the restroom.

Some kinds of *E. coli* can be good for you. One kind of *E. coli* helps your gut. It helps to make certain vitamins. It can also prevent bad bacteria from taking over. Good gut microbes can keep bad microbes from making their home in your gut and getting you sick.

Probiotics are good gut microbes. They change the way food tastes, help preserve it, and provide a source of good bacteria for the gut. You can find probiotics in foods like yogurt and sauerkraut.

The Good Gut Microbes

Many foods and pills have labels that say they contain *probiotics*. Probiotics are microbes you can eat that can act as helpful gut microbes. Sometimes the probiotics you eat are the same kind of gut microbe that you already have. Other times, the probiotics are a little different. Probiotics are like siblings to the gut microbes that already live in your body.

The probiotics might help make vitamins. They also help keep the gut healthy by making it harder for bad microbes to survive there. Probiotics in your gut take up space and prevent bad microbes from living in your gut. They help reduce the number of bad microbes in the gut.

People have used probiotics for a long time. A lot of different foods contain probiotics, like yogurt, sauerkraut, and sourdough bread. People originally added them to food as a way of preserving the food. They added probiotics to plain milk to form yogurt. The yogurt would last longer than milk. Sauerkraut can keep longer than raw cabbage. Sourdough bread can last longer than many other types of bread because of the probiotics.

Today, we know that probiotics do more than keep food fresh. They also keep our bodies healthy.

Best Friends Forever

Probiotics and other gut microbes can help keep you healthy. Many people eat food with probiotics for this reason. They also eat probiotics to prevent bad bacteria from living in the gut. But what if you do not eat food with probiotics? How will you keep your gut healthy?

Babies share their gut microbes with their mother. But it turns out that a family actually shares similar gut microbes! When you are young, your gut microbes are the same as your parents' and siblings' gut microbes. Scientists are not sure how this happens. They think that it might be from touching each other and living with each other.

The microbes you pick up from your parents and siblings might stay with you for your entire life. Scientists have started studying the microbes in a person's gut as they grow older. They take samples of the microbes that live in a person's gut every few months. They found that the microbes did not change over time! The gut microbes you have when you are born can stay with you for your entire life. Bacteria really are some of the best friends you can ever have!

A family has the same types of gut microbes. The mircrobes you pick up from your parents and siblings might stay with you for your entire life.

What Animal Structures Are Used for Support, Movement, and Protection?

Science Vocabulary

bone

exoskeleton

feather

fin

joint

muscle

scale

skeleton

Different animals have different structures that they use for support, protection, and movement. Many animals, such as this deer, have skeletons made of bones inside their bodies. Other animals have exoskeletons, a hard outer shell. Structures called muscles interact with an animal's skeleton for movement. Many animals use movement for protection, by running away from other animals that want to eat them.

 NGSS **4-LS1-1.** Construct an argument that plants and animals have internal and external structures that function to support survival, growth, behavior, and reproduction.

LS1.A. Plants and animals have both internal and external structures that serve various functions in growth, survival, behavior, and reproduction.

Systems and System Models A system can be described in terms of its components and their interactions.

 **Engaging in Argument from Evidence**

1. Bones Make up the Skeleton

If you put your hand on your chest, you can feel hard structures underneath your skin. Those are your ribs, a set of bones inside your body. Why do you and many other animals need bones?

A **bone** is a hard structure inside some animals' bodies. Bones and other structures that provide support to the body make up the **skeleton**. A skeleton also contains *cartilage*, a strong and flexible material. Together, bones and cartilage support an animal's body. The skeleton also helps protect soft parts inside the body. For example, your ribcage protects your heart and lungs.

Many bones make up the skeleton. A backbone is a row of small bones that runs along the inside of these animals' backs. Arms and legs contain long bones. A skull protects the brain inside the animal's head. Smaller bones make up the ribs of the chest. Bones grow and change like other parts of the body. The skeleton also helps these animals move.

Two or more bones come together at a **joint**. Several kinds of joints allow different kinds of movement. For example, the elbow and knee are *hinge joints*. The bones in a hinge joint move back and forth like a door hinge. *Ball and socket joints* in the shoulders and hips let the bones move in a circle.

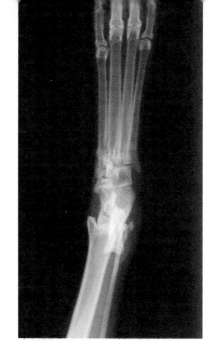

This is an X-ray of a dog's foot. Dogs have many different bones in their bodies, and those bones support their body weight.

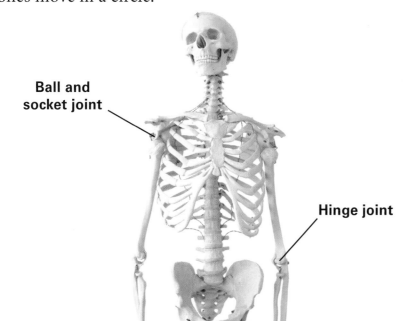

Ball and socket joint

Hinge joint

This is what the skeleton inside your body looks like. Each bone is connected to other bones at joints.

2. Muscles Move Bones

The bones in your arm move to straighten or bend your arm. But bones cannot move by themselves. What structures in animals helps them move?

A **muscle** is a structure that contracts and relaxes to produce movement. When a muscle contracts, it gets shorter. When it relaxes, it gets longer. When a muscle pulls on a bone, it moves. Muscles often work in pairs. When one muscle in a pair contracts and gets shorter, the other muscle in the pair relaxes and gets longer. Muscles work closely with bones to allow animals to move. For example, an animal with legs can walk by contracting and relaxing the muscles attached to its leg bones.

A snake's bones and muscles work together to cause movement. Snakes move in an S-shaped pattern.

You may have watched a snake move. Snakes have no legs, but they move by contracting the muscles on the right side and the left side of their body back and forth. The snake's body first is pulled to the right and then to the left in an S-shaped motion. Each contraction moves the snake forward.

Some muscles in the body are not attached to bones. For example, recall that the heart is made of muscles. When the heart muscles contract, blood is pumped through the body. The muscles in the stomach and throat contract and relax to push food through the body.

Muscles often work in pairs. When one muscle contracts, the other usually relaxes.

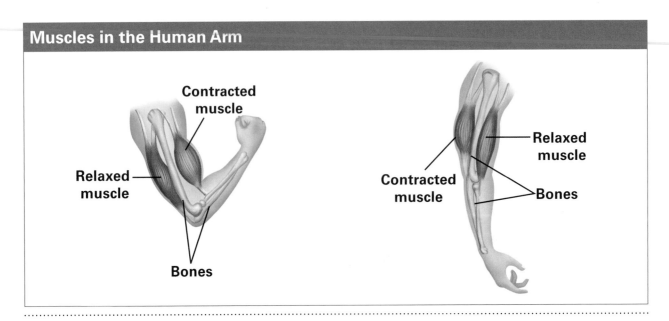

Muscles in the Human Arm

Contracted muscle

Relaxed muscle

Bones

Relaxed muscle

Contracted muscle

Bones

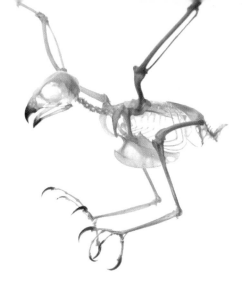

This is a bird's skeleton. Most birds have very flexible, strong, and hollow bones, so they can fly.

3. Bird and Fish Structures for Movement

Birds and fish have muscles, like other animals. But what unique structures do they use to move?

Most birds have unique structures that help them fly. A bird has a skeleton, like you, but its bones are very different. Bones inside a bird's wings are hollow. Hollow bones are very strong and more flexible. Having flexible bones helps keep a bird in the air.

Most birds are also covered in feathers. A **feather** is a lightweight, flat structure that forms the outside covering of a bird's body. Even though they feel soft, feathers are made of the same strong material as your fingernails. They make a bird's body smooth, so it can glide through the air easily. Long tail-feathers help a bird balance and steer.

Fish also have unique structures, but not to fly. Fish have fins and a tail to move through the water. A **fin** is a flattened structure on the outside of a fish. Fins help the fish move, steer, and balance, and the tail fin pushes water to propel the fish forward.

Like birds, fish must also have a smooth body. Most fish are covered with hard, slippery scales. A **scale** is a stiff flattened plate. Many scales together form a protective covering on the outside of a fish. But not all fish have scales. For example, catfish have no scales.

This is a giant clam. Its body is very soft, with no bones. But it is protected and supported by hard, outer shells.

4. Animals Without Backbones Need Support

All the animals you have read about have bony skeletons inside their bodies. But many kinds of animals have no bones. How can an animal support its body without bones?

Land animals without bones cannot grow very large. Many of these boneless animals are insects. Insects have a kind of skeleton, but it is not made of bone, and it is not inside the insect's body. An insect's skeleton, called an **exoskeleton,** is a hard cover and is on the outside of its body. The cover protects the insect's soft body parts and gives it support. Unlike bones, an exoskeleton cannot grow. When an insect gets too big, a new, larger cover forms under the old one. Then the insect sheds the old cover. The new cover is soft at first, but it quickly hardens.

Many animals with no bones live in water, like squid. The water pushes against the animal's body and supports its weight. Other animals have a water-filled structure inside their bodies. The water pushes outward and supports the animal from the inside.

Have you ever seen shells on a beach? The shells are the remains of clams and oysters. Hard shells protect and support their soft bodies and make it harder for other animals to eat them.

This is an insect's exoskeleton. It is the hard outer covering that protects and supports the insect.

This is a snail. Most of its body that you can see in this picture is a muscle, called a foot. It moves by contracting and relaxing its foot.

5. Other Structures Allow Movement

Most animals without bones can still move. They just do not move the way you do.

Insects have six jointed legs, which allow the insect to walk and jump. An insect's muscles are inside its body, and are attached to its exoskeleton. Many insects also have wings and can fly. Muscles move the wings up and down over and over very quickly.

The body of an earthworm contains water-filled structures and muscles throughout the worm's body. When the worm's muscles contract, they pull against the water-filled structures. That part of the worm moves forward. An earthworm also has stiff hairs on the bottom of its body. The hairs attach to a surface so the worm does not slide backwards when it moves forward.

Snails move with a single foot. The foot is a muscle that contracts and relaxes to move the snail forward. A snail also has a structure that produces slime. The slime helps the snail glide along the ground.

Squids and octopuses move in two ways. They crawl along the ocean floor, using the suckers on their eight arms to grab rocks. When a squid needs to move quickly, it pulls water into a structure in its body and then pushes the water out through a tube. The force of the squirting water pushes the squid backward through the water.

This earthworm uses muscles and water-filled structures to move. The water-filled structures work like a skeleton, and the muscles can contract and relax against them to move the worm forward.

There is a pygmy seahorse in this picture. It has pink and white skin, covered with bumps, so it looks very similar to the coral around it. Can you find the seahorse?

6. Animal Structures for Protection

You learned that plants protect themselves with things such as thorns, chemicals, and waxy leaves. But how do you think animals protect themselves?

Many animals protect themselves by moving. If a snake is trying to eat a mouse, that mouse will run away as fast as it can. The mouse's muscles and bones move in ways that protect it from animals like snakes.

Like some plants, other animals protect themselves with chemicals. Some insect caterpillars have structures that produce poisonous or bad-tasting substances. If a bird tries to eat a poisonous caterpillar, it will get sick. That bird will learn not to eat that species of caterpillar.

Some animals have structures that let them hide. For example, a pygmy seahorse has skin that is bumpy, pink, and white. It looks very similar to coral where it lives, so if the seahorse stays still, other fish cannot see it.

Other animals, such as porcupines, have sharp structures on the outside of their bodies for protection, called *quills*. A quill is a type of hair that is hard and sharp. Porcupines are hard to eat because these quills can be very dangerous.

This is a porcupine. Those white and black hairs growing out of its body are sharp quills. If a fox or a wolf tries to eat it, the porcupine will turn its quills toward the attacker to defend itself.

What Animal Structures Are Used for Support, Movement, and Protection?

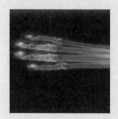

1. Bones Make up the Skeleton   Some animals have a skeleton, or a set of bones, inside their bodies. Bones are hard structures that support the weight of the rest of the body. Bones also protect the soft insides of many animals' bodies.

2. Muscles Move Bones   Animals have muscles attached to their bones. When muscles contract and relax, they move the bones, causing the animal to move.

3. Bird and Fish Structures for Movement   Birds have hollow bones and feathers. Both structures help them fly. Fish have fins that allow them to move quickly and steer through water.

4. Animals Without Backbones Need Support   Animals without bones have other structures for support. Insects have exoskeletons, hard outer coverings that supports their bodies. Clams have hard outer shells.

5. Other Structures Allow Movement   Animals without skeletons have different structures for movement. Insects' muscles are attached to their exoskeletons. Snails move with a single large muscle. Some squids and octopuses move with suckers.

6. Animals Structures for Protection   Most animals move for protection. They move to run away from other animals that want to eat them. Some animals produce poisonous substances or grow sharp quills for protection.

Robo-Motion

Movie robots often look and move just like people. But, of course, many of those movie robots have people inside them! And those people have body structures that let them move. In real life, human-like robots are rare. Why don't most robots move like humans?

Suppose that you had a robot that would do whatever you wanted. What would you have the robot do? Perhaps you would make it do chores like making your bed or washing the dishes. Or maybe you would want it to play with you. It could pitch a softball so you could practice hitting. When most people think of robots, they think of a machine that looks and moves like another person. Real robots rarely do, but it is not from a lack of trying.

Scientists and engineers have been working for years to make robots that move like humans. They have learned that it is not easy. Even seemingly simple motions, such as walking, are hard for a robot. When you walk, your feet and legs move a certain way to help you keep your balance. Your arms move, too. And you shift your weight from side to side with each step. An engineer making a robot walk has to program the robot to make each little movement involved in walking. That is just for a walking on a flat floor. Even more work is needed to make the robot walk on uneven ground or use stairs without tumbling!

Engineers worked for more than ten years to build this robot. It can walk and run like a human.

Robots in Space

Making a robot walk is an interesting challenge for engineers. But teaching a robot to do other things is often more important. After all, you want a robot to *do* something, not just move around. So, one problem engineers are working on is teaching a robot to use its hands like a human.

Having a robot use its hands to do work may seem out of this world—and it is! Robonaut 2, or R2, is a robot made by NASA to help astronauts in space. An R2 robot on the International Space Station can do chores for the astronauts living there.

R2 is shaped like the top half of a person. It has a chest, arms, and a head. But instead of legs, it just has a pole. The pole is long enough to make R2 the height of an average person. Having a robot that is the same size and shape as a person is important. It can use and reach the same controls that a person can.

Although R2 can do tasks just like a person can, it can also do some things better than a human. For one thing, R2 does not need to breathe. So, it can easily do things outside of the Space Station. It also never gets tired or bored when it does the same thing over and over!

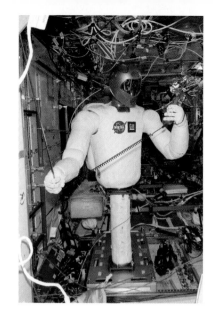

Robonaut 2 uses a tool to check the air inside the International Space Station.

Is that a secret robot handshake? Probably not, but R2 could do one because it has hands just like a human.

The muscles and bones of astronauts who spend a lot of time in space eventually become weak. NASA is designing the X1 to help astronauts exercise. Right now, astronauts in space must exercise by strapping themselves into a bungee harness like this one.

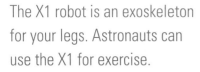

The X1 robot is an exoskeleton for your legs. Astronauts can use the X1 for exercise.

This Robot Has My Back

R2 is not the only robot that NASA is working on. They are also making a robot called X1. The X1 robot does not look like R2 or like a human at all. Instead it is designed to fit onto a person. The robot is made up of a backpack and parts that fit around a person's legs. The parts that fit around the legs give the legs support much like the exoskeleton of an insect.

The X1 can be used in different ways. One way is to help astronauts exercise in space. When astronauts are in space, they do not feel gravity pulling their bodies down. So, the astronaut's muscles and bones do not have to hold the astronauts up. As a result, the muscles and bones of astronauts who spend a lot of time in space eventually become weak.

To keep their bones and muscles strong, astronauts can put on the X1 robot and set it to resist their movements. The astronauts' legs then have to push against the X1 robot. This pushing exercises the leg muscles and bones to keep them healthy. The robot's computer can keep track of how each astronaut is doing and change the exercises as needed. So, the X1 will be like a personal exercise coach for astronauts—one that you wear.

Space-Age Technology on Earth

Of course, getting help from a robot that moves like a human does not require going into space. NASA's X1 robot has a use on Earth. Instead of having the X1 work against the motion of the person wearing it, it can be set to help the person move. The X1 is being tested on people who cannot walk on their own. These people can strap on an X1 and have the robot help them stand up and walk. The robot exoskeleton gives a person's legs the support they need to hold the person's body up. It also acts as muscles to move the person's legs.

Robot designs have improved a lot over the years. But some people would like them to improve faster. So, they started competitions to encourage engineers to spend more time working on robots. One such contest is RoboCup. The overall goal of RoboCup is to design a team of robots that can play against professional soccer players and win. It will still take a long time before robots can beat human athletes. For now, engineers competing in RoboCup must build two or three robots that can play soccer together. The teams of robots that they have designed compete against each other to win.

RoboCup challenges are not just for adults. There is a division for people under 20 years old. Age does not have to stop you from building a prize-winning robot!

Robots can play soccer, but they cannot beat humans . . . yet!

What Animal Structures Are Used for Reproduction?

Science Vocabulary

egg

sperm

Animals have different structures that help them reproduce. Some animals have structures that help them find and attract a mate. This frog has an air sack under its mouth that will help it make sounds to attract a mate. Animals also have structures that help them reproduce. Male and female animals have different structures that interact to produce offspring. Finally, some animals have structures that help their offspring grow and develop. These different structures all work together to help an animal reproduce successfully.

NGSS

4-LS1-1. Construct an argument that plants and animals have internal and external structures that function to support survival, growth, behavior, and reproduction.

LS1.A. Plants and animals have both internal and external structures that serve various functions in growth, survival, behavior, and reproduction.

Systems and System Models A system can be described in terms of its components and their interactions.

Engaging in Argument from Evidence

1. Structures for Finding and Choosing a Mate

When a male firefly needs to find a mate, he uses a structure on his body that produces light. He flashes the light in a specific pattern that a female of the same species will recognize. She responds with similar flashes, and the male flies to her.

Many animals have structures inside their bodies that produce substances for attracting a mate. For example, many female moths release substances that male moths can detect. This helps the moths find mates.

Some animals have structures used to make sounds that attract a mate. Woodpeckers use their beaks to drum on tree trunks in specific patterns of sound. Some male beetles rub parts of their bodies together to make a squeaking sound that attracts females.

Several males of one species may attract the same female. How does she decide which one to choose? Most females are attracted to structures on the males. For example, male peacocks have a beautiful tail that they display to an interested female. The best looking tail usually belongs to the male that is healthiest and will make the best mate. Some male frogs have large red throat pouches. The frog with the biggest pouch is probably the healthiest male and the best mate. Other male animals have horns or antlers on their heads. Males may use them to fight other males or to attract a female.

Fireflies have a structure that gives off light in a pattern. Female and male fireflies recognize the pattern and can find each other to mate.

These male deer are fighting with their antlers. Many species of deer do this to attract females.

This female frog just laid hundreds of eggs in the water. Soon, a male frog will spread sperm over the eggs, fertilizing them.

2. Structures for Reproduction

When you read about plants, you learned that reproduction takes place when a male structure and a female structure combine in a cone or a flower. A very similar process happens in animals.

Animals Form Sperm and Eggs

Like plants, animals make male and female structures, too. A male structure is called a **sperm**. Sperm are made in body parts inside a male animal. A female structure is called an **egg**.

Fertilization

When a sperm and an egg meet, they combine. The egg is now *fertilized*. The fertilized egg develops into a new baby animal. Two parents are needed for reproduction in most animals—a male father to produce sperm and a female mother to produce eggs.

Fertilization can take place either outside or inside the mother's body. Female frogs lay eggs in the water where they live. A male spreads sperm over the eggs in the water, and the eggs are fertilized. The fertilized eggs develop into offspring that live in water during the early part of their lives. Insects, lizards, snakes, birds, and deer are all animals in which the eggs are fertilized inside the female's body. The male places sperm in the female, where they can combine with the egg.

Development

A fertilized egg can develop either outside or inside the mother's body. Birds and most reptiles lay eggs with a shell. Bird eggs have hard shells. Most reptiles lay eggs with soft, leathery shells. A shell protects the egg and keeps it from drying out while it is outside the mother's body. When the offspring can live outside the egg, it cracks open the shell and climbs out. In most mammals, such as dogs and mice, the fertilized egg develops in a structure inside the mother's body. When the offspring can live outside its mother, it is born. A few snakes and fish also give birth to live offspring.

Animals Without Skeletons

You have read that many animals without bones live in water. They also reproduce there. Eggs are laid in the water and are fertilized by sperm. Earthworms and some other land animals have both male and female structures in the same animal. Each worm makes both eggs and sperm but they cannot combine with each other. A second worm is needed. Both worms make eggs that are fertilized by the other worm's sperm. Thus, two worms can produce twice as many offspring than they could if each worm was either male or female.

Many animals, like most reptiles, lay eggs. These snake eggs are soft and leathery. If you look closely, you can see two snakes hatching out of the eggs.

Some animals care for their offspring. Kangaroo babies are cared for in their mother's pouch. The mother provides milk inside the pouch so the baby can eat and grow.

3. Structures for Taking Care of Offspring

Have you ever seen a baby human crawling down the sidewalk alone? Of course not! Adult humans take care of their young.

Animals differ in how much they care for their young. Many animals whose eggs are fertilized in water do not take care of their offspring at all. For example, fish and frogs usually produce large numbers of eggs because only a few offspring survive. So, a frog or fish might lay hundreds or thousands of eggs, but only a few live to become adults.

Animals whose eggs are fertilized in the mother's body make fewer eggs, but the offspring are often cared for until they can live on their own. For example, birds and reptiles lay their eggs in nests that the parents build, and most birds take care of their offspring after the eggs hatch. Most reptiles do not. Most bird parents find food and feed their young. They also protect their offspring and keep them warm.

Mammals feed their young with milk that the mother produces from her body. Rabbits, cats, and mice are examples of mammals. After they are born, kangaroo babies crawl into a pouch. A pouch is a structure on the front of their mothers' body. Milk is provided in the pouch so they can develop and grow.

Some fish can lay hundreds or thousands of eggs. Each orange tube is one fish egg. Many will be eaten and, of the offspring that hatch, most will not survive.

What Animal Structures Are Used for Reproduction?

1. Structures for Finding and Choosing a Mate   Before animals reproduce, they need to find mates. Different animals have different structures to find and attract mates. Some animals produce flashing lights. Some animals make specific sounds. Still others may have colorful feathers. Some male animals fight to attract a female.

2. Structures for Reproduction   Reproduction in most animals requires a male and a female. A male animal produces structures called sperm, and a female animal produces structures called eggs. When a sperm and egg combine, the fertilized egg can grow into a new animal.

3. Structures for Taking Care of Offspring   Only some animals take care of their offspring after they are born. Those animals usually have special structures to help them. Mammals, like cats and mice, have structures to produce milk to feed their offspring. Other animals will also feed their offspring until they can find food on their own.

Vet Tech

In the wild, animals take care of themselves. But pets depend on people to stay healthy. Pet owners do most of the work themselves. But sometimes they need help from an expert. What is it like to take care of animals as your job?

Amy hears the alarm go off. Time to get up! Amy must walk the Wus' three dogs before her job at the animal clinic. While at the clinic, Amy will tend to many other pets. After work, she will tend to her own two cats. A lot of different animals will depend on her today!

Amy loves her job because she gets to work with animals every day. She has wanted to work with animals since she was a young child. After graduating from high school, Amy enrolled in a program that teaches people how to care for animals in a veterinarian's office or an animal hospital. After two years of studying and taking classes, she had to take a test. After passing the test, Amy earned a certificate that shows she is trained to be a veterinary technician, or vet tech.

When a pet arrives at a clinic, a vet tech collects and writes down information about its health. Here, a vet tech is helping a family fill out information about their pet.

As a vet tech, Amy works under a veterinarian, or animal doctor. When a pet arrives at the clinic, Amy collects and writes down information about its health. She weighs the pet and may take the pet's temperature. Next, she helps to perform medical tests. These duties may include helping to collect blood and urine for testing. Amy may take the pet's blood pressure. She may help to take and develop X-rays.

A vet tech may work in an animal clinic. Being kind to pets and their owners is an important part of the job.

After the vet has determined what treatment is needed, Amy may help give the pets medicine. Amy will explain to pet owners how to take care of their pets and give medicines at home.

Amy will assist the vet if the pet needs surgery. An animal might swallow something dangerous like a bottle cap and need surgery to have the object removed. Amy prepares the animals and instruments. She also monitors the pet after surgery.

Some pets require ongoing care at home. Amy visits pets at home, too. Treatments at home are often less stressful for the pet. Amy gives medicine and shots when they are needed.

Vet techs help perform medical tests, such as taking and developing X-rays. Once an X-ray is developed, a vet-tech will study it to help animals get better.

Amy works in a clinic. But some vet techs work in labs, hospitals, shelters, or kennels. No matter where they work, one thing that all vet techs share is a love for animals. A vet tech must be gentle with the pet and kind to its worried owner. The ability to communicate well with the vet and other staff is important, too.

When you love animals like Amy does, being a vet tech is more than just a way to earn a living. A friendly lick or a purr from a grateful pet is her biggest reward!

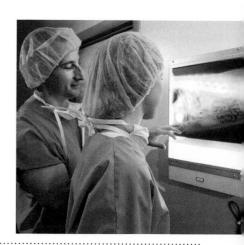

What Animal Structures Are Used for Sensing the Environment?

Science Vocabulary

antenna

ear

eardrum

eye

sense receptor

taste bud

Animals have many different structures, such as eyes, ears, and mouths. They can be used to sense things like light, sound, touch, and substances in their environment. These structures work together to give an animal information about its surroundings. If a human has problems with their structures that sense their surroundings, engineers can sometimes design solutions to enable them to see or hear better.

 NGSS

4-PS4-2. Develop a model to describe that light reflecting from objects and entering the eye allows objects to be seen.
4-LS1-2. Use a model to describe that animals receive different types of information through their senses, process the information in their brain, and respond to the information in different ways.

PS4.B. An object can be seen when light reflected from its surface enters the eyes.
LS1.D. Different sense receptors are specialized for particular kinds of information, which may be then processed by the animal's brain. Animals are able to use their perceptions and memories to guide their actions.

Cause and Effect Cause and effect relationships are routinely identified.
Systems and System Models A system can be described in terms of its components and their interactions.

 **Developing and Using Models**

1. Sense Organs Detect Stimuli

Have you ever watched a snail? It waves two long stalks as it glides along. How do you think those stalks help it survive?

Snails do not have the same sense organs humans do, but they can still sense similar things. At the end of each stalk is an eye that senses changes in light. Two short stalks detect smells. Light and smells are *stimuli*, a word that means more than one stimulus.

An animal detects stimuli with **sense receptors,** structures that can detect information about the environment. There are many types of stimuli. Light, sound, smells, and touch are some examples. Different animals can detect different stimuli. For example, dogs can hear sounds that humans cannot.

Sense receptors detect stimuli from both inside and outside the body. A receptor detecting the substances in a rat's blood might tell the rat that it needs more water or food. Other receptors collect data about the outside of the body. They are specialized for sensing different kinds of stimuli. All these receptors work together in a system that gives an animal information about its environment. A bee has receptors that detect the color of a flower. Receptors in the skin detect pressure that an animal feels as touch. Other receptors in the skin sense pain and heat.

Animals have structures for sensing different kinds of stimuli. A snail has stalks on its head to detect light and scents.

This bee has sense receptors that detect flower color. It knows to look for brightly colored flowers and to ignore other parts of a plant.

2. Structures for Detecting Sound

Think of some very loud sounds, like a rock concert. And think of some quiet sounds, like a whisper. How do you and other animals sense sound?

Many animals have ears. An **ear** is a sense organ that contains receptors for detecting sound. The outer ear, the part that you can see, collects sound. The sound travels into the ear and vibrates the *eardrum*. The **eardrum** is a thin elastic membrane in the ear. The vibrations then go to three tiny bones in the middle ear that magnify the sound. Finally, they go to the inner ear. A coil-shaped structure in the inner ear contains tiny hairs with receptors that detect vibration.

Many animals hear sounds using organs similar to your ears. Frogs have eardrums on each side of their heads. Insects, such as grasshoppers, have different structures for detecting sound on their legs or other parts of their body. In each case, the animal's sound receptors are part of these structures.

Animals detect sounds with different kinds of structures. An **antenna** is a long, stalk-shaped sense organ on the head of an insect. Each antenna on a mosquito's head has tiny hairs with sound receptors. These receptors detect sounds when the hairs vibrate. Other receptors on the antenna detect smells.

This is a mosquito. Those thin hairs on each antenna can detect sound. That helps the mosquito avoid predators and find animals to bite.

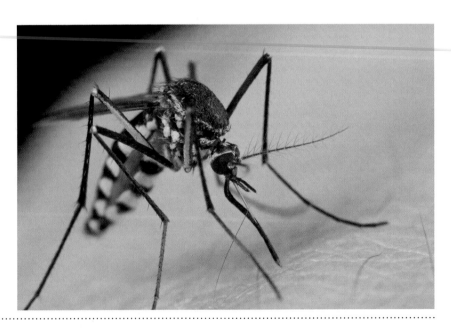

The whiskers on a lion connect to receptors that can detect moving air. This helps lions hunt in the dark.

3. Structures That Are Sensitive to Touch

If you touch a hot stove, you will be glad that your skin contains sense receptors. Heat and pain receptors detect these stimuli. You jerk your hand away so that you do not get burned.

Different kinds of receptors in skin detect touch, pain, heat, and cold. They keep you from being hurt because they alert you to danger. The number of each kind of receptor varies with the part of the body. For example, the skin on your fingertips has many more touch receptors than the skin on your back does.

An animal senses touch when something pushes on its body. Touch receptors respond to pressure changes. The skin at the base of whiskers and other hairs contains touch receptors. They detect air moving near the animal's body. Cats, lions, and tigers use their whiskers to feel their way around in the dark. Their whiskers detect other animals nearby. This helps them to hunt in the dark.

Insects have touch receptors in structures on their bodies and on each antenna. For example, crickets have two large pointy structures at the back of their bodies. These structures detect air movement caused by animals that might want to eat the crickets.

Snakes have structures to detect substances in the air. Their tongue gathers substances in the air and presses those substances into its mouth so that it can detect food and enemies.

4. Structures for Detecting Substances

Your senses of smell and taste depend on sense receptors in your nose and on your tongue. Receptors in your nose detect substances in the air. Receptors on your tongue and nose detect substances in food.

All animals have receptors that sense substances. They are found in snail stalks, octopus arms, insect antennae and mouthparts, insect legs, and fish fins.

Many animals have *taste buds* on their tongues. A **taste bud** is a structure that has sense receptors for taste. These receptors allow an animal to taste sweet, sour, salty, and bitter substances. Taste buds are located on and around the small bumps on the tongue. An animal must have a sense of taste so that it knows what foods are safe to eat.

The sense of smell is important to animals that hunt for food. Snakes do not have noses, but they can smell using their tongues. The tongue gathers substances in the air and passes them to receptors in a smell organ inside the snake's mouth.

Bears have the sharpest sense of smell of any animal. They have large noses that contain thousands of smell receptors. These receptors detect smells in the air that let them find food. In addition, bears have the same sense organ in the roof of their mouths that snakes have.

Bears have a very good sense of smell. They smell both with their noses and structures like those of snakes.

Almost all animals can detect light. This hummingbird has eyes that are very sensitive to red, orange, and purple. This helps it find flowers with nectar it can eat.

5. Structures for Detecting Light

Suppose there was no light in the world. You and other animals would not be able to see anything. How does light help you see?

Most of the kinds of animals you know of have eyes. An **eye** is a sense organ that contains light receptors. Animals that hunt for food, such as eagles and wolves, must have very sharp eyesight so that they can clearly see other animals they want to eat. Hummingbirds are attracted to red, orange, and purple flowers. Their eyes have receptors that can detect these colors because these flowers are rich in the nectar the birds drink for food.

Other kinds of animals that have no eyes can still sense light. These animals use simple structures called *eyespots*. Eyespots are not eyes, but they contain light receptors. Sea stars have an eyespot at the tip of each of their arms. The eyespots allow the sea star to sense shadows and changes in light brightness. Animals with eyespots cannot see objects.

Some animals have light receptors in their skin. Earthworms must live in soil, which is dark and moist. A worm avoids light because its skin would dry out if it were not in soil. If the worm's skin senses light, the worm will respond by moving away from the light toward the dark.

This sea star doesn't have any eyes, but it can still detect light. It has eyespots at the end of each arm. They can detect light brightness.

Animals can only see objects that have light reflected off of them. Owls cannot see their prey without at least small amounts of light.

 Nature of Science

6. Scientists Studying Light

When you look around your classroom, what objects can you see? How do you think you can see them?

Objects Reflect Light

Light coming from an object and entering your eyes is what causes the object to be seen. Light can *reflect* off of an object, like a ball can bounce off a wall. Light comes from a light source, such as the sun or the light bulb in your classroom. The light travels from that light source to different objects, such as books, desks, and pencils. The light bounces off those objects and into your eye.

When there is more light coming from an object, you can see it more clearly. That is why when you go outside in the middle of the day you can see trees, other students, and buildings very clearly. But at night there is much less light. If you are outside at night you cannot see objects very well. If you are ever in a room with no light, you could not see any objects.

No matter what kind of eye an animal has, it can only see objects if light is reflecting from them. Birds such as owls can see very well in the dark. But they still cannot see if there is no light at all. They hunt at night because there is still enough light from the moon and stars.

You have now learned that to see an object, light has to bounce off of it. When you are in a dark room, you cannot see well. If you turn on a light, you can see the objects in the room.

Scientists Study Light

How do you think scientists figured out that this is true for all objects on Earth? Scientists have not shined a flashlight on every object in the world. That would take way too long! Instead, science assumes that if one thing is true in one place, it is true everywhere. Scientists assume that the basic laws of nature are the same everywhere in the universe.

That means that some scientists studied how light bounces off objects. Other scientists studied how our eyes work. Now, scientists assume that if we can see an object, light is bouncing off of it or coming from it.

The same is true for other animals. Scientists have not studied every animal's eye. But they assume that other animals can only detect objects if light is coming from them.

Whenever scientists discover something that is different from what they assume, they change their explanations. That means that if scientists ever found an animal that had an eye that worked differently, they would change their assumptions about how animals see.

These three eyes are from three different animals— a cat, a frog, and a fly. Though the eyes are very different, scientists assume that they all sense reflected light.

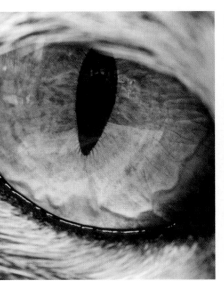  

7. Engineering Sense Organs

You may have some friends that cannot hear. Maybe some members of your family cannot see well. Do any of them use tools to help them hear or see better?

Engineers have designed many different tools that help people see and hear better. One of the most common examples is eyeglasses. You probably know someone who wears glasses. People who need glasses cannot see very well without them. Everything is blurry. But with glasses, they can see very well.

Over time, engineers have made glasses better and better. Hundreds of years ago glasses were heavy, and did not work very well. Now, engineers have tested many different types of glasses and designed pairs that can fix most vision problems.

Engineers identified the problem of bad eyesight and developed solutions to fix it. Other solutions include contact lenses and even laser eye surgery that changes the shape of the eye. These are all different solutions for the same problem.

Engineers have also done this with hearing aids. Hearing aids are tools that help people hear better. There are many different kinds of hearing aids, but most go inside the ear.

Engineers test many different solutions for poor vision. This engineer is making a new lens for a pair of glasses.

What Animal Structures Are Used for Sensing the Environment?

1. Sense Organs Detect Stimuli   Animals have many different sense receptors. These sense receptors detect different stimuli in their environments.

2. Structures for Detecting Sound   Sense receptors for sound can feel the vibrations that sound makes. An ear and an antenna are examples of organs used to sense sounds.

3. Structures That Are Sensitive to Touch   Many animals have sense receptors for touch. In humans, these are located on the skin over the whole body. In addition, some animals have whiskers which are very sensitive to touch.

4. Structures for Detecting Substances   Animals have receptors that can sense different substances in the air or their food. In humans these senses are called smell and taste. Snakes gather substances on their tongues and bring the substances to a receptor in their mouths.

5. Structures for Detecting Light   Almost all animals have receptors for detecting light. Some animals are able to see light in detail and many different colors. Other animals can simply detect whether they are in the light or in shadow.

6. Scientists Studying Light   Scientists discovered that objects that do not produce light can only be seen when light bounces off of them and travels into an eye. They studied several animals and used the laws of nature to reach this discovery about all animals on Earth.

7. Engineering Sense Organs   Some people's sense receptors for light and sound do not work very well. Engineers can sometimes design solutions that help people see and hear better. These include eyeglasses, contact lenses, and hearing aids.

Super Senses

A bee zooms toward a flower, wings buzzing. Faster than you can blink, it lands right on target—in the middle of the flower! It can't be luck, because the bee does the same thing flower after flower. It makes you wonder: does the bee see something you can't see?

You have various sense structures that allow you to detect light, sound, smell, and touch. You can see the words on this page. At school, you can hear the bell ring and smell food cooking in the cafeteria. On a windy day, you can feel a breeze on your face.

Many animals sense things that humans cannot. Have you ever observed a dog raise its head and become suddenly alert when it seems there is no reason to? You do not hear anything, but the dog does. After a couple of minutes, you hear the doorbell ring. The dog predicted the arrival of the visitor, because it was able to hear footsteps from a long way off. The dog sensed something that you could not.

A bee also senses something that you cannot. When you glance at a flower, the first thing you notice might be its bright yellow petals. However, a bee sees the center of the flower as a dark area that stands out from the rest of the flower. This ability helps the bee to find the center of the flower quickly every time.

Humans see this flower as it appears on the left. Bees might see the same flower as it appears on the right.

Reindeer can see UV light. This ability lets them get around in the frozen Arctic and find food.

The Eyes Have It

What allows the bee to see the flower the way it does? The answer is: the bee can see ultraviolet, or UV, light, a type of light humans cannot see. UV light makes the dark markings in the flower's center stand out. These dark markings are called "nectar guides." They guide the bee to the nectar located at the flower's center. Nectar is food for bees.

How do scientists know that bees can see UV light? Scientists showed bees different colors next to food sources. Then scientists took away the food and the bees flew toward the colors they could see trying to find the food.

Bees are not the only animals that see UV light. The ability to see UV light helps butterflies find mates. Butterflies recognize mates by patterns on their wings, which stand out in UV light. In birds, detecting UV light helps them to recognize the patterns on their eggs.

Reindeer live in the Arctic where the ground is white with snow most of the year. Their ability to see UV light allows them to see any unevenness in the land. Thus, the land doesn't look like one vast white sheet to them. This ability helps them get around without becoming lost. The ability to see UV light also lets them find food that might otherwise blend in with the environment.

Birds travel thousands of miles to meet their needs. They use Earth's magnetic field to find their way.

Animal Magnetism

It is one thing to have more sensitivity in one of the five senses. It is another to have an extra sense beyond those that humans have. Many different kinds of animals have a sixth sense that allows them to sense magnetic fields. These animals have to travel long distances to meet their needs. Birds fly thousands of miles from their nesting grounds in the north to their warm winter homes in the south. Sea turtles swim thousands of miles from their nesting grounds to their feeding grounds and back. While on these long trips, the animals use Earth's magnetic field to find their way.

Scientists are now working to find out how this sense works. Scientists studied the noses of trout, a kind of fish. They noticed that there was something in the nose that would respond to magnets! They used microscopes to look really closely at parts of the nose. They discovered that these parts were shiny. What could be making these parts of the nose shiny? The scientists discovered that there was a material that was rich in iron, a metal that can be pulled by a magnet.

This material is most likely what allows trout to sense Earth's magnetic field. Scientists are not sure exactly how. So, they are doing more experiments to get to the bottom of this mystery.

My, What Big Ears You Have

Some humans have excellent hearing, yet, many animals hear things that no person ever could. Dogs, of course, can hear sounds that are too high-pitched for your ears. What other animals have better hearing than you do?

Bats make sounds that are too high-pitched for people to hear, though the bats can hear them just fine. In fact, they use this super hearing to find things at night. The high-pitch sounds bats make bounce off objects and back to the bat's ears. The returning sounds tell the bat where things are located. This method of finding things is called *echolocation*. Using echolocation, bats can find their way in the dark. Bats also use echolocation to find insects, their favorite food.

Whales use sound to communicate with each other and find their way around in the sea. It helps that sound travels five times faster underwater than in air. Also, whales make low-pitched sounds, which can travel farther than high-pitched sounds. Thus, whales can communicate very long distances by sound. Like bats, many whales use echolocation to find their way around.

Too bad you aren't a whale, because echolocation could help keep you from stubbing your toe in the middle of the night. Of course, if you were a whale, you wouldn't have toes to stub!

Bats can hear sounds that are very high-pitched. Whales can hear very low-pitched sounds. Both use echolocation to help them find their way around.

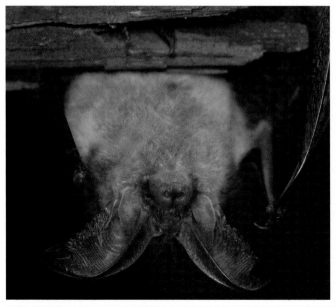

How Do Animals Respond to Their Environment?

Science Vocabulary

behavior

brain

instinct

memory

nerve

reflex

spinal cord

You may have seen birds flying to warmer areas during winter. Why do birds migrate as seasons change? Most animals, like birds, respond to their environment as they receive signals from it. Sometimes they respond quickly, and other times they respond more slowly. You will learn why some responses take longer than others.

4-LS1-2. Use a model to describe that animals receive different types of information through their senses, process the information in their brain, and respond to the information in different ways.

LS1.D. Different sense receptors are specialized for particular kinds of information, which may be then processed by the animal's brain. Animals are able to use their perceptions and memories to guide their actions.

Systems and System Models A system can be described in terms of its components and their interactions.

Developing and Using Models

1. The Brain Controls the Body's Activities

Suppose a wolf sees a deer. Its eyes send messages to its brain, and the brain responds by sending messages to the rest of its body. The wolf chases the deer, pounces, and brings down its prey.

An animal can respond to stimuli because its sense organs work closely with its brain. The **brain** is the organ that is the control center of the body. The brain is very important, so it is protected by bones that make up the wolf's skull. Messages travel from the sense organs to the brain. The brain interprets them and sends messages to the muscles that tells them how to respond.

Wolf brains have three main parts. Each part has its own functions. The largest part of the brain is the *cerebrum*. It controls muscles in body parts that the wolf wants to move, such as its legs or jaws. This part of the brain also controls memory, learning, and thinking. Information from the sense organs goes here.

The second part of the brain controls the wolf's balance. It is called the *cerebellum*. It also lets the wolf stand up and walk around without needing to think about it.

The third part of the brain, the *brain stem*, controls all the functions the wolf's body needs to stay alive, such as breathing and digesting food. The wolf does not have to think about these functions. They happen automatically.

This wolf is standing up and breathing. Its cerebellum and brain stem control these actions so the wolf does not have to think about them.

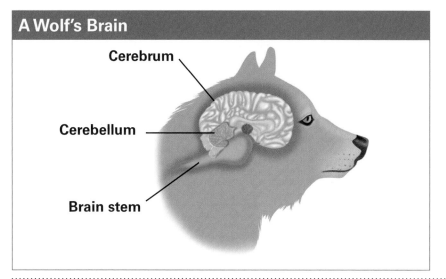

A Wolf's Brain

Cerebrum

Cerebellum

Brain stem

A wolf's brain is very similar to yours. Different parts of its brain control different activities.

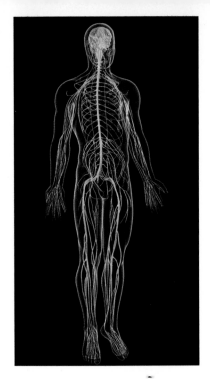

This is a human nervous system. Nerves run throughout the whole body, so the brain can receive and send messages to every part of the body.

2. Nerves and the Spinal Cord

Since a wolf's brain controls its body, how do you think it sends messages to the muscles? How does it receive messages from sense organs?

A **nerve** is a structure that carries messages from one part of the body to another. Some nerves carry messages from sense organs to the *spinal cord* and brain. Other nerves carry messages from the brain and spinal cord to muscles.

The **spinal cord** is a long bundle of nerves that ties the brain to the rest of the body. It runs inside the backbone, which protects it. Many nerves branch off from the spinal cord. The nerves, spinal cord, and brain are all parts of the *nervous system*.

The nervous system helps animals react to stimuli, such as when a wolf hunts a deer. Receptors in the sense organs collect stimuli from the environment. Nerves carry messages from the wolf's sense organs to its brain and spinal cord. If a wolf smells a deer, nerves carry a message about the deer to the wolf's brain. Other nerves then carry messages from the wolf's brain and spinal cord to its legs. The messages tell the leg muscles to move the legs toward the deer. Then the brain sends messages to the wolf's jaw muscles to bite the deer. The wolf's nervous system and muscles work together to hunt the deer.

A wolf's nervous system is composed of its brain, spinal cord, and nerves. The brain can send and receive messages from the whole body.

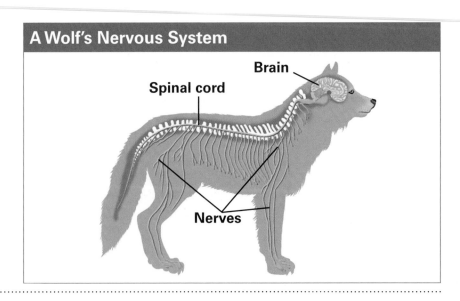

A Wolf's Nervous System

Brain

Spinal cord

Nerves

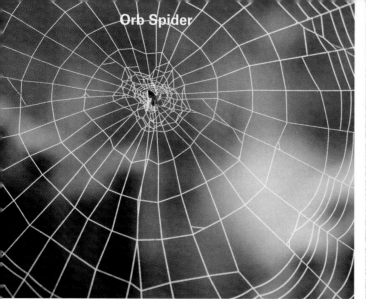

Orb Spider

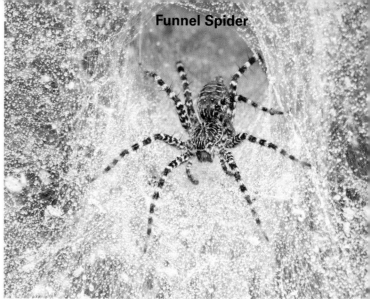

Funnel Spider

3. Instincts

If someone throws a ball at you, you react without thinking. Your body knows what to do to keep you from getting hurt.

Behavior is the way an animal acts. A behavior can be a response to a stimulus, such as hunting for food when hungry. Most behaviors that help an animal survive do not have to be learned. A behavior that an animal is born knowing how to do is called an **instinct**. For example, a mouse is born knowing how to run away from a snake. The mouse also knows that it should eat fruit and insects, even if it has never seen them before.

Many birds are born with the instinct of knowing that they should fly to warmer areas when it gets cold outside. Ducks living in Canada are born knowing they should fly south when it starts getting cold, even if it is their first winter.

Many spiders spin webs to trap insects. Each kind of web-spinning spider spins a web with a different shape. A funnel spider spins a web that is shaped like a tube. An orb spider's web has circles with lines crossing them. Each spider knows how to build only one type of web, and they know how to build this web when they are born—it is an instinct.

Spiders are born with the instinct of knowing how to spin one type of web. A funnel spider spins a funnel-shaped web and an orb spider spins a round web. Neither spider can spin the other's kind of web.

4. Reflexes

All instincts involve the brain. Sense receptors pick up stimuli from the surroundings. They send messages to the brain. The brain must figure out each message before sending a message to the muscles. This process takes time.

But not all behaviors involve the brain. A **reflex** is a behavior that does not involve the brain. Many reflexes keep animals out of danger. For example, if someone throws a ball at your face, you blink. Blinking is a reflex that protects your eyes. Your brain is not involved in blinking. Another common reflex is sneezing. Reflexes are usually simpler than instincts.

How does a reflex work? If you touch a hot object with your hand, heat and pain receptors in your skin detect the stimuli. The receptors send messages to the spinal cord. The spinal cord quickly sends a message to your arm muscles, and you pull your hand away. Because the messages do not have to be processed in the brain, a reflex is much faster than an instinct. A reflex occurs before the brain is aware of what happened. Your brain learns of the movement of your hand after the response takes place. However, your brain cannot control the movement.

When you touch a hot object, a reflex moves your hand. Your receptors in the skin send a message about the object to your spinal cord, which sends a message to your arm muscles to move your hand back.

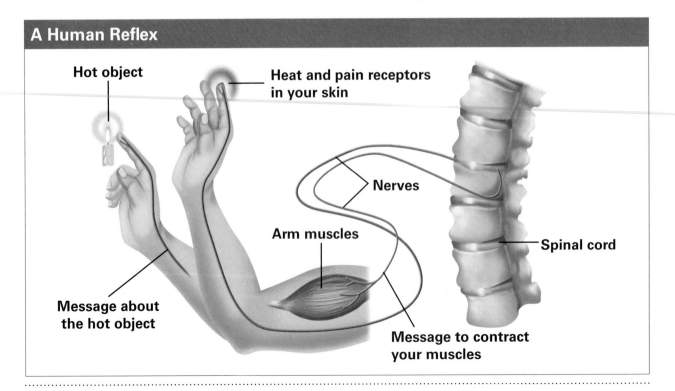

A Human Reflex

Hot object

Heat and pain receptors in your skin

Nerves

Arm muscles

Spinal cord

Message about the hot object

Message to contract your muscles

5. Learned Behavior

When you were young and first held a book, you could not read the words. It took a long time before you learned to read. You had to practice before you could read as well as you do now. Reading is a learned behavior.

Many behaviors and responses have to be learned and practiced. Baby chimpanzees are born with few skills. As the baby chimpanzee grows and develops, it must learn how to find food and feed itself. It must learn how to take care of itself. It learns how to use a rock as a hammer to break open nuts and how to use a stick to dig insects out of the ground.

Both you and the chimpanzee learn by watching others or by being taught. A teacher probably taught you how to read in school. You learned how to read from the teacher. You probably learned other skills from your parents or friends. Learning happens in the brain.

Animals must practice a learned behavior until they can do it well. For example, young tigers practice sneaking up on prey. They learn from their parents to be good hunters. Animals can also learn by trial and error. A mouse in a maze makes many wrong turns before it learns the right path out of the maze. Next time, it goes through the maze faster because the mouse has done it before.

This chimp is using a stick as a tool. It learned how to use this tool from its parents.

This salmon has spent many years living in the ocean, but it still remembers where it hatched. When it is older, it returns to the very same river where it hatched.

6. Memory

Have you ever seen a mouse in a maze? Each time the mouse goes through the maze, it can solve it faster. Why do you think that is?

Each time an animal senses something, it forms a memory. Each time an animal does something, it also forms a memory. **Memory** is any information stored in the brain. For example, animals might remember what a plant smells like. They might also remember where they like to hunt. Forming and using memories is very complicated. Many structures work together to make memories, like the brain and other structures of the nervous system.

When an animal repeats the same behavior, it is forming stronger memories. The behavior improves with each practice. For example, a baby lion is not very good at hunting. But every day, the lion practices hunting. Soon, it has hunted many times. Each time it went hunting, it used its memories to become a better hunter.

Some animals can remember exactly where they hatched, even then they are old. For example, Pacific salmon are born in rivers near the ocean. When they are a few years old, they swim to the ocean. As adults, the salmon return to the exact same river where they hatched. Salmon can remember exactly what the river they were born in smells like!

How Do Animals Respond to Their Environment?

1. The Brain Controls the Body's Activities   Many animals have brains that are divided into different parts. Each part controls different functions. Some parts control actions such as walking and biting, while others control actions such as breathing.

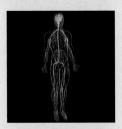

2. Nerves and the Spinal Cord   Messages throughout the body are transported by nerves. Nerves send messages from sensory receptors to the brain, and those receptors send messages from the brain to muscles throughout the body.

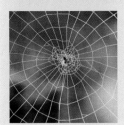

3. Instincts   Behavior is the way an animal acts. Instincts are behaviors that animals are born knowing how to do, like spiders spinning their own kind of web. That is an instinct. These behaviors help an animal survive and do not have to be learned.

4. Reflexes   Reflexes are responses that happen without involving the brain. They are an automatic response to some stimuli that happen very quickly. Blinking and sneezing are examples of reflexes. Many reflexes keep animals out of danger.

5. Learned Behavior   Animals are able to learn different behaviors. Some animals learn behaviors from their parents or other members of their species. Sometimes animals learn from trial and error. Animals must practice a learned behavior to do it well.

6. Memory   Animals can form memories of behaviors they do and of stimuli in their environments. Animals use these memories to perform the same behaviors over and over and to find the same stimuli in their environments.

Elephant Smarts

One important way that animals respond to their environment is through learning. Elephants are no exception. In fact, they are quite intelligent. What can elephants learn to do?

A female elephant steps into a river. She dips her trunk into the water and lifts it up over her head. She blows out a stream of water, spraying her back until it is completely wet. Next to her, a baby elephant follows her example. Ah, that feels good! What's next, Mom?

Baby elephants are not born knowing how to take a bath. Instead, they learn important life skills from the adults around them. Elephants must learn how to use their trunks, find food and water, and get along with each other.

Elephants live for about 60 years. They grow up in families that have 2 to 25 members. Elephant families consist largely of female elephants and have female leaders. A family includes a mother, her babies, her grown daughters, her sisters, and her aunts. Sisters and aunts help bring up the babies. When the babies are grown, females stay with their families while male elephants leave when they are 12 to 15 years old. The male elephants join a group of other males and only come together with females when it is time to mate. There is so much for an elephant to learn during its entire life that it never stops learning!

Come on in! The water's fine! A mother elephant leads her baby into a river to bathe.

Hand Me That Screwdriver

Having a trunk is handy, but only if you know how to use it. Elephants spend their days searching for food and water. They eat grass, roots, leaves, and fruit. To become as large as they are, elephants must eat a lot. To do that, they must learn to use their trunks. A baby elephant begins to practice using its trunk when it is about four months old. It watches other elephants use their trunks and copies what they do. It takes a lot of practice because a trunk is long and has more than 100,000 muscles.

An elephant can use its trunk like you use your arm and hand. Elephants use their trunks to dig holes and find water. If the elephant wants to come back to the hole later, it might use its trunk to rip bark off a tree and chew it into the shape of a ball. Then it uses the ball to cover the water hole and save the water and save the water. Later, the elephant may return to the water hole for another drink.

Elephants are master tool users—only they don't have hands, so they must use their trunks. Elephants sometimes use sticks as tools. An elephant might use its trunk to pick up a stick to scratch its itchy back with. Elephants have even been seen dropping rocks onto electric fences to break them and shut off the electricity!

An elephant can use its flexible trunk to grasp objects. This baby elephant is learning to use its trunk.

This young elephant is trumpeting. Elephants can communicate through sounds like trumpeting and rumbling.

Ready to Rumble

Another important skill elephants must learn is how to communicate with one another. They communicate by sound, sight, smell, and touch.

Have you ever heard an elephant trumpeting? It sure is loud! Elephants make other kinds of sounds, too, many of which are low-pitched rumbles. An elephant rumble can travel through the ground, much like an earthquake wave. The rumbles allow elephants to communicate with each other over very long distances.

An elephant can communicate visually by holding its head and ears a certain way. When an elephant is in command, it holds up its head and spreads its ears. Other elephants know not to challenge it, and they keep their heads down and their ears in.

An elephant has a keen sense of smell. It can pick up the smell of an enemy from two kilometers away. Elephants can also tell the difference among the scents of their many different relatives. This ability helps elephants to stay together when traveling in a large herd.

Elephants communicate a lot by touch. They touch each other to show how they are feeling. Mothers touch babies with their trunks to reassure them. They brush each other with their ears to show affection. They use their tails to swat each other when feeling annoyed.

Elephants use different methods, such as touching, to communicate with each other.

Remember Me?

Because elephants live in family groups, it is important for everyone to learn to get along. One way elephants learn to get along with each other is through play. Babies play with each other and with adults. Adults play with each other, too. Elephants may play together by rolling around on the ground or in mud. These activities help elephants in a family bond with one another.

Elephants have pretty complex lives. How do they keep everything straight? Elephants are great at remembering things. They may be large animals, but they also have large brains. Their good memory helps them protect each other. An elephant alerts the group when she remembers familiar dangers or when she recognizes familiar feeding locations. She can remember friends and enemies from what they smell and sound like. Elephants show signs of remembering and grief when they come upon a dead relative. They pause and then gently touch the bones with their feet and trunks. Elephants are always learning new things throughout their lives.

Playtime! Elephants play in the mud together. This helps them to bond with and remember each other.

Energy

Keeping your eyes on the pins, you steadily roll the ball down the lane. You watch the moving ball crash into the pins. The pins then start to move and fall over. You score a strike! You will learn that moving objects have energy. Energy is the ability to cause objects to move or change. You will also discover that energy can transfer between objects causing many effects.

Unit Contents

Unit 2 Overview

Graphic Organizer: This unit is structured to first define simple properties of **energy**, then explore the diverse ways **energy is transferred**, and finally discuss how people **use energy**.

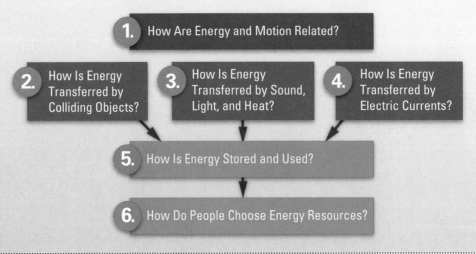

1. How Are Energy and Motion Related?

2. How Is Energy Transferred by Colliding Objects?

3. How Is Energy Transferred by Sound, Light, and Heat?

4. How Is Energy Transferred by Electric Currents?

5. How Is Energy Stored and Used?

6. How Do People Choose Energy Resources?

NGSS Next Generation Science Standards

Performance Expectations

4-PS3-1. Use evidence to construct an explanation relating the speed of an object to the energy of that object.

4-PS3-2. Make observations to provide evidence that energy can be transferred from place to place by sound, light, heat, and electric currents.

4-PS3-3. Ask questions and predict outcomes about the changes in energy that occur when objects collide.

4-PS3-4. Apply scientific ideas to design, test, and refine a device that converts energy from one form to another.

4-ESS3-1. Obtain and combine information to describe that energy and fuels are derived from natural resources and their uses affect the environment.

Disciplinary Core Ideas

PS3.A: Definitions of Energy • The faster a given object is moving, the more energy it possesses. • Energy can be moved from place to place by moving objects or through sound, light, or electric currents.

PS3.B: Conservation of Energy and Energy Transfer • Energy is present whenever there are moving objects, sound, light, or heat. When objects collide, energy can be transferred from one object to another, thereby changing their motion. In such collisions, some energy is typically also transferred to the surrounding air; as a result, the air gets heated and sound is produced. • Light also transfers energy from place to place. • Energy can also be transferred from place to place by electric currents, which can then be used locally to produce motion, sound, heat, or light. The currents may have been produced to begin with by transforming the energy of motion into electrical energy.

PS3.C: Relationship Between Energy and Forces • When objects collide, the contact forces transfer energy so as to change the objects' motions.

PS3.D: Energy in Chemical Processes and Everyday Life • The expression "produce energy" typically refers to the conversion of stored energy into a desired form for practical use.

ESS3.A: Natural Resources • Energy and fuels that humans use are derived from natural sources, and their use affects the environment in multiple ways. Some resources are renewable over time, and others are not.

ETS1.A: Defining Engineering Problems • Possible solutions to a problem are limited by available materials and resources (constraints). The success of a designed solution is determined by considering the desired features of a solution (criteria). Different proposals for solutions can be compared on the basis of how well each one meets the specified criteria for success or how well each takes the constraints into account.

Crosscutting Concepts

Cause and Effect • Cause and effect relationships are routinely identified and used to explain change.

Energy and Matter • Energy can be transferred in various ways and between objects.

 Asking Questions and Defining Problems

 Planning and Carrying Out Investigations

 Constructing Explanations and Designing Solutions

 Obtaining, Evaluating, and Communicating Information

Have you ever wondered...

When a moving ball hits a still pin, you will observe the pin move. Similarly, if you kick a still ball, your moving foot will make the ball move. This unit will help you answer these questions and many others you may ask.

Why does a ball move when I kick it?

Why does eating give me energy?

What causes an instrument to make a sound?

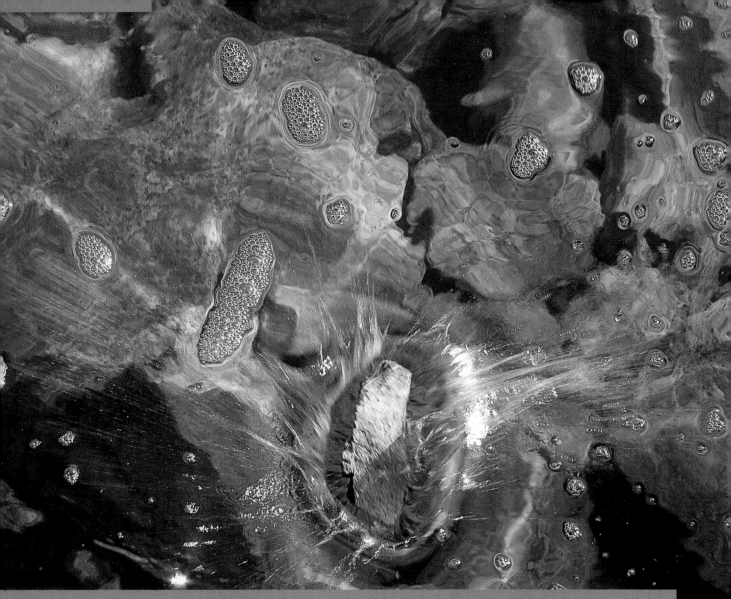

How Are Energy and Motion Related?

Science Vocabulary

conserved

energy

transfer

What does a rock falling into water have to do with energy? You will learn how scientists use the word *energy* to describe an ability to move or cause change. All objects have energy, and energy can even be passed from one object to another. Different factors, like weight and speed, can affect an object's energy.

NGSS   **4-PS3-1.** Use evidence to construct an explanation relating the speed of an object to the energy of that object.   **PS3.A.** The faster a given object is moving, the more energy it possesses.   **Energy and Matter** Energy can be transferred in various ways and between objects.    **Constructing Explanations and Designing Solutions**

1. Moving Objects Have Energy

When you use the word *energy*, you might say, "I don't have much energy today. I can't get out of bed!" A scientist will agree that it does take energy to move your body out of bed. But what is energy?

In science, **energy** is the ability to make an object move or to cause a change. All moving objects have energy, which is called energy of motion. A basketball has energy when it bounces on a court. Water has energy as it flows in a river, and air has energy when it blows by as wind.

How does an object get its energy of motion? One way is when a moving object *transfers* its energy to another object. To **transfer** means to shift or to move from one object to another. Suppose you have a rock in your hand. When you throw the rock, you transfer energy from your moving arm to the rock. Your moving arm is the source of the rock's energy. When the moving rock lands in a pond, it makes a splash because the rock's energy is transferred to the water. The drops of pond water that make up the splash are now flying through the air. Their energy came from the energy of the rock.

When a rock is thrown into water, the person's moving arm transfers energy to the rock. The moving rock then transfers energy to the water, which makes it splash.

2. Heavier Objects Have More Energy

You just learned that all moving objects have energy. But not all moving objects have the same amount of energy. One factor that affects the amount of energy that a moving object has is weight.

A heavier object has more energy than a lighter object that is moving at the same speed. Suppose that you have two rocks and that one rock is much larger than the other. The larger rock is also much heavier than the smaller rock. If you dropped them into a pond from the same height, they would land in the water at the same time since they have the same speed. But even though their motion is the same, they have different amounts of energy. You can see this difference in energy because the larger rock would cause a much bigger splash than the smaller rock. The heavier rock makes a bigger splash because it transfers more energy to the water.

Another example is if a bowling ball and a soccer ball are rolling at the same speed. Both are about the same size and shape. But the bowling ball is much heavier. Even though it moves at the same speed as the soccer ball, it has much more energy. You would not want the bowling ball to run into your foot! It has more energy to transfer to your foot and cause pain.

A large rock is heavier and has more energy than a small rock that is moving at the same speed. The rock that weighs more makes a bigger splash. This is because the heavier rock transfers more energy to the water.

Weight Affects An Object's Energy

Light rock

Heavy rock

3. Objects Moving Faster Have More Energy

Suppose you are playing baseball with your friends. One ball moves slowly, and your hand only moves a little when you catch it. But another ball moves much faster, and when you catch it, your hand moves back a lot. Both balls move your hand because they transfer energy. Why did the fast-moving ball transfer more?

Speed is another factor that affects how much energy of motion an object has. Picture a golf ball slowly rolling toward your bare foot. If it hits you, you would hardy feel it. Now picture that same ball moving very fast when it hits your foot. This time, it would hurt more because as an object moves faster, its energy of motion increases. This is why the fast-moving baseball made your hand move more than the slow-moving baseball.

Another example of how speed affects energy of motion is if you throw a rock twice into a pond from the same height but at different speeds. First, you might throw the rock very slowly. It would make a small splash when it hits the water. But if you throw the same rock much faster, it would make a much bigger splash. This is because the rock travels at a greater speed when it hits the water, so it has more energy. So, it transfers more energy to the water, which makes a bigger splash.

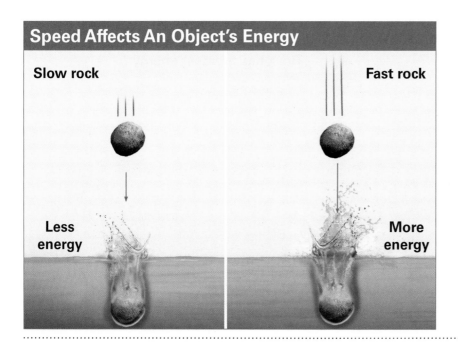

Speed Affects An Object's Energy

Slow rock

Less energy

Fast rock

More energy

The more speed an object has, the more energy it has and transfers. This is why a slow-moving rock creates a much smaller splash when it hits the water than a fast-moving rock does.

4. Energy Can Be Gained and Lost

You now know that objects can transfer their energy to other objects. But what happens to the energy of the moving object after it is transferred?

An object's energy does not just appear and disappear. It must come from somewhere, and it must go somewhere. So, objects can gain and lose energy.

Recall that when you throw a rock into a pond, it has energy of motion, but the rock's energy does not just appear out of nowhere. It comes from the energy of your moving hand. When you throw the rock, your moving hand transfers energy to the rock. When this happens, the rock has more energy than it did before, and your hand has less energy.

When the thrown rock hits the water, most of its energy is transferred to the water when it pushes the water up in a splash. At the same time, the rock slows down as it enters the water. Because the rock's speed decreases, it has less energy. Eventually, the rock sinks to the bottom of the pond. At the bottom of the pond, the rock is no longer in motion. It no longer has energy of motion because it has all been transferred to the water.

When this rock is thrown, it gains speed and energy. When it hits the water, it has less speed and its energy is transferred to the water. So, it loses energy when it hits the water.

Objects Can Lose Energy

Rock has greatest energy

Rock has less energy

Rock has no energy

5. Energy Can Be Stored

You learned that a moving object has energy of motion. But can a still object have energy, too?

A still object can also have energy. Instead of having energy of motion, it has *stored energy*. Any object that is lifted off the ground has stored energy since gravity is pulling on it. These objects have the *potential*, or ability, to move or cause a change without another object touching it. If you drop the object, gravity will make it fall. You do not have to transfer energy to the object for it move.

An object on the ground can also have stored energy, depending on its position. For example, when you stand in your room, you have the potential to fall over even though you are on the ground. But if you lie flat on the floor, you do not have stored energy since you cannot change positions without moving yourself.

Stored energy can be transferred. A rock you hold has stored energy. If you let go of it, its stored energy changes into energy of motion as it falls. When the rock hits the ground and stops moving, it has lost all of its energy of motion. It has also lost its stored energy. The energy has been transferred to the floor and other nearby objects.

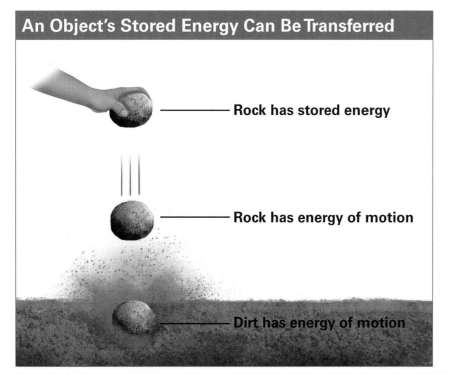

An Object's Stored Energy Can Be Transferred

Rock has stored energy

Rock has energy of motion

Dirt has energy of motion

When the rock is still, it has stored energy that is changed into energy of motion as it falls. Some of the rock's energy of motion is transferred to the ground when it lands.

6. Energy Is Conserved

Objects can gain and lose stored energy, just like how they can gain and lose energy of motion.

Energy moves from object to object, but no matter what, the total energy always stays the same. So, for example, when you throw a rock into a pond, the amount of energy that the rock loses is equal to the energy gained by the water and air around it. Or the energy of motion can become stored energy. But no amount of energy is created from nothing and no amount of energy is destroyed. The total amount of energy stays the same before and after each change in motion.

Because energy cannot be created or destroyed, scientists say that energy is *conserved*. **Conserved** means having the same total amount before and after a change happens. Another way of saying that energy is conserved is to say that energy cannot be created or destroyed. It can only transfer from one object to another during a change or become stored energy. For instance, suppose you kick a ball up a small hill. The ball has energy of motion as it rolls up the hill. As it rolls up the hill, most of its energy of motion becomes stored energy since the ball slows down and has the potential to roll down the hill. In this interaction, like all interactions, the energy is conserved.

Energy cannot be created or destroyed, which means that when energy is transferred, the total amount of energy always stays the same. So, scientists say that energy is conserved.

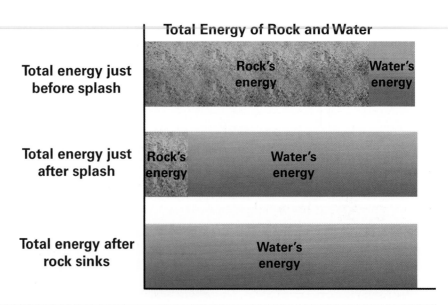

Total Energy of Rock and Water

Total energy just before splash — Rock's energy | Water's energy

Total energy just after splash — Rock's energy | Water's energy

Total energy after rock sinks — Water's energy

How Are Energy and Motion Related?

1. Moving Objects Have Energy   Energy is the ability to make an object move or cause change. All moving objects have energy of motion. An object can get energy when one moving object transfers its energy to another object.

2. Heavier Objects Have More Energy   If you drop two different-sized rocks into water, the heavier one will create a bigger splash. It has more energy. Heavier objects have more energy than lighter objects moving at the same speed.

3. Objects Moving Faster Have More Energy   As objects move faster, the amount of energy they have increases. If you drop a rock into water twice at different speeds, the faster-moving one will create a bigger splash.

4. Energy Can Be Gained and Lost   An object's energy can be gained or lost. When an object transfers energy to another object, it loses that energy. But that energy does not simply disappear. The other object gains that energy.

5. Energy Can Be Stored   Moving objects are not the only objects that have energy. Still objects can have energy that is called stored energy. Any object that is lifted off the ground has stored energy because gravity is pulling on it.

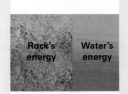

Rock's energy   Water's energy

6. Energy Is Conserved   All objects can gain and lose energy through an energy transfer. When energy transfers to another object, the amount of energy stays the same because energy is conserved.

Coaster Energy

You hear the riders scream as the roller coaster train races around the track! The train speeds up and gains energy as it goes down a hill. How does energy make a roller coaster more exciting?

You see it in the distance as you walk across the hot pavement to get in line. The track loops through the air, and the towering hill looks several stories tall. Are you really going to ride that monster of a roller coaster?

You start to feel scared. Your stomach hurts. Finally, you are at the front of the line. You still have time to change your mind, and you wonder if maybe you should run away! Then you see that the people who just finished their ride are smiling. Well, most of them are smiling.

You sit down in your seat and pull down your harness. A worker comes by to make sure you are locked in. Then the roller coaster slowly begins to pull out. There is no turning back now!

You see the sky as the roller coaster train slowly climbs up a steep hill. You hear the clink of the chains that are pulling the train, transferring energy to it as it moves up the hill. As the train climbs, it gains stored energy. What will happen to all this energy?

A roller coaster is able to move because of energy transfers. As a roller coaster moves up a steep hill, it gains stored energy.

The slow ride up the first hill may be the least exciting part of the roller coaster ride. But it is the most important. Roller coaster trains do not have engines to move them around the track. Instead, the train uses the stored energy that the train gets as it climbs the first hill. This is what allows the train to speed through the rest of the ride. The stored energy will change into the train's energy of motion as the train goes downhill.

Once you reach the top of that first hill, the train is at a slow crawl. Most of its energy is stored energy. Then gravity begins to pull the train downhill. Its stored energy starts changing into energy of motion. Whoa! You let out a scream as the train goes faster and faster. Its energy of motion increases. It might be moving more than 80 kilometers per hour (about 50 miles per hour) when you to reach the bottom of the hill. Now, most of the stored energy that the train had at the top of the hill has changed into the energy of motion.

Roller coaster engineers know that if a roller coaster started on a small hill, it would be a boring ride. The first hill needs to be tall enough to give the train enough stored energy to make it all the way around the track. And to make it around with speed! So, the first hill is usually the tallest in the whole ride.

The roller coaster train speeds up as it goes down the first hill. The stored energy changes to energy of motion.

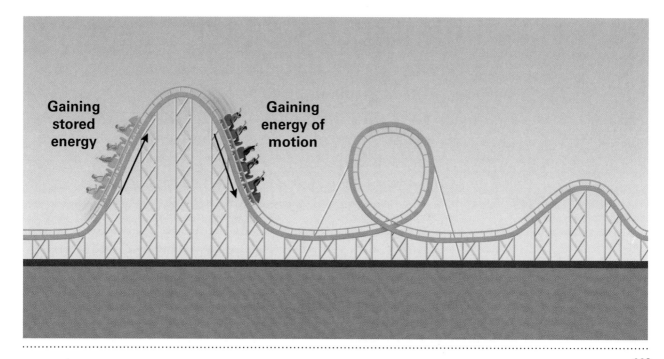

Gaining stored energy

Gaining energy of motion

When you go around a loop, your stored energy is highest when you are hanging upside down at the top.

Through the Loop

Your heart is racing as the train speeds around the track. The train slows a little as a small hill causes some of its energy of motion to change back into stored energy. But it quickly changes back to energy of motion as the train speeds down the small hill.

The roller coaster goes through twists and turns, which makes your stomach turn. Is the train going to fall off the track? You don't have to worry about that. Roller coaster engineers designed trains that have three sets of wheels. Every car has wheels that sit on the top, bottom, and side of the track to keep it moving smoothly along. Thank goodness, because the track forms a loop and you are about to be turned upside down!

As you zoom toward the top of the loop, your speed decreases. Some of your energy of motion once again changes into stored energy. This stored energy changes back into energy of motion as you zip down the other side of the loop. Of course, all of this happens so fast, you do not have time to think about

Losing Steam

As you race around the hills, loops, and curves of the track, the train's energy is constantly changing. You speed up when stored energy changes to the energy of motion. You slow down when energy of motion changes to stored energy. But you also slow down little by little all along the way. Some of the train's energy is lost, or transferred, when the wheels rub against the track. Some of the energy is also transferred to the air. These transfers make the train lose energy. The roller coaster train is always losing some of its energy. Yet, the overall energy is always conserved.

Engineers design roller coasters so that you are moving the slowest at the end of the ride. But the train needs to lose even more energy to stop. Roller coaster engineers add brakes that can quickly stop the train. The brakes are actually part of the tracks at the end of the ride. The energy of the train is transferred to the brakes as they clamp down on the side of the train.

The train stops right at the platform. Its energy of motion is finally zero. Your harness unlocks. You hop out of the train and run back into line. You want to experience the energy transfers of a roller coaster again!

You transfer some energy to the air that pushes against your skin as you zoom around the track.

How Is Energy Transferred by Colliding Objects?

Picture you and your friend giving each other a *high five*! When your moving hands touch, they collide, or come into direct contact. You will discover what happens to energy of motion when objects collide. Some energy transfers to another object or to air during a collision. Some energy produces sound or heat. But no matter how energy changes, its amount always stays the same.

NGSS **4-PS3-3.** Ask questions and predict outcomes about the changes in energy that occur when objects collide.

PS3.A. Energy can be moved from place to place by moving objects or through sound, light, or electric currents.
PS3.B. Energy is present whenever there are moving objects, sound, light, or heat. When objects collide, energy can be transferred from one object to another, thereby changing their motion. In such collisions, some energy is typically also transferred to the surrounding air; as a result, the air gets heated and sound is produced.
PS3.C. When objects collide, the contact forces transfer energy so as to change the objects' motions.

Energy and Matter
Energy can be transferred in various ways and between objects.

 Asking Questions and Defining Problems

1. Energy Is Transferred and Conserved

After soccer practice, you collect soccer balls from the field. You roll one ball straight at another ball that is still. The rolling ball hits the still one, and a curious thing happens. The two balls seem to trade motions. The rolling ball stops moving at the exact spot where the two balls meet. The ball that was still rolls in the direction that the other ball had been rolling. What caused this to happen?

The two balls moved the way they did because they *collided*. To **collide** is to touch something while moving. Energy transfers from one object to another when objects collide. Recall that all moving objects have energy of motion. So, the first ball, which is rolling, has energy of motion, but the second ball, which is still, has none. At the moment when the balls collide, the forces between them cause the first ball to slow down, and the second ball to move. When this happens, the first ball's energy shifts to the other ball. The second ball now has energy, while the first no longer has energy of motion. So, its motion has stopped.

Because of the collision, the speeds of both balls changed, and so did their energy. However, the total amount of energy did not change because energy is always conserved, even during a collision.

The energy of the moving ball transfers to the still ball when they collide. With the energy it gains during the collision, the ball that was still now is set in motion. The ball that was moving now is still.

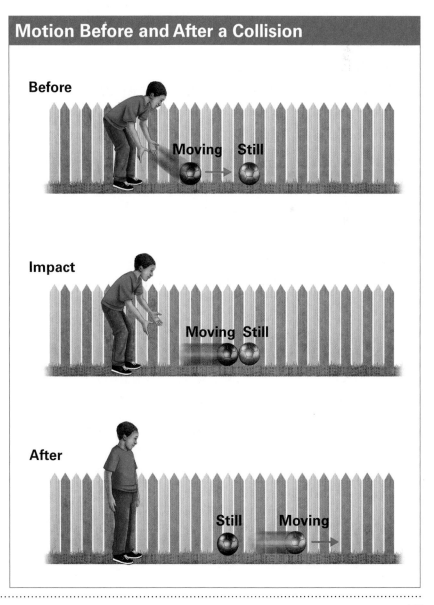

Motion Before and After a Collision

Before — Moving Still

Impact — Moving Still

After — Still Moving

A bowling ball has a greater weight than a bowling pin. So, when a slow bowling ball collides with pins, they will move at a faster speed. This is because weight and speed affect how energy transfers during a collision.

2. Collisions and Motion

It is your last chance to knock over the final bowling pin and win the game. You roll the heavy bowling ball toward the still pin, and it moves slowly down the lane. When the objects collide, the pin quickly shoots away from the collision. You win the game!

Not all collisions result in the same changes in motion. The collision of the bowling ball and a bowling pin is different from the collision of two soccer balls. Even though the bowling ball hits the pin at a slower speed, the pin moves at a faster speed after the collision. Recall that the amount of energy a moving object has relates to its weight and speed. So, weight and speed also affect what happens when objects collide and transfer energy.

Colliding with a Still Object of the Same Weight

When a moving object collides with a still object of the same weight, the energy transfer causes the still object to move at the speed of the object that hit it. So, if a rolling soccer ball collides with a still soccer ball of the same weight, the still ball will gain the same energy of motion that the rolling ball lost. Since both balls are the same weight, the second ball will move at the same speed as the ball that collided with it did.

Colliding with a Still Object of a Different Weight

When a moving object collides with a still object of a different weight, the energy transfer can affect the objects' speeds differently. A bowling ball is heavier than a bowling pin. When the ball collides with the pin, it transfers energy. The pin weighs less, so this energy makes it move faster than the ball.

Colliding at the Same Speed

When two objects moving at the same speed with the same weight collide head on, they each bounce back in the direction they came from at the same speed. Suppose you and a friend kick soccer balls toward each other at the same speed. After colliding, each ball will return toward its kicker at the same speed it was traveling.

Colliding at Different Speeds

When two objects of the same weight traveling at different speeds collide head on, they bounce backward. They each travel at the original speed of the other object. Think about kicking a soccer ball hard. Your friend kicks his ball gently. Your ball will move quicker and thus have more energy. After they collide, your ball will roll back to you with less energy and slower. Your friend's ball will roll back to him with more energy and quicker.

These soccer balls have different speeds before they collide. After they collide, the ball that was faster now moves at the slower speed. The ball that was slower now moves at the faster speed.

3. Collisions and Sound, Light, and Heat

You hear a loud "whack"! A softball goes flying as the batter drops the bat and runs toward first base. The batter slides into second base before her opponent can get the ball and tag her. She is safe. What happens to the energy during these collisions?

Energy Produces Sound

Some of the energy transferred during a collision produces sound. For example, the ball and the bat both have energy of motion because they are both moving. Energy transfers between the ball and the bat when they collide, so the ball's motion changes direction. However, during a collision, some of the energy transfers to the surrounding air and produces a sound. This is why you hear a whack when a ball hits a bat.

Energy Produces Light

Sometimes light is produced when objects collide. This light transfers some energy away from the objects. For example, people can start fires by hitting a kind of rock called flint against a piece of steel. This collision produces a bright spark. Some of the flint's energy transfers to the steel and air, but some of the energy can also be carried away by the light.

Flint is a rock that can be used to start a fire when it is struck against steel.

Energy Produces Heat

When objects collide, some of the energy is transferred and produces heat. For example, when the softball player slides into second base, she is colliding with the ground. As she slides along the ground, energy moves from her to the ground. Both the player and the ground are warmed up because some of her energy of motion became heat during the collision.

Energy moves between any moving object and the surface it touches. When the energy moves, it creates heat and makes both objects warmer. That is why quickly rubbing your hands together warms them. Some of the energy of motion is changed into heat.

A moving object will keep moving unless its energy changes. Changes in energy are what make a moving object stop moving. Think about dropping a rubber ball on the ground. When you first drop it, it might bounce up very high. But each time it bounces, it rises to a lower height since it transfers energy to the air and ground with each bounce. Some is carried by sound. Some also becomes heat. All of these changes make the ball lose energy. Eventually, the ball will lose all of its energy of motion and stop moving. All of the ball's energy will have transferred to the ground and air, making sound and heat.

A moving object stops moving because of changes in energy. Some of its energy transfers to other objects, and some produces heat and sound. That is why this ball keeps bouncing lower each time it hits the ground, until it eventually stops moving.

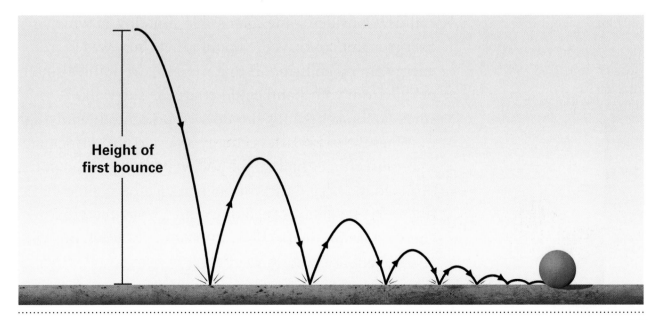

Height of first bounce

If energy were not conserved, you could not predict what would happen during a collision. A small collision, like a paintbrush touching paper, could cause a lot of damage.

4. Imagining Collisions Without Conserved Energy

Recall that scientists say that energy is conserved since it cannot be created or destroyed. An object's energy is still conserved during collisions. So, although energy moves during a collision, the total amount of energy stays the same. Scientists investigate where energy goes during collisions. It helps them better understand what happens when objects run into one another. It also helps them predict how objects will move or how they will stop moving.

If energy were not conserved, you, or even scientists, could not predict what would happen when objects collide. Consider some impossible situation in which energy is not conserved. Suppose that there was more energy after a collision. If that were so, dropping a small pebble from your hand could crack the sidewalk. A small tap on someone's shoulder could send them flying.

What if there was less energy after a collision? If that were so, a rubber ball might not ever bounce when you dropped it. Or rubbing your hands together would cause them to get colder instead of warmer. You know that energy does not work this way. It does not work this way because energy is conserved.

How Is Energy Transferred by Colliding Objects?

1. Energy Is Transferred and Conserved Sometimes a moving object collides with another object. When this happens, some of an object's energy of motion transfers to the other object. But when energy transfers, the total amount of energy always stays the same. This is because energy is conserved.

2. Collisions and Motion Not all collisions result in the same changes of motion. The amount of energy a moving object has relates to its weight and speed. So the speed and weight of objects when they collide affect what happens when energy transfers.

3. Collisions and Sound, Heat, and Light Not all the energy in a collision transfers to an object. Some of it transfers to the air and produces sound. Some also produces heat and warms up the objects in the collision. Some energy may also be transferred away by light. A moving object will keep moving in the same direction unless its energy changes.

4. Imagining Collisions Without Conserved Energy Because energy is conserved, you can predict what will happen to energy of motion when objects collide. Scientists study where energy transfers and goes during a collision. It helps them understand what happens when objects run into each other.

Dummies Keep Getting Smarter

One of the first things you do when getting into a car is buckle your seat belt. You want to be safe in case the car crashes. Other parts of a car also keep you safe during a collision. How do engineers make sure a car is safe?

A car speeds toward a steel and concrete wall. Look out, it's going to crash! It smashes into the wall at almost 65 kilometers per hour (about 40 miles per hour). There is a loud sound as its front end crumples. Broken bits of metal and glass fly in all directions. The passenger's head is flung towards the hard dashboard, but the impact is stopped by the airbag that pops open.

Car collisions happen in this spot every week. Luckily, this place is a crash testing lab. Engineers who test cars for safety crash cars here over and over. They use crash tests to learn how energy is transferred during a car crash so they can design safe cars.

Engineers use important technology at the crash testing lab—crash test dummies. To test how safe a car is, it helps to have someone inside. But real people could be hurt in a test crash. So, engineers strap crash test dummies into a test car. The car crashes only once, but test dummies go through crashes for many years. Their parts can be replaced if they break. They also collect data about how energy is transferred to the passengers during the crash.

Engineers crash test cars to learn how energy is transferred in collisions. They use technology to learn what happens to passengers during a crash.

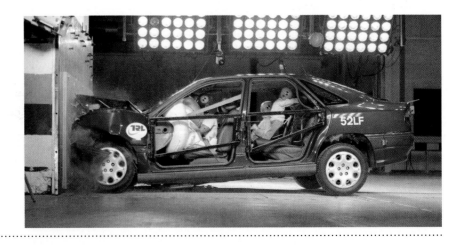

Cars are heavy and can move very quickly. So, they can transfer a large amount of energy during a collision. Energy is transferred to the object the car hits. It is also transferred to the passengers when they collide with the inside of the car. These collisions can cause bumps, broken bones, and even death.

Modern cars have seat belts and air bags to keep passengers from colliding with objects inside the car. Engineers know that the way energy is transferred between a passenger and objects inside of the car depends on the weight of the passenger. Size is also important. A seat belt fits you a little differently than it fits a grownup. So, engineers use crash test dummies of different sizes and weights to make sure that all sizes of people are safe.

The most common crash test dummy is the size of an average adult. It weighs about 78 kg (172 lbs). But dummies come in different sizes. Some dummies are even child-sized. These dummies help engineers make sure that safety belts and air bags are safe for people of different ages and sizes. Infant-sized dummies are even used to test child safety seats.

Engineers have designed crash test dummies in several sizes so they can make cars as safe as possible for all kinds of passengers.

A Good Head on Its Shoulders

Modern crash test dummies may look like simple, oversized dolls. But they are much more. Their parts are designed to move the way real people would move during a crash. This helps engineers predict how people could be injured in a car crash.

The parts of crash test dummies are designed to move like a human's. The ankles, knees, and hips of crash test dummies can bend and rotate just like a person's. The design of a crash test dummy's head and neck is also very important. Head and neck injuries are common in car crashes. A crash test dummy's neck may not look much like your neck. But it moves just like a real person's neck would during a crash.

Crash test dummies are not empty-headed either. They have *sensors* inside. A sensor is a device that takes measurements. It measures the amount of force a crash has on certain parts of a dummy. Engineers use the sensors in a dummy's head and neck to find out how energy is transferred during the crash. This information helps them predict whether the crash would hurt a real person's head or neck.

The neck of a crash test dummy may look very different from a real person's neck. But it moves in a similar way that a real person's would during a crash.

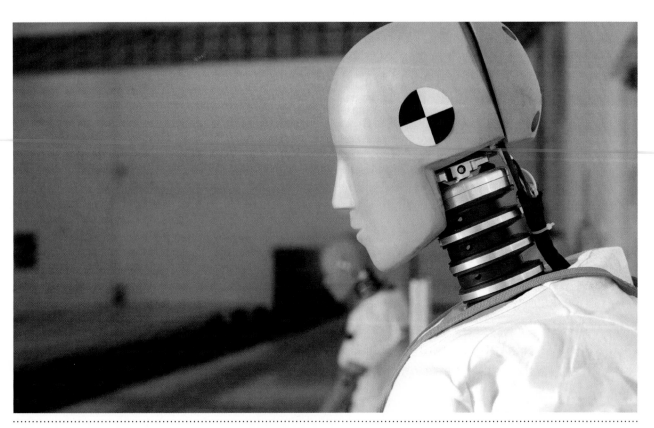

This crash test dummy is used to test crashes that happen when a car is hit from the side. It has sensors that collect information about how the dummy moves during the crash.

Advanced Dummies

The head is not the only part of a crash test dummy that is like a human's. Its skeleton may be made of metal. But it is designed to resemble real bone. This skeleton helps engineers predict which bones may break during a car crash.

Crash test dummies may often all look alike on the outside. But, depending on their job, they have different parts on the inside. This is because they need to be able to test different types of car crashes. Some dummies are used for head-on collisions. Other dummies are used to test what happens when a car is hit from the side. Different dummies are used to test what happens when a car is rear-ended by another car. Energy is transferred differently in each of these types of car crashes. And the dummies are specially designed to test each type of crash.

Engineers are continuing to improve crash test dummies. They are adding more sensors so they can learn more during each crash test. They are even redesigning the skeleton so they can better predict injuries. These new and improved dummies can be crashed again and again to make cars safer for you. So, the next time you buckle your seat belt, say a special thank you to crash test dummies.

How Is Energy Transferred by Sound, Light, and Heat?

Science Vocabulary

absorb

reflect

vibrate

This picture of camping cowboys shows energy being transferred in many different ways. Even the hot, glowing fire and the strumming guitar are transferring energy. You will find out that energy can be transferred without a moving object. Energy can be transferred by sound, light, or heat, even though you don't see anything moving.

NGSS **4-PS3-2.** Make observations to provide evidence that energy can be transferred from place to place by sound, light, heat, and electric currents.

PS3.A. Energy can be moved from place to place by moving objects or through sound, light, or electric currents.
PS3.B. • Energy is present whenever there are moving objects, sound, light, or heat. When objects collide, energy can be transferred from one object to another, thereby changing their motion. In such collisions, some energy is typically also transferred to the surrounding air; as a result, the air gets heated and sound is produced. • Light also transfers energy from place to place.

Energy and Matter Energy can be transferred in various ways and between objects.

Planning and Carrying out Investigations

1. Sound, Light, and Heat Transfer Energy

You know that when you kick a ball or throw a rock into a pond, a moving object collides with another object and transfers its energy. But energy can also be transferred without moving objects.

Three ways that energy transfers without moving objects are when it is carried by sound, light, and heat. A sound starts when an object, such as a guitar string, **vibrates**, or quickly moves back and forth. The vibration causes nearby air to also vibrate. This vibrating air then makes surrounding air vibrate, too. Energy transfers from each area of vibrating air to the next.

Energy transfers also happen when light carries energy. Unlike sound, light can move through empty space. This is why light can carry energy from the sun to Earth. Light can also travel through air. It moves energy away from its source in all directions. A light bulb can light up an entire room because it moves energy in all directions around the room.

Heat is a third way that energy transfers without moving objects. Your hand becomes cooler when you hold a cold cup of water, and it becomes warmer when you hold a hot cup of tea. These changes in temperature tell you that energy is moving because of heat. Energy is transferring from the hot cup to your hand.

When an object, like a guitar string, vibrates, it transfers energy.

Heat is a transfer of energy when there is a difference in temperature. The energy can be transferred to other objects. This is why holding a hot drink can warm up your hands.

2. Sound Carries Energy

All sound starts with a vibration. A soccer ball vibrates when you hit it. The floor vibrates when you stomp on it. Drums and guitars vibrate when you play them. What happens to energy when an object vibrates?

Vibrations Cause Sound

When you pluck a guitar string, you transfer energy to the string. The string then vibrates and collides with the air that surrounds it. As it does this, it transfers energy to the surrounding air, which produces sound. The sound also carries energy as it moves through the air. Objects, as well as air, transfer energy when they collide with each other. In this way, the energy carried by sound spreads out away from the guitar string. You hear the sound when this vibrating air reaches your ear.

A vibrating object loses energy as it produces sound, but this energy is not destroyed because energy is always conserved. The sound carries the energy away from the object that is the sound's source. For a plucked guitar string, the string has lost all of its energy when it stops vibrating. That energy is not gone. Instead, it has been transferred to the air and other objects.

A reed is a small piece of wood on the mouthpiece of some instruments.

All sounds begin with a vibration. When you blow into a clarinet, the air makes a reed vibrate, which then transfers energy to surrounding air. This produces sound.

Sound Causes Vibrations

You now know that the energy of vibrating objects causes sound. But sound can also make objects vibrate by transferring energy. This is why when sound from vibrating air hits other nearby air, that air also begins to vibrate. The energy carried by the sound is transferred to more of the surrounding air. If you watch a concert with drums, you might feel the ground vibrating below you. Loud music in a nearby car can cause your car's windows to rattle. All of these vibrations happen because the energy that causes the air to vibrate is transferred. It is transferred from the sound's source to the ground and to the windows of your car. The transferred energy makes the ground and window vibrate.

Again, when sound causes an object to vibrate, energy is still conserved. It is not destroyed and has simply moved from object to object. The energy moves from the sound's source to the vibrating air that surrounds it. Then after the sound travels away from the source, the energy moves from the vibrating air to all the objects that the air is touching. In this way, sound carries energy and transfers it to different objects, such as your car windows.

If you hear a loud sound, like the sound of these taiko drums, you can sometimes feel the ground move. This happens because energy from the sound transfers to other objects.

Some energy is carried by light. When this energy is transferred to other objects, different things can happen. It can pass through materials that you can see through, like glass.

3. Light Carries Energy

Energy transfers also happen when energy is carried by light. When light bounces off an object and into your eye, the object looks a certain way. Black construction paper looks dull but a mirror looks shiny. Some materials, like glass and water, you can see through. The differences in how these objects appear has to do with what happens when energy carried by light hits them.

When light carries energy and transfers it to an object, three things can happen. One thing that can happen is that light **reflects**, or bounces off. All materials that you can see reflect some light. But materials that you cannot see, like air, do not reflect much light. A second thing that can happen is that the light passes through the materials. The energy carried by light passes through clear materials like air, glass, and water. A third thing that can happen when light hits material is that the material can **absorb**, or take in, the light.

When material absorbs the energy carried by light, the material heats up. For example, when you wear a black shirt on a sunny day, the shirt becomes hot. This happens because the energy transferred by light is absorbed by the material that makes up the shirt. The energy carried by light absorbed by the shirt gets changed into heat.

4. Heat Carries Energy

When energy is transferred as heat to other objects, it warms the objects up. Consider how you make toast. You put a piece of bread in a toaster and push the knob down. The wires in the slot of a toaster begin as gray and cool, but when they heat up, they start to glow with an orange light. What makes these objects glow when they get hot?

Energy transferred as heat can produce light. You cannot always see it, but the material that makes up objects is always moving. Adding energy as heat to an object can cause its material to move faster. This makes its temperature rise, too. The more energy added to an object, the faster its material moves and the higher its temperature rises. If you add enough energy to an object, it makes more heat and light. For example, energy is added to the metal wires in a toaster. The material moves so fast that it gives off light and glows.

As an object gives off light, it loses energy. But since energy is always conserved, this energy is not destroyed. The light carries the energy away from the object. In a toaster, the heat produces light. The energy carried by light transfers to the bread and heats it up.

The wires in a toaster use heat to produce light and toast bread.

Metal can get so hot that it gives off light. Here, a horse shoe is being heated by a blacksmith. The horseshoe is glowing because energy transferred as heat is producing light.

If energy was not conserved, a flashlight might burn a piece of paper when it shined. But this situation is impossible because all energy is conserved.

5. Imagining Sound, Light, and Heat Without Conserved Energy

Sound, light, and heat are different ways that energy can move from place to place. The energy they carry is always conserved. An object's energy was not created from nothing. It came from the original source of the heat, light, or sound. When an object loses energy as heat, light, or sound, the energy is not destroyed. It is simply transferred to a new object.

What would happen if energy were not conserved? Consider some impossible situations in which energy is not conserved. When you speak, vocal folds inside of you vibrate and transfer energy to the air, which vibrates and produces sound. The air then has the energy lost by the vocal cords. What if energy carried by sound was destroyed? Energy might not transfer to air. So, you could shout as loudly as you can, but you might not make a noise.

Consider what would happen if the energy carried by light was not conserved. The light of a flashlight carries energy away from the bulb to other objects. You might hold a notebook in front of a flashlight. If more energy hit the paper than came out of the flashlight, the paper would burn from all the extra energy. This does not happen because energy is conserved even when it is carried away from a flashlight bulb.

How Is Energy Transferred by Sound, Light, and Heat?

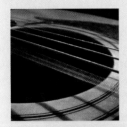

1. Sound, Light, and Heat Transfer Energy   Energy can be transferred without a moving object. It can be carried by sound, light, and heat. Energy that transfers with sound, light, and heat do not need collisions between objects.

2. Sound Carries Energy   All sounds start with a vibrating object. The object transfers energy to nearby air, which vibrates, producing sound. The energy is then transferred to more of the surrounding air. Sound can also transfer energy to objects and make them vibrate.

3. Light Carries Energy   When light carries energy, three things can happen. Any object that you can see reflects light. Light passes through objects that you can see through. Light can also be absorbed by an object.

4. Heat Carries Energy   Like light, heat can carry energy. When energy is transferred to an object, the object gets warmed up. Energy transferred as heat can also make material move so quickly that it produces light.

5. Imagining Sound, Light, and Heat Without Conserved Energy   Sound, light, and heat can all move energy. The energy that they carry is always conserved. If energy were not conserved, you could shout as loudly as possible and not make a sound.

Energy from Smartphones

Heat carries energy away from your warm hands to a cool glass of water. Sound carries energy away from your hands when you snap your fingers. But when do light, sound, and heat transfer energy from the palm of your hand all at the same time? When you use a smartphone!

"LOL! What a fun game—you have to try it! Mom is calling. TTYL." Every time you send or open a text message, the smartphone transfers energy. The same is true when you look at pictures on a tablet computer. The screen lights up and sound comes out because of all the tiny working parts inside.

Think of everything you can do on a phone. Of course, you can call your friend. You can also send text messages and look at pictures. You might even play games and listen to music on your phone. That is pretty amazing for a machine that can fit in your pocket!

So, how do a microphone, speaker, lights, and even a small computer all fit inside a phone? Engineers keep finding ways to make all of the parts that make up a phone smaller and smaller. They not only have to be small, but they have to work well. And, they all have to transfer energy well.

You can use a smartphone to send messages, talk to someone far way, and even play games. The phone transfers sound and light energy when you use it.

Light It Up

The screen is one of the most important parts of smartphones. You see images on the screen because light from the screen carries energy to your eyes. You need the screen to look at photos, play games, and send a text message.

When you look at a picture on a phone, it seems like the screen lights up. The light of some smartphone screens comes from tiny lights called LEDs. The LEDs are behind the screen. Only three colors of light can pass through. Yet, you see many colors on the screen. That's because the screen allows only certain amounts of each color of light to pass through at a time.

The screen is divided into thousands of squares called pixels. Each pixel is red, blue, or green. When you choose which photo you want to see, the computer inside the phone changes how much light passes through each pixel. When light passes through a red pixel, red light carries energy to your eyes. When light passes through a blue pixel, blue light carries energy to your eyes, and so on. Think about different colors of paint. Even if you only have three colors of paint, you can mix them to create many other colors. In the same way, the colors from pixels that are close together can combine to make almost any color imaginable.

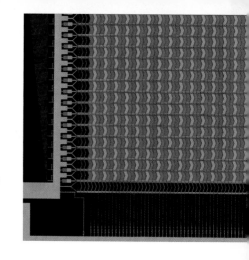

The screen of a smartphone is divided up into red, blue, or green pixels

Behind a smartphone screen are three colors of lights called LEDs. The screen only lets certain amounts of light pass through at a time, so you can see many colors.

A signal from the mp3 player travels up the wire to the headphones. The speakers in the headphones vibrate, causing sound that carries energy into your ears.

Sound It Out

Ring! Ring! That used to be the only sound all phones made. Now, a phone might play part of your favorite song when someone is calling you. Many phones will let you store and listen to all of your favorite music. So do all computers and mp3 players. How do all these devices produce sound?

Phones and computers have small speakers and microphones inside them. Suppose you are calling your best friend. The sound of your voice transfers energy to a microphone inside of the phone. The phone changes the vibrations of the sound into a signal that it sends away from your phone.

Far away, your friend's phone receives this signal. The signal causes a speaker inside the phone to vibrate. The vibrations of the speaker make the air vibrate. This vibration produces the sound of your voice. And finally, the sound carries energy out of the phone to your friend's ears.

Headphones and earbuds are also speakers that you can plug into your mp3 player. When you press the play button, a signal travels up the wire to each speaker. The speakers vibrate to produce sound. The sound needs to carry energy only a short distance because the speakers are very close to the inside of your ears.

Heat It Up

Do your hands ever feel warm after you have been using a smartphone for a long time? That happens because heat transfers energy from the phone to your hands. Why does a smartphone produce heat?

Like many devices you use, a smartphone is powered by a battery. The battery has stored energy. The battery transfers its energy through wires to other parts inside of the phone. These parts, such as the screen and the speakers, do not work until energy is transferred to them. Some of this transferred energy is carried by light and sound. But some of this energy is also carried as heat. So, when you hold a phone, energy transfers to your hand. This is why a phone might feel warm after you use it for a long time.

Energy carried by light and sound are useful for a smartphone. Light helps you see a phone's screen and sound helps you listen and talk on a phone. But energy transferred as heat is not useful. In fact, if too much heat is produced, it can destroy a phone.

Energy carried by light, heat, and sound exist all around you. Energy is carried by all three of these when you use a smartphone. Next time you use a phone, notice all the ways that energy is transferred. It might make you feel very smart!

When you hold a smartphone, you might feel your hand become warm. This happens because the phone transfers energy carried as heat to your hand.

How Is Energy Transferred by Electric Currents?

Every time you turn on a light or use a phone, you are using an electric current. An electric current is a steady flow of electric charges. You will learn that an electric current carries energy to a machine. It can also be used to produce motion, sound, light, and heat. So, there are many different machines that use electric currents to transfer energy.

NGSS **4-PS3-2.** Make observations to provide evidence that energy can be transferred from place to place by sound, light, heat, and electric currents.

PS3.A. Energy can be moved from place to place by moving objects or through sound, light, or electric currents.
PS3.B. Energy can also be transferred from place to place by electric currents, which can then be used locally to produce motion, sound, heat, or light. The currents may have been produced to begin with by transforming the energy of motion into electrical energy.

Energy and Matter Energy can be transferred in various ways and between objects.

Planning and Carrying out Investigations

1. Electric Currents Transfer Energy

You use electricity every day. Whenever you turn on a light or a computer, you use electricity. Electricity powers phones and tablet computers. But what is electricity?

Electricity is interactions between *electric charges*, or tiny objects that push or pull on one another. When electric charges move, they can be used to transfer energy to other objects. This energy can move and change objects.

When the same kind of electric charges, or "like" charges, move in the same direction, they form an electric current. An **electric current** is a flow of electric charges. The charges do not flow just anywhere. They can only flow through some materials, such as metal. Usually a metal wire forms a path for an electric current.

Electric currents carry energy to machines. This is why you might see wires attached to some machines. Electric currents can be used to produce motion, sound, light, and heat. For example, light bulbs use electric currents to produce light. Radios use currents to make sound, but fans use them to make motion. Heaters and freezers use them to make spaces warmer or cooler.

Electric currents carry energy to machines. Here, electric charges flow from the battery through the metal wires and transfer energy to the light bulb.

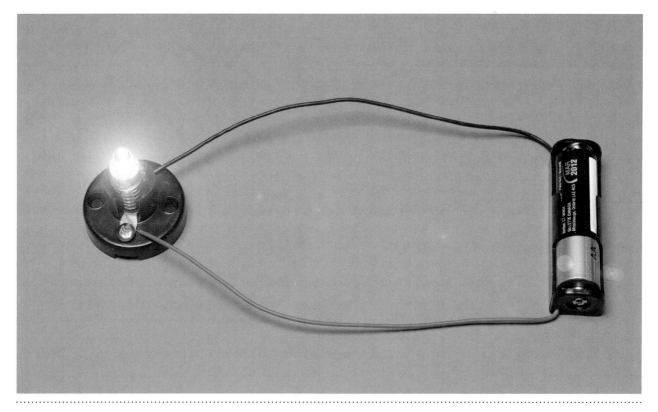

A solar cell takes in energy carried by light. It uses the light to produce an electric current. Some people put solar cells on their roof to provide electricity to their home.

2. Light and Heat Can Make Electric Currents

You just learned that electric currents can produce sound, light, and heat since they can carry energy. But, light and heat can also make electric currents.

Light Can Transfer Energy to an Electric Current

Light can transfer its energy to an electric current. To transfer energy carried by light to an electric current, you need a *solar cell*. A **solar cell** is a flat board made of thin layers of different materials, including silicon. The top layer lets light pass through and traps the light. A middle layer absorbs the light. As it takes up energy from the light, electric charges begin to flow through other layers of the cell. Because the energy from the light is transferred to the solar cell, the energy that was carried by light is now carried by an electric current.

Sunlight often provides the energy that a solar cell uses to produce an electric current. Sunlight shines on Earth every day. As long as there is light, a solar cell works without stopping. But energy is still conserved. Once the source of light goes away, the solar cell stops making an electric current. There is no longer a source of energy for the solar cell. If the sun sets, the solar cell will stop working. You will need another source of an electric current to do your work.

Heat Can Transfer Energy to an Electric Current

Like light, energy carried by heat can transfer to an electric current. So, heat can also be used to power devices.

Some power plants use a *steam engine*, or an engine that uses steam to move some of its parts. When steam is heated, it expands. The expanding steam moves part of the engine, giving the engine energy of motion. This is because steam is a gas. So, like all gases, when the temperature of steam goes up, it *expands*, or takes up more space. As the steam in a power plant heats and expands, it pushes on the fan-like blades of a spinning wheel called a *turbine*. The more hot gas that flows past the turbine, the faster the turbine moves. In this way, the energy of heat causes the motion of an object. The turbine spins a part inside of a generator, which produces an electric current.

The turbine's energy is not created from nothing. The energy of the turbine's motion comes from the energy of the steam expanding. The energy of the steam comes from the heat produced by the burning fuel. In this way, the energy of the system is conserved.

A power plant burns fuel to heat water and make steam. The fast-expanding steam flows past a turbine. A turbine is like a pinwheel. When steam flows past the turbine, it spins.

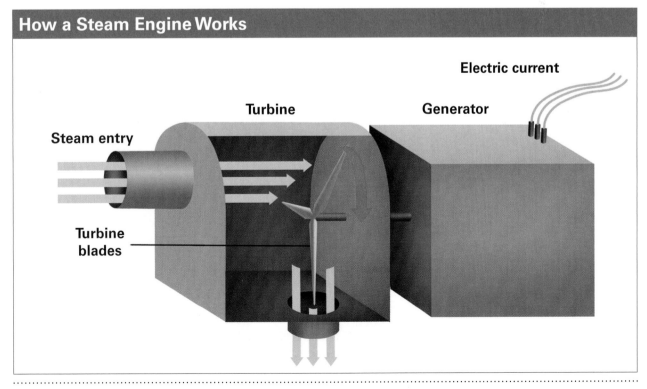

How a Steam Engine Works

Electric current

Turbine

Generator

Steam entry

Turbine blades

This toy car has a motor that gets energy from batteries.

A motor is a device that uses an electric current to produce motion. Inside of a motor is a magnet that curves around a coil. When an electric current flows through the coil, the magnet makes the coil spin and move parts in the motor.

3. Electric Currents and Motion

You and your friend are racing toy cars. When you switch on your car, its wheels spin, and it speeds away! A toy car is powered by batteries that produce an electric current. The energy in the electric current powers the motor, which moves the car.

A **motor** is a device that uses an electric current to produce motion. You can find motors in machines that use electric current to make parts spin. Clothes dryers and fans have spinning parts powered by motors.

A motor uses a magnet and a coil of wire to make parts spin. The magnet inside of a motor curves around the coil. You know that magnets can push or pull on one another. But, in a motor, magnets push on the coil. When there is an electric current in the coil, the magnet pushes on it, which makes the coil spin. In this way, an electric current in a coil can cause a spinning motion, like the motor in a toy car.

The energy of a motor comes from an electric current. Some motors, like a fan's, use an electric current from a wire connected to an outlet. Others, like a toy car's, use batteries. If you leave the toy car running for a long time, its batteries will run out. This happens when the motor has used up all the stored energy in the battery.

How a Motor Works

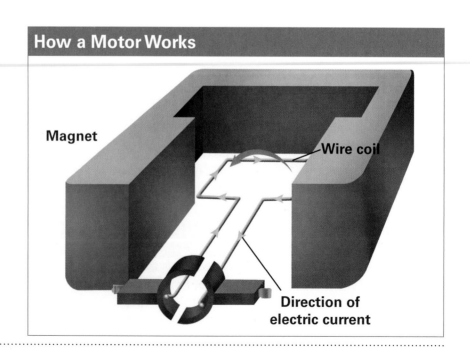

Magnet

Wire coil

Direction of electric current

4. Electric Currents and Sound

You now know how an electric current can be used to make motion. What are other ways that electric current can be used?

Many devices have speakers that use an electric current to produce sound. Think about a music player. Music players have both a source of an electric current and a speaker. One common type of speaker uses a magnet and a coil of wire. The coil is attached to a flat cone. The electric current in the coil changes, which makes the coil and magnet push and pull on each other and vibrate. This movement causes the cone to vibrate and push on the air next to it. The vibrations move through the air. In this way, sound is produced.

The energy of the electric current is changed into the energy that vibrates the air. These vibrations transfer to other nearby air, so the energy is conserved. What if you used a music player for a long time? In time, the battery would run out of stored energy. All of its energy would be transferred to the air, so the player would stop running.

A speaker uses an electric current to transfer energy to air by sound. The electric current moves the flat cone-shaped part of the speaker, which vibrates the surrounding air.

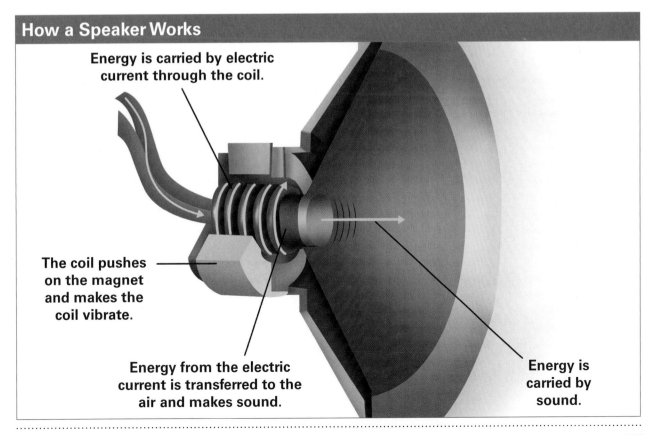

How a Speaker Works

Energy is carried by electric current through the coil.

The coil pushes on the magnet and makes the coil vibrate.

Energy from the electric current is transferred to the air and makes sound.

Energy is carried by sound.

Incandescent lights were invented in the 1800s. An incandescent light bulb transfers the energy of an electric current carried by a wire to its surroundings. Light then carries the energy away from the wire of the light bulb.

5. Electric Currents and Light

At night, you turn on lights so that you can see. At home, you might turn on a reading lamp or kitchen light. Outside, you might use a flashlight. What do all of these light sources have in common?

Lamps, kitchen lights, and flashlights all shine because they produce light from an electric current. One type of electric light is the incandescent light bulb. These lights are made of a round glass bulb. Inside is a very thin, coiled wire called a *filament*. When you switch on a lamp, electric charges flow through the filament inside of the bulb. But the filament does not let moving electric charges pass through it easily. When they pass through the filament, some of the energy is converted to heat. The hot wire then glows and gives off light. So, energy is carried away by light. This light travels away from the light bulb in all directions.

Just like when energy in an electric current causes sound, when it causes light, the energy is conserved. So, the total amount of energy after the bulb lights up is the same as the energy before it lights up. The energy of the electric current has not been destroyed by the bulb. It has simply been carried away.

6. Electric Currents and Heat

You watch your neighbor turn on an electric stove and place a pan on top of the burner. Within moments, the burner changes from black to a glowing orange. The pan then starts to heat and your neighbor places peppers on the hot pan. The smell of cooked peppers fills the air as they cook.

An electric stove heats a pan by changing energy carried by an electric current into heat. The stove is plugged into an outlet, its source of energy. When you turn on the stove, it completes the path that carries an electric current. The burner of an electric stove is made of metal that does not let electric charges pass through it easily. So, when the charges flow through the metal, they lose some energy as heat and light. The metal becomes hot. When you place a pan on the burner, heat energy moves from the hot metal to the cool pan. This heats the pan and cooks whatever food is placed inside of it.

The energy carried by electric current becomes heat as it transfers to the metal of the stove. The burner's energy is conserved since the energy lost by electric current becomes heat that warms the pan.

The burner of an electric stove is made of metal that gets hot when it carries an electric current. The metal changes the energy into heat, which can warm a pan.

7. Imagining Electric Currents Without Conserved Energy

You want to watch your favorite television show. You press the buttons on the controller, but nothing happens. Oh, no! The batteries have run out of energy! Where did the energy go?

Even the energy of moving electric charges is always conserved. Batteries may run out of stored energy because their energy is transferred to objects in the machine that they power. Some types of batteries can be charged again, which means that energy can be added back to them. They can store, lose, and gain back energy over and over again. But that energy has to come from somewhere. It is not just created. It comes from the energy of an electrical outlet.

Consider impossible situations in which energy is not conserved. If energy could be created from nothing, a battery might be able to last forever. If energy could be destroyed, even an entire power plant might be unable to light up a light bulb. Since energy is conserved, you can often predict what will happen when energy transfers to an object. For instance, you can predict how brightly a bulb will shine if you know how much current can flow through the wire.

Batteries can run out of stored energy, but that energy is still conserved. It is not destroyed. Instead, the devices that use batteries convert that energy into other forms of energy.

How Is Energy Transferred by Electric Currents?

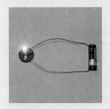

1. Electric Currents Transfer Energy   Electric charges are tiny objects that push or pull on each other. Electricity is the interactions between electric charges. An electric current is a steady flow of electric charge. It can transfer energy to other objects.

2. Light and Heat Can Make Electric Currents   Energy carried by light or heat can become energy carried by electric currents. Solar cells use use sunlight to make electric currents.

3. Electric Currents and Motion   Machines that have parts that spin get their motion from a motor. A motor uses an electric current to produce motion.

4. Electric Currents and Sound   Many devices use electric currents in speakers to change energy into sound. An electric current makes parts of a speaker vibrate, which vibrates the air, producing sound.

5. Electric Currents and Light   An electric current can produce light. In an incandescent light bulb, an electric current moves through a filament producing heat and light.

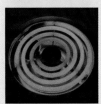

6. Electric Currents and Heat   Electric currents can produce heat. An electric current passing through the metal of an electric stove burner produces heat.

7. Imagining Electric Currents Without Conserved Energy   Like all energy, the energy of moving electric charges is always conserved. Since the energy of moving electric charges is conserved, it is possible to predict what will happen when energy transfers to an object.

The Business of Creativity

Light bulbs, motorized toys, telephones, and calculators—all these objects have something in common. They all use electric current. They also all came from the minds of inventors. What makes someone a good inventor?

It was 1866, and the American Civil War just ended. American homes did not yet have electric power. It would be almost 15 years before Thomas Edison would invent a light bulb that could be used in homes. Inventors were still designing and improving generators that could be used to produce electric current. That year, Granville T. Woods finished school.

Woods would become a great American inventor, but he was only 10 years old in 1866. At that time, many children worked on farms or in factories. Some, like Granville Woods, became apprentices to learn the skills they needed for a job while working.

After finishing school, Woods worked at a machine shop. He learned the skills of a blacksmith. He learned how to shape hot metal into parts for machines. He also learned how to fix machines. He was curious about how things worked and learned as much as he could about the machines he fixed. His understanding of how machines worked is part of what made him a great inventor.

Granville T. Woods worked as a blacksmith. There, he learned how to fix machines, which is part of why he became a great inventor.

Knowing how machines work was not the only skill that made Granville Woods a great inventor. He also had a passion for learning. While he was working, he took classes at night. He also took private lessons and read about topics that interested him. Besides only being able to learn during his free time, Woods had other obstacles to overcome. There was segregation in the United States at the time. As an African American, this meant he could not go to many places that white people could, including libraries. He sometimes had to ask friends to check out books for him.

At the age of 16, Woods left the machine shop to become a fireman on a railroad. Then, he became an engineer of a steam locomotive that pulled the train. He also spent some time traveling the ocean as an engineer on a steamship. All this time, he continued to learn. Woods was especially excited about electricity. He learned everything he could about it.

Granville Woods' experience with steam engines would help him design one of his first inventions. He invented a new steam boiler furnace. This invention would be the first of many creative inventions.

Granville T. Woods learned about trains when he was younger, which helped him design his first invention.

Granville T. Woods used what he knew about electricity and machines to become a great American inventor.

A telegraph sent messages using a different wire than a telephone.

Electrifying Inventions

Woods had many ideas for inventions, but he did not have the time and money to work on them. Yet, he did not give up on his dream of being an inventor. Just like inventors today, he tried to find people who would pay him money for his ideas. He also sold the *patents* to his inventions. A patent is a license from the government to make or sell an invention. Woods made money by selling patents.

Woods sold one of his first inventions to the company of Alexander Graham Bell. Bell had become famous for inventing the telephone. The telephone changes voices to electrical signals that carry energy sent through wires. At the time, telegraphs also used electric current to send messages. But telegraph messages traveled on a different system of wires than telephones did. Woods invented a device that could be used as a telephone or as a telegraph on the same wire. He called this device a *telegraphony*. He sold the patent for this device to Bell's company.

With the money he made by selling patents and getting paid by others, Woods became a full-time inventor. Many of his inventions combined his interests in both electricity and railroads. He used these interests to solve a big problem for railroads.

Telephone and telegraph messages were sent through different wires using electric current. Granville Woods invented a device that could be used as a telephone or a telegraph.

During the 1800s, train stations sent messages using telegraphs. They could send messages to another station, but the signals had to travel through electric wires. The electric wires could not be attached to moving trains. Once a train left the station, there was no way to tell where it was until it reached the next station. Trains sometimes collided because the engineers did not know another train was on the same track!

Woods came up with a solution. Instead of attaching the wire to the trains, he put it next to the tracks. The wire threaded through a coil of wire that was attached to the trains. When the trains moved, the wire moved through the coil. This made electric charges move through the wire by the tracks. The resulting electric current could be used to send telegraph messages to moving trains. Woods' invention helped prevent train crashes and made railroads safer.

Woods kept inventing his whole life. Many of his inventions helped make it possible for others to invent newer kinds of trains, such as subways and elevated trains. He also came up with other creative ideas. He even invented a machine that used electricity to incubate thousands of eggs. You just never know what kinds of ideas will hatch in an inventive mind!

Subways and elevated trains use electric current. Granville Woods' inventions helped make the invention of these trains possible.

Woods even invented a machine that uses electricity to incubate eggs.

How Is Energy Stored and Used?

Science Vocabulary

efficient

Anytime you drop a ball or use an electronic device, these objects release stored energy. You will learn how stored energy can be useful in different ways. Some stored energy can be easily moved and transported. Some stored energy is efficient, or does not create much wasted energy. Engineers often use stored energy to solve problems. Stored energy can also solve everyday problems.

NGSS

4-PS3-4. Apply scientific ideas to design, test, and refine a device that converts energy from one form to another.

PS3.B. Energy can also be transferred from place to place by electric currents, which can then be used locally to produce motion, sound, heat, or light. The currents may have been produced to begin with by transforming the energy of motion into electrical energy.
PS3.D. The expression "produce energy" typically refers to the conversion of stored energy into a desired form for practical use.
ETS1.A. Possible solutions to a problem are limited by available materials and resources (constraints). The success of a designed solution is determined by considering the desired features of a solution (criteria). Different proposals for solutions can be compared on the basis of how well each one meets the specified criteria for success or how well each takes the constraints into account.

Energy and Matter
Energy can be transferred in various ways and between objects.

Constructing Explanations and Designing Solutions

1. Energy Is Stored

A person can bring a music player anywhere by just putting it in his or her pocket. All he or she has to do is turn it on to hear a favorite song. This is because a music player has stored energy.

There are many ways to store energy. The music player stores electric energy in its battery. This stored energy makes an electric current, which goes to a speaker to produce sound.

Food you eat has stored energy. So does the gasoline that you put in a car. The energy in food and gasoline are stored and released when the food and gasoline break down. So, the stored energy in food becomes energy that you use to do things. The stored energy of gasoline becomes energy that the car uses to move.

You might have heard somebody say, "We need to produce more energy." You've learned that energy cannot be created. So, what does this expression mean? To produce energy means to change energy into a useful form. For example, dams store water so that they can produce electric current whenever they need to. Dams hold back lots of water that has stored energy. When the water is released, it falls into a river and spins a turbine that produces an electric current.

Stored energy can be used at a different time or place than where it started out. Batteries, gasoline, and the dam are all objects that have stored energy.

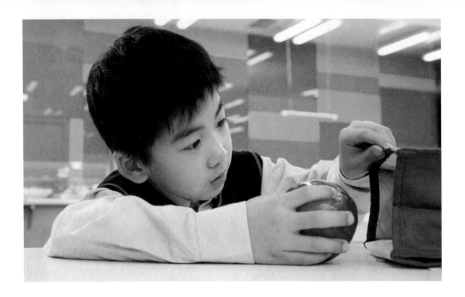

You might need energy in between lunch and dinner. You can carry an apple in your bag. The stored energy of an apple is easier to carry around than a lot of other foods.

2. Stored Energy Is Useful

Energy cannot be created or destroyed. Yet, you might hear people say that the energy was "used up." What do you think they mean?

Stored energy can be used at a different time or place from where it started out. When someone says they are "using energy," they are talking about releasing stored energy. When stored energy is released, it is transferred from one object to another object. This transfer can cause motion, sound, heat, light, or electric current. When you exercise, you are changing food's stored energy into energy of motion. When you use the energy in a battery, the energy is transferred to a wire, causing an electric current. That current can transfer energy to other objects.

Stored Energy Can Be Useful in Different Times and Places

Some kinds of stored energy are useful because they can easily move to different places. You are not always near an electrical outlet, but you can easily bring batteries wherever you go. Batteries let you move energy to other objects in different places. Food and gasoline can also be moved to where they are needed. A car carries gas in its gas tank that stores the gas until the car needs it to move. You might carry a snack in your bag so that you can eat later when you are not near a kitchen.

Some Stored Energy Is Less Wasteful

Some kinds of stored energy are more *efficient* than others. To be **efficient** means to be useful without creating a lot of wasted energy. Consider a car that runs on energy stored in gasoline. When the car releases its energy, some of that energy heats the engine and road. That heat does not help the car move. But now think about a car that runs on electricity stored in a battery. This car might release less heat than the other car, so less of its stored energy is wasted. More of its stored energy is used to move the car. In this case, the car that runs on electricity is more efficient, and the car that runs on gasoline is less efficient.

Some Stored Energy Is Less Expensive

Some kinds of stored energy are useful because they do not cost very much to buy. These days, a car that runs on gasoline is often less expensive to buy than a car that runs on energy stored in batteries. As people invent ways to make cheaper car batteries, this might change. The same is true for buying and setting up solar cells. It is often more expensive to put solar cells on a home than to connect to a power plant using power lines. But once they are set up, solar panels can be much cheaper to use.

A car that runs on energy stored in a battery is called an electric car. Electric cars can be more efficient than cars that run on gasoline.

The new ranger's station needs electricity. It also needs to be small so that it does not harm living things nearby. So, engineers must design a solution to this problem.

 Engineering Design

 Nature of Science

3. Engineers Use Energy to Solve Problems

Suppose that rangers at a national park need a new ranger station. So, during the summer, the park hires an engineering company to design a plan for meeting the energy needs of the new station. The company assigns several engineers who, like most engineers, work as a team.

Defining the Problem

The first step the team of engineers takes is defining the problem. The rangers who will use the new station have many needs. They need heat to cook food and light to be able to see at night. They also need radios to communicate with rangers at other stations. The best way to power all of these activities is with electricity. But the challenge is that there are no power lines near this part of the park. So, the engineers need to solve the problem of bringing power to the cabin.

The engineers have several limitations for their design. The first limitation is that they cannot spend more money than the park can afford. A second is that the cabin must be built before the harsh winter weather comes. The third is that the rangers want to keep the land as natural as possible so that they do not harm nearby living things. The engineers can only make small changes to the land. What is the best way to get electricity to the new station?

Proposing Solutions

Each engineer on the team chooses a kind of energy resource to think about using at the new station. One person considers using the same energy source used at the old ranger's station. That station uses electricity from a power line that came from a nearby city's power plant. Another person thinks about ways to use gasoline and a small generator to produce an electric current. Other choices the team considers are solar cells and a wind turbine. There is a creek nearby, so someone also looks into a way to use water power.

Choosing the Best Solution

The team meets to discuss the advantages and disadvantages of each energy source. Building power lines from the other station to the new station would change the land too much. So would building a large wind turbine or a dam on the creek. Burning gasoline in a generator would make too much noise and smoke.

Solar cells are one of the most expensive choices to build. But they would meet all of the energy needs of the new station. They would also not take up too much space. They could be placed on the roof of the station. And, they would use the energy of sunlight, which is easy to come by in the park. So, the team decides that solar energy is the best way to power the station.

Each kind of energy resource has pros and cons. The best solution for powering the new ranger's station has to have pros that outweigh the cons. So, each engineer on the team has to think about the different resources they can use.

When designing something, you define the problem, think of ways to solve the problem, and select a design. After, you build and test your design, like these students testing a solar oven, you see if it works and if it needs to be improved.

 Engineering Design

 Nature of Science

4. Energy Can Solve Everyday Problems

You and a friend are excited about the contest you are entering. To win, you must design and build a way to cook food without fire. Your limitations are that you cannot spend more than $30, and you only have six weeks to create your design.

Like engineers, first you define the problem you are trying to solve. You know you need to cook food without using the stored energy of wood and other fuels. You also have cost and time limits.

You decide to design a solar oven that will transfer energy from sunlight to food, heating it. Your friend goes to the library to find out how other people have made solar ovens. You go to the store to buy tools and materials. Together, you build a working solar oven so that you can test your design. Days before the contest, you test the oven. It is very sunny, so it works perfectly.

But on the morning of the contest, you see a problem. It is cloudy, so there is not enough sunshine for the oven to work. Thinking quickly, you come up with a way to improve the oven. You add a battery powered lamp to use on cloudy days. The lamp produces light and heat so that the oven can cook the food even when there is no sunlight. It uses stored energy instead of sunlight. Problem solved!

How Is Energy Stored and Used?

1. Energy Is Stored Objects have stored energy, which is energy that can be used a different time or place than where it started out. Food and gasoline are examples of objects containing stored energy. To produce energy means to change stored energy into a useful form.

2. Stored Energy Is Useful When stored energy is released, it is transferred from one object to another. This transfer can cause motion, sound, heat, light, or electric current. Stored energy can be used at different times and in different places. Some kinds of stored energy are very efficient, or useful without creating a lot of wasted energy.

3. Engineers Use Energy to Solve Problems Suppose that rangers hire engineers to design a station. First, the engineers define their problem. Then, they consider different resources and the advantages and disadvantages of the resources. Finally, the engineers choose a solution that has the most advantages and the least disadvantages.

4. Energy Can Solve Everyday Problems Consider that you and a friend must design a way to cook food without fire. Like engineers, first you define your problem. You define it as not being able to use materials that burn. You decide to design a solar oven that you then build and test.

Blackout!

You use stored energy each day. Much of the energy you use comes from electric currents from electrical outlets. What happens when the current stops flowing from these outlets?

Rain pounds against the roof, and a loud clap of thunder makes the windows rattle. Good thing you are safe inside reading your favorite book. Then suddenly, the lights go out, leaving you in total darkness. Through the rain streaked window, you can see that all of the lights across the street are out, too. It's a blackout!

Power plants produce electric current far away from where most people live. The electric current flows long distances to towns and cities through wires called *power lines*. The energy in the electric current is not stored energy. When the electric current stops flowing through the wires, the power goes out. Any machines or lights that use electric current from power lines stop working during a blackout.

You cannot turn on lights or watch TV during a blackout. But you can turn on a flashlight to use the energy stored in its batteries. Usually, the power will come back on again shortly. You can get through a blackout pretty easily at home. But, what happens in the rest of the city during a blackout?

When the power goes out, electric current stops flowing through wires into your house. Anything that plugs into the wall stops working. But you can still use stored energy in batteries to make light.

Getting around a city during a blackout is difficult. Cars still work, but streetlights and traffic lights do not.

People who are out during a blackout might have trouble getting home. The streets will be dark because the streetlights will be off. Cars and buses can move down the streets because they use stored energy from gasoline in their tanks. Yet, none of the traffic lights will be working. The subways use electric current, too. So, they will come to a halt. People will not even be able to use elevators to get to the bottom floor of a tall building.

Blackouts also affect people in some unexpected ways. The water that comes out of your faucet might not seem to depend on electric current, but it does. Electric current is used to pump water from where it is stored through pipes into buildings. No flowing electric current may also mean no flowing water.

For places such as hospitals, losing the energy carried by electric currents is very dangerous. Many patients depend on machines that use electric current. Doctors need light to operate. That is why hospitals have generators that turn on during an emergency. Generators use the stored energy in fuel to produce electricity.

Power Down

Some blackouts affect only one neighborhood. Sometimes, though, a big problem can cause a blackout in many whole cities at once. The number of people left in the dark depends on the cause of the blackout.

Weather is often to blame. Thunderstorms, snow storms, and hurricanes can cause blackouts. Lightning strikes can damage equipment that helps electric current flow through power lines. Strong winds and heavy snow can knock down power lines. When the wires are broken, electric current will not flow. Large storms may knock down many power lines at once. People in the storm's path may be without power for days until the power lines are fixed.

Workers may stop electric current from flowing through power lines on purpose, for safety reasons. Electric currents carry a large amount of energy through power lines. They are dangerous if they flow from the wires to other objects. Normally, the power lines do not touch anything that can carry the electric current. However, power lines sometimes sag and can touch a tall tree if one is nearby. Then, the electric current can flow through the tree. If that happens, the flow of electric current to that line automatically shuts off. If it did not, the tree might catch on fire.

Large storms, like Hurricane Sandy in 2012, can cause blackouts. Winds knock down power lines. Flooding can damage equipment needed to keep electric current flowing through power lines.

Reducing Blackouts

Have you ever seen power lines passing through the forest in the country? They follow a path that has been cleared of trees. There is a reason for that. Many blackouts are caused by trees touching power lines. Power companies are supposed to cut the trees along the path of the large power lines that carry energy to cities. Within cities, workers keep tree branches trimmed so that they do not touch smaller power lines. Keeping the trees away from power lines is one simple way to reduce blackouts.

Engineers also use new tools to measure the electric current flowing through power lines. These tools help them detect problems with the electric current early. Then, they may be able to fix the problem before it causes a blackout.

Even with trimmed trees and engineers keeping watch over power lines, there will still be some blackouts. There is no way to stop a storm. Strong winds and lightning strikes will very likely cause blackouts from time to time. So, make sure you are prepared with a supply of stored energy. You don't need a generator. But a flashlight and some extra batteries will keep you from being in the dark.

Workers keep trees trimmed so that they are far away from big power lines. That way, even if the power lines sag, they will not touch a tree.

How Do People Choose Energy Resources?

Science Vocabulary

natural resource

nonrenewable resource

renewable resource

You may have heard that it is important to turn off lights so that you do not waste electricity. This is because electricity is produced from the energy of natural resources. You will discover that some natural resources can easily be replaced and some cannot.

NGSS **4-ESS3-1.** Obtain and combine information to describe that energy and fuels are derived from natural resources and their uses affect the environment.

ESS3.A. Energy and fuels that humans use are derived from natural sources, and their use affects the environment in multiple ways. Some resources are renewable over time, and others are not.

Cause and Effect Cause and effect relationships are routinely identified and used to explain change.

 Obtaining, Evaluating, and Communicating Information

1. Everything Uses Energy

When you are at home, you might turn on lights or open a refrigerator. The lights and refrigerator both require energy to run. Most of the energy people use in their homes was produced far away from where they live.

Some of the energy people use comes from fuels, like gasoline and natural gas that are burned to produce heat and, from the heat, motion. If you walk, ride the bus, or take a car to school, you use energy. Farms use energy to grow and harvest foods. It takes a lot of energy to move people, materials, and products from place to place. It even takes energy to move fuel from place to place.

Cities and towns need a large amount of energy since they have lots of people. Much of this energy is carried by electric currents. Electric currents power many devices that people use. A radio uses electric current to make sound, a lamp uses it to make light, and a stove uses it to make heat. Electric currents are useful because they can easily flow through wires to homes and devices. So, they can be produced far away from people and brought to them easily through power lines.

People use energy for many different activities. Electricity is an efficient way to deliver energy to lots of people.

2. Energy Comes from Natural Resources

If you are outside and look up, you might see power lines. These wires carry electric current to homes and businesses. Where does the electric current come from?

How Power Plants Produce Electricity

Since energy cannot be created or destroyed, it has to come from the energy of another object or place. Many homes get their energy from a power plant, or a station where electricity is produced. Many power plants use machines called generators.

Generators use the energy of motion to produce an electric current. A generator has a large metal wire coil and a strong magnet. A magnet can move electric charges. So, when the magnet in a generator moves near the wire, it makes electric charges flow. As they move through the wire, they create an electric current.

In a generator, a *turbine* can move a magnet near a coil of wire to produce electric current. A turbine is a device that uses the energy of a moving gas or liquid to spin a rod. The rod is attached to the coil or the magnet. The rod turns and makes the electric charges move within the wire coil. This is how a generator uses turning motion to produce electricity.

All energy has to come from another object or place. Many homes get their energy from power plants that use generators. A generator produces electricity using the energy of its moving parts.

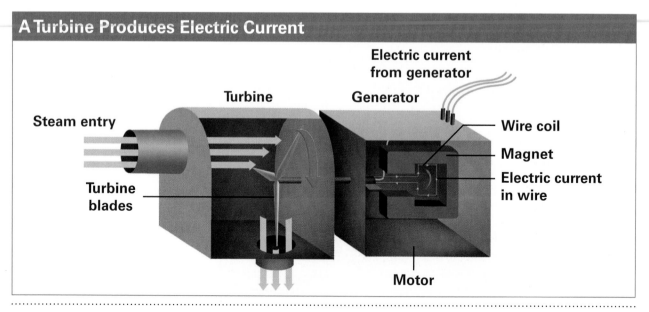

A Turbine Produces Electric Current

Electric current from generator

Turbine

Generator

Steam entry

Wire coil

Magnet

Electric current in wire

Turbine blades

Motor

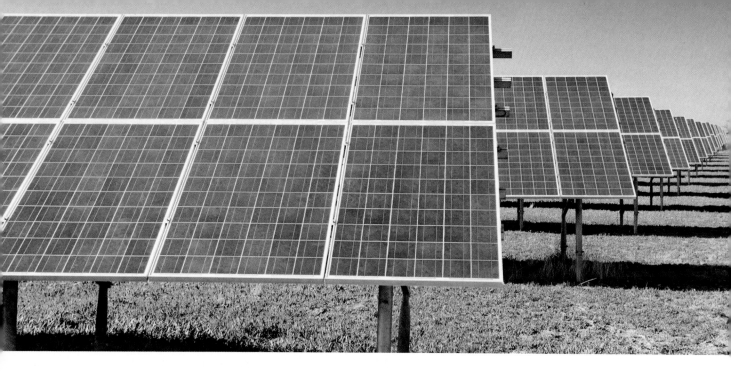

Power Plants Use Natural Resources

Many power plants use generators with turbines to produce electric current. They can differ in how they get the turbines to turn. Some burn fuels to produce heat, which makes steam that spins the turbine. Common fuels are oil, coal, wood, and natural gas. Nuclear power plants use special fuels that, when they break down, give off lots of energy. Other power plants use the stored energy of water behind a dam. When gates open, water spills from the dam. As it flows past, it turns the turbine. Still others use the energy of wind to make a turbine turn.

Even the energy of a power plant is not created from nothing. It comes from the natural world. Power plants use natural resources to produce energy. A **natural resource** is a material or source of energy found in nature that is useful to people. Oil, coal, wood, and natural gas are natural resources. So are wind and moving water. Materials such as uranium that are sources of nuclear energy are also natural resources. Even sunlight is a natural resource. In fact, some power plants do not use generators. Instead, they use solar cells. They absorb sunlight to produce electricity directly.

Many different kinds of natural resources are used to produce electrical energy. Here, solar cells are producing electricity using sunlight.

3. Energy Resources Have Advantages and Disadvantages

The kind of energy resource that is most useful for a place depends on factors such as its location, its effect on the environment, and if it can be replaced.

How Easy Is It to Get the Resource?

Some places have lots of one type of resource nearby, but other places might not have any. For example, a windy area is a good place to build a wind farm. An area that gets lots of sunshine year round would be a good place to build a solar power plant. You are more likely to find a power plant that runs on coal near a coal mine because coal is a plentiful resource in the area.

How Will Using the Resource Affect the Environment?

Most energy resources have disadvantages. Using some energy resources can cause problems for nearby living things. A dam causes the level of water in an area to change, which can lead to flooding and habitat loss. These changes can cause some types of plants and animals to die off. The dam can cause other types of living things to grow out of control. Power plants that burn fuels can give off heat, smoke, or other forms of air pollution that harm living things. Nuclear power plants produce wastes that are dangerous to all living things for thousands of years.

Some natural resources are easy to get, but they might cause problems for the environment. This excavator is used for coal mining. Coal mining causes habitat loss and can harm living things.

Wind turbines create electrical energy from wind energy. Wind is an example of a renewable energy source because it does not get used up.

Can the Resource Be Replaced?

Not all energy resources will be around forever. A **nonrenewable resource** is a natural resource that cannot be replaced as quickly as it is used by people. Coal, oil, and natural gas are nonrenewable resources that are found underground. They come from the ancient remains of living things. It takes millions of years for them to form. So, when people burn them for energy, they cannot easily be replaced. There might be many of these fuels on Earth today. But people cannot easily make more. Once they are used up, they are gone.

Some natural resources can be replaced as quickly as they are used. These are called **renewable resources**. Water, sunlight, and wind are renewable resources. For example, people can use solar cells to produce electric current from sunlight. No matter how much sunlight is used, it cannot be used up because the sun continues to shine and produce more sunlight.

When people design power plants, they have to think about all of these factors. They have to understand how energy transfers. They have to consider how the energy will be used and which energy resource is the best for an area. They think about the pros and cons of each resource. Then they choose the best one for their needs.

4. Energy Use in the Past and Present

What do you do when the power goes out at night? You might have to use a flashlight to find your way around. But before electricity was discovered, using a flashlight would not be an option.

People have not always used the same natural resources for energy. In the past, the only light people could use at night was from burning candles and oil lamps. Candles were made from animal oils or fats. Oil lamps used a type of oil called kerosene. Then scientists discovered electricity and found ways to use it to produce light. People could use electric lamps to light up their homes at night. They used oils and animal fats less often, but they used other natural resources more.

Engineers are always looking for ways to improve how we get our energy. They look for cheaper ways to get energy. They also look for ways of producing and using energy that does not create too much waste or cause pollution. Engineers also look for ways to cut down on the ways that power plants harm living things. To improve how we get energy, engineers must have a strong science background and understanding of the effects of using natural resources.

Before electricity, people used oil lamps like this one to see at night.

The way that people use natural resources for energy has changed over time. Nowadays, people use electric lamps instead of oil lamps to provide light at night.

How Do People Choose Energy Resources?

1. Everything Uses Energy   Much of the energy that people use in their homes comes from fuels. Fuels such as oil and natural gas are burned to produce heat and, from the heat, to produce motion. Much of this energy is carried by electric currents. Many devices use energy carried by electric currents.

2. Energy Comes from Natural Resources   All energy has to come from another object or place. Many homes get energy from power plants that use generators to produce electric current from energy of motion. Power plants produce energy from materials or sources of energy found in nature that are useful to people.

3. Energy Resources Have Advantages and Disadvantages Many factors determine how useful an energy resource is. If there is a lot of a resource nearby, then it is useful to be used for energy. Some resources have disadvantages, such as causing problems for living things. Some resources can be easily replaced as they are used and some cannot.

4. Energy Use in the Past and Present   Inventions have changed how people use energy. Engineers are looking for ways to improve how we get energy. Improvements can make energy cheaper to obtain. Improvements can also make obtaining energy less harmful to living things.

Your Energy Future

The ways people use energy resources change over time. Your grandparents probably did not use solar cells when they were young. Engineers were still developing that technology then. How do you think you will get the energy you use in future?

Have you ever thought about your dream car? Maybe it will be a small car that's painted your favorite color. Perhaps it might even be able to drive itself! One thing is for sure, it will use energy.

Engineers are always developing new cars, computers, and other machines. More and more people around the world are also using these machines. With more machines and more people using them, the amount of energy people use is growing. Engineers are thinking of new, creative ways to solve this problem, too.

Engineers are already developing new ways to power cars. For your dream car, you might have pictured filling up its tank with gasoline. But, you could also choose an electric car that plugs into an outlet to charge its battery. Or you could choose a hybrid car that uses both gasoline and a battery.

Some cars even run on hydrogen gas. Cars that use hydrogen produce little pollution. But, hydrogen is a gas, like air. Engineers are still trying to find safer ways to store the hydrogen fuel in a car.

Today, most people fuel their cars with gasoline. In the future, people may use hydrogen gas as fuel, as this car does.

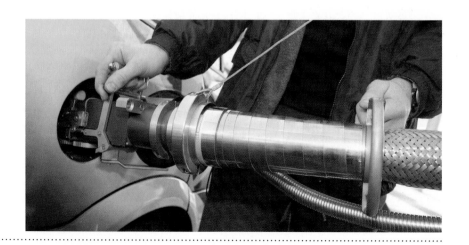

Turning Tornadoes into Electricity

Engineers are always looking for new sources of energy for power plants. Some are even turning to an unlikely source—tornadoes!

A tornado is a column of whirling air. That fast moving air has a huge amount of energy. It can have enough energy to tear down buildings. Most tornadoes are hard to predict and only last a few minutes. So, how can engineers use them to generate electricity?

The answer is: make your own tornado! Some engineers are doing just that. They have made a tornado in a tube. At about 100 m (328 ft) tall, it is much smaller than a real tornado. But it is the first step in using tornadoes to produce electricity. Now they need to make a tornado big enough so that the moving air has enough energy to turn a turbine. The tornado would suck air through the turbine. The turbine would then turn the energy of motion into electricity.

No one is sure yet if using a tornado will work. Engineers need lots of hot air to make a big tornado, and it takes energy to heat the air. However, they might be able to use heat that is otherwise wasted at fuel-burning power plants. There is a chance that the tornado could get out of control. Yet, it's possible that someday you may safely be using energy from a tornado.

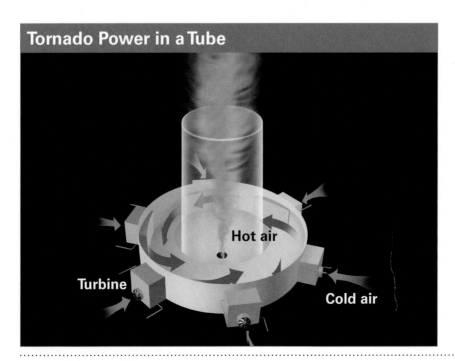

Tornado Power in a Tube

Hot air

Turbine

Cold air

Engineers can make tornadoes in a tube. The energy of the moving air in the tornado could someday be used to turn turbines that would generate electricity.

This power plant uses heat from the rocks in inactive volcanoes to heat water underground. This makes steam that moves a turbine.

Volcano Boiling Pot

Tornadoes are not the only force of nature that could one day generate electricity. Inactive volcanoes may also be an energy resource of the future.

An inactive volcano may seem like any other mountain. It does not spit ash, and no hot lava runs down its sides. However, the rocks inside Earth below the volcano are often still hot enough to turn water into steam. And, steam is very useful for producing electricity. It can turn the turbines in power plants.

Some power plants, including many in Iceland, already use hot underground water to generate electricity. But some volcanoes do not have much water below ground. This has not stopped the creative minds of engineers. Near a volcano in Oregon, they are pumping millions of gallons of water deep underground. There, the hot rocks heat the water to make steam. The steam moves a turbine at a power plant before going back into the ground as hot water.

Power plants that use this energy do not burn fuels that pollute the air. But they have another problem. Pumping water underground can cause earthquakes. So far, most of these earthquakes have been too small to feel. Engineers are studying what causes them so they can prevent bigger ones.

Ocean Wave Power

Off the coast of Scotland, engineers have designed a clever way to get at another source of energy: ocean waves. When waves roll onto the shore, their energy moves sand and other objects on the beach. This movement could be used to generate electricity.

Engineers put machines with big flaps underwater near the shore. When a wave passes by a machine, it transfers energy to the flap and makes it move back and forth.

The energy of the moving flap is still offshore. How can people on land use it? To solve this problem, engineers connected the machines to a power plant that has pipes filled with water. The moving flaps push the water in the pipes to the power plant. The pushed water then turns a turbine and generates electricity.

As with all ways of producing electricity, using ocean waves has advantages and disadvantages. It does not produce pollution. But wave power machines are useful only where and when ocean waves have enough energy to move the flaps. The machines could also affect the animals that live near them in the ocean.

It is hard to say which energy sources will be in your future. Engineers have already designed several choices. Perhaps you might even think of a new one!

In Scotland, engineers created machines that use energy from waves to produce electricity.

Earth's Changing Surface

If you look closely around you, you will see evidence of Earth's changing surface. You might see rainwater flowing down a hill. Or you might see wind blowing across sand. Ocean waves beating against a shore can break up rock and deposit sand. Some changes are slow. Others happen quickly. Some changes happen in patterns that scientists study and map. In this unit, you will learn how Earth's surface is changing. These changes can tell us about Earth's past.

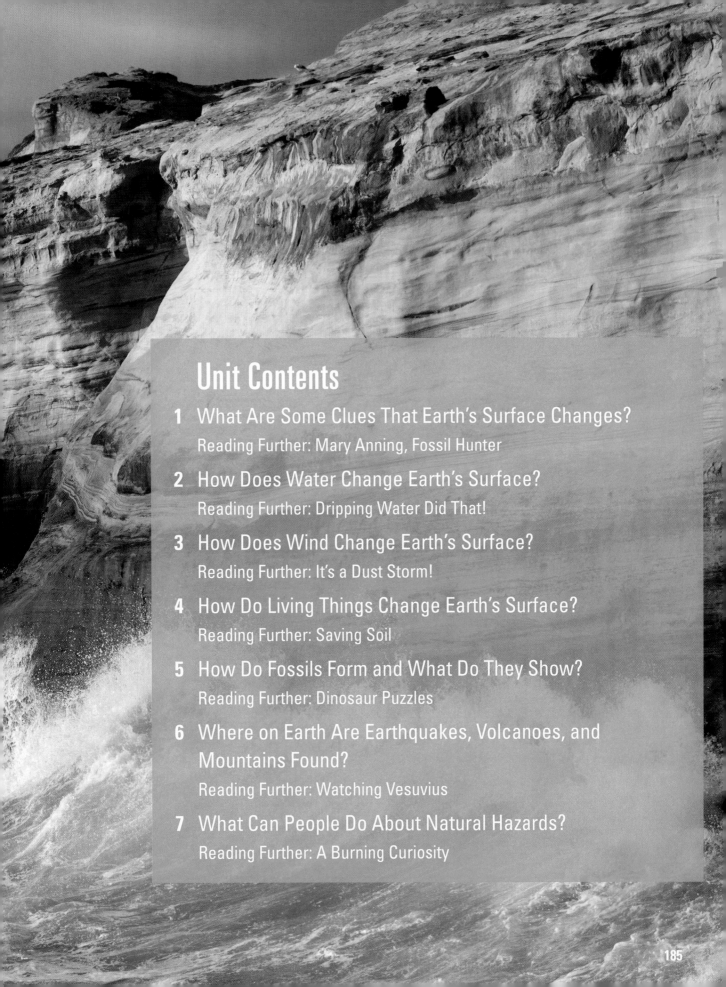

Unit Contents

Unit 3 Overview

NGSS Next Generation Science Standards

Performance Expectations

4-ESS1-1. Identify evidence from patterns in rock formations and fossils in rock layers to support an explanation for changes in a landscape over time.

4-ESS2-1. Make observations and/or measurements to provide evidence of the effects of weathering or the rate of erosion by water, ice, wind, or vegetation.

4-ESS2-2. Analyze and interpret data from maps to describe patterns of Earth's features.

4-ESS3-2. Generate and compare multiple solutions to reduce the impacts of natural Earth processes on humans.

Disciplinary Core Ideas

ESS1.C: The History of Planet Earth

• Local, regional, and global patterns of rock formations reveal changes over time due to earth forces, such as earthquakes. The presence and location of certain fossil types indicate the order in which rock layers were formed.

ESS2.A: Earth Materials and Systems

• Rainfall helps to shape the land and affects the types of living things found in a region. Water, ice, wind, living organisms, and gravity break rocks, soils, and sediments into smaller particles and move them around.

ESS2.B: Plate Tectonics and Large-Scale System Interactions

• The locations of mountain ranges, deep ocean trenches, ocean floor structures, earthquakes, and volcanoes occur in patterns. Most earthquakes and volcanoes occur in bands that are often along the boundaries between continents and oceans. Major mountain chains form inside continents or near their edges. Maps can help locate the different land and water features areas of Earth.

ESS2.E: Biogeology

• Living things affect the physical characteristics of their regions.

ESS3.B: Natural Hazards

• A variety of hazards result from natural processes (e.g., earthquakes, tsunamis, volcanic eruptions). Humans cannot eliminate the hazards but can take steps to reduce their impacts.

ETS1.B: Designing Solutions to Engineering Problems

• Testing a solution involves investigating how well it performs under a range of likely conditions.

Crosscutting Concepts

Patterns

• Patterns can be used as evidence to support an explanation.

Cause and Effect

• Cause and effect relationships are routinely identified, tested, and used to explain change.

 Planning and Carrying Out Investigations

 Analyzing and Interpreting Data

 Constructing Explanations and Designing Solutions

Have you ever wondered...

Rain, ocean waves, ice, wind, and living things constantly change Earth's surface. These changes can reveal clues about Earth's past. This unit will help you answer these questions and many others you may ask.

How do fossils form?

Are mountains found all over the world?

Why do some places on Earth have different colored layers?

What Are Some Clues That Earth's Surface Changes?

Science Vocabulary

deposition

erosion

weathering

If you go outside and observe your surroundings, you can find evidence of how Earth's surface has changed. You might find layers of dry mud, ripples in sand, or cracked rocks. Evidence like this shows changes to Earth's surface. Scientists study this kind of evidence to learn about Earth's surface and predict future changes.

NGSS

4-ESS2-1. Make observations and/or measurements to provide evidence of the effects of weathering or the rate of erosion by water, ice, wind, or vegetation.

ESS2.A. Rainfall helps to shape the land and affects the types of living things found in a region. Water, ice, wind, living organisms, and gravity break rocks, soils, and sediments into smaller particles and move them around.

ESS2.E. Living things affect the physical characteristics of their regions.

Cause and Effect Cause and effect relationships are routinely identified, tested, and used to explain change.

Planning and Carrying Out Investigations

1. Earth's Changing Surface

The surface of Earth is always changing. Sometimes, these changes happen so slowly you might not notice them. And other times, these changes happen quickly. Three processes change Earth's surface: *weathering*, *erosion*, and *deposition*.

Water, ice, wind, and living things can all cause these processes. **Weathering** is the natural process of breaking down rock. Moving water or wind can weather rock by breaking it down into smaller and smaller pieces like sand and soil. A growing plant can also break apart rock. Sometimes, the weathered pieces are then moved by a process called *erosion*. **Erosion** occurs when weathered bits of rock or soil are loosened and moved from one place to another. Eventually, the eroded pieces stop moving and settle. This process is called **deposition**.

How can you tell what changes have happened around you? You can see evidence in many different places, like the bend of a river, a windy beach, or the roots of a tree. Scientists study evidence to learn about how Earth has changed. They look for patterns in the evidence that help predict changes. You might see some of the same evidence in the Earth's surface near you. You can use it to learn how Earth's surface has changed. You can also use it to predict what changes might happen in the future.

Earth's surface is always changing. During a storm, the force of raindrops falling on the ground loosens small bits of soil. This is called weathering. The water then moves some of this material as it flows to different places in a process called erosion.

Rainwater can erode soil, rocks, and other objects and then deposit them in new places. When rainwater dries, it leaves behind dried mud that crumbles when you touch it. Mud is evidence of how Earth's surface has changed.

2. Water Leaves Evidence of How It Changes Earth's Surface

Water can cause weathering, erosion, and deposition. You can observe evidence all around you that shows how water has caused these changes.

If you've seen how the ground changes during and after a rainstorm, then you've seen how water can change Earth's surface. Think about a garden and sidewalk when it is warm and dry outside. The soil is evenly distributed around the plants, and the sidewalk is clean. Then, suddenly, there is a rainstorm! Water flows from the garden to the sidewalk, carrying bits of soil. This is erosion. The water leaves behind a layer of soil on the sidewalk. This is deposition. Some of the water soaks into the ground and some collects in puddles.

A few days after the storm, you notice that the puddles have dried up. Where the puddles had been is a thick layer of dried mud deposited by each puddle. You can even pick up the mud and crumble it.

Compare how the sidewalk looks before and after the rain. Can you observe how rain caused erosion and deposition? The layer of dried mud left from the puddle was not on the sidewalk before it rained, but it was afterward. This is evidence that water caused Earth's surface to change.

3. Wind Leaves Evidence of How It Changes Earth's Surface

Wind can also cause Earth's surface to change through weathering, erosion, and deposition. You can find evidence left by wind that shows these changes.

In deserts, you can often observe changes in the sand caused by wind. Suppose you visit a desert. The landscape is covered in sand with few plants or animals, and the sand is smooth and flat. When you crouch close to the sand, you observe that it is still.

The next day you return to the same area, but it looks very different! You might have seen how wind changes water when it blows over a pond. The wind makes tiny waves, called ripples, which move the same direction as the wind. In this same way, the wind has formed ripples in the sand that look just like the ones in water. If you bend down to observe the ripples, you may notice the wind is still blowing tiny bits of sand, moving them along.

Sand ripples are often formed in deserts by wind, far from any water at all. If you observe the sand ripples, can you see how wind caused weathering, erosion, or deposition? The sand ripples were not in the sand before the wind started blowing. The wind eroded the sand, moving it to new places. Ripples are evidence that wind changed Earth's surface.

Blowing winds in the open desert can erode and deposit large amounts of sand. Ripples in the sand are evidence that the wind has blown here.

4. Living Things Leave Evidence of How They Change Earth's Surface

Like wind and water, living things can change Earth's surface through weathering, erosion, and deposition. But they can also prevent these processes from happening.

The roots of a tree can speed up or slow down weathering, erosion, and deposition. Suppose you are hiking in a park, and you stop to observe a river. There are no trees on the river's edge, but there are large rocks. Soil and bits of rock look like they will fall into the water.

As you continue to hike along the river, you come to an area that has many trees that line the river's edge. You notice that the roots of some trees are sticking out of the soil. You see roots that have pushed through rocks and cracked them. But they also look like they are holding soil in place and stopping it from falling into the water.

Living things, like the growing roots of a tree, can affect weathering, erosion, and deposition and change Earth's surface. Compare the part of the river without trees on its edge to the part with trees on its edge. Can you observe how the roots have affected weathering, erosion or deposition? The roots sticking out and the broken rocks are evidence that Earth's surface has changed.

Living things, like the roots of a tree, can cause weathering, erosion, and deposition. At other times, like these trees holding soil on a riverbank, they slow down these processes.

What Are Some Clues That Earth's Surface Changes?

1. Earth's Changing Surface Earth's surface is always changing. The different types of changes are weathering, erosion, and deposition. Water, wind, and living things can all cause these processes. They leave evidence that scientists study to find out what Earth used to be like and how it is changing today.

2. Water Leaves Evidence of How It Changes Earth's Surface The water from a rainstorm can cause weathering, erosion, and deposition. If you observe the sidewalk before and after a storm, you can find evidence of how these processes have changed Earth's surface. Finding mud is evidence that water was once there.

3. Wind Leaves Evidence of How It Changes Earth's Surface Wind can cause weathering, erosion, and deposition. The wind can pick up weathered material and move it. In a desert, the wind creates ripples in the sand by first eroding and then depositing it. Sand ripples are clues that wind has changed Earth's surface.

4. Living Things Leave Evidence of How They Change Earth's Surface Living things can cause weathering, erosion, and deposition. Living things can also slow down these processes. The roots of a tree can crack rocks into smaller pieces. But they might also prevent water erosion by holding soil and rocks in place.

Mary Anning, Fossil Hunter

Mary Anning has been called "the greatest fossilist the world ever knew." She was very young when she found the first known fossil of a huge reptile that once lived in the ocean.

Try repeating this saying several times quickly without getting tripped up: *She sells seashells by the seashore.* This tongue twister is fun to say, and it is also about a real person—Mary Anning. However, the "seashells" she sold were fossils. Some actually were the fossils of shells. Other fossils she found were what people at first called "sea monsters."

Anning was born in 1799 in an English town called Lyme Regis, located on the southwest coast of England. All along this coast are high cliffs containing many fossils. Anning's father made furniture for a living. However, his real passion was hunting for fossils. He introduced Mary and her brother to fossil hunting along the beach near their home, and they loved it.

Anning earned money by selling small fossils to tourists.

The cliffs along the Lyme Regis coast are made of rock layers. These layers formed from clay, mud, and a rock called limestone. Chunks of cliff continually erode. They break off and fall to the beach. When Anning and her brother went fossil hunting with their father, they used hammers to dig into the cliffs or break open fallen rocks. The fossils they found were known as "curiosities." They were one of the reasons many people were inspired to visit Lyme Regis.

Finding the "Fish Lizard"

During Mary Anning's life, girls and women rarely went to school or worked outside the home. Her father earned all the money for the family. They were poor. So, when he died in 1810, the family had no money coming in.

A few months after her father's death, Anning went looking for fossils alone. A powerful storm had just hit the coast. Storms cause landslides that expose new fossils. These fossils have to be collected quickly before they are lost to the sea. Anning had a skilled eye for finding these fossils. She found several beautiful, newly exposed fossils.

Anning and her brother started earning money again by hunting for fossils. Then they sold them to tourists. In 1811, when she was 12, they made an unusual find. It was a large, strange skull. Her brother had started working by then, so Anning uncovered the rest of the fossil skeleton herself. It took months of extremely slow, careful work.

As Anning worked, word spread of the discovery. No one had ever seen anything like it before. The skull looked like a crocodile, but it had huge, round eyes. The skeleton looked like a lizard except it was shaped like a fish. The creature was later named *Ichthyosaurus*, which means "fish lizard." It was the first such fossil skeleton ever found.

This fossil is a complete skeleton of another kind of ichthyosaur, known as *Ichthyosaurus communis*. It also was found in Lyme Regis.

Gaining Acceptance

After finding and selling the "fish lizard," Anning started teaching herself geology. She also learned how to make scientific drawings of the fossils she found. She kept searching the rocky cliffs for fossils. And she studied how fossil animals compared to living animals.

Anning continued to find many small and large fossils. She sold them to tourists, collectors, and scientists. In 1823, Anning made another major discovery. She found the first complete skeleton of a *plesiosaur*. Plesiosaurs were another type of reptile that lived in the oceans. Anning's discovery showed that plesiosaurs had paddle-like limbs and very long necks.

After the plesiosaur find, Anning became increasingly well known as a fossil hunter. However, she was still poor, despite her experience and knowledge. Because she was a woman, she could not go to college. For many years, the male scientists who bought and studied Mary Anning's fossils got all the credit for these discoveries.

Fortunately, Anning had friends among the successful scientists of the time. They began to help inform the world that she had discovered so many important fossils. Many shared information with her through letters. Some came to visit her and see the cliffs of Lyme Regis for themselves. They also helped her sell her fossils to museums.

A visitor at the Natural History Museum in London, England, views Anning's first plesiosaur find.

Mary Anning's discoveries were very important. During the 1800s, scientists were just beginning to understand what fossils tell us about Earth's history. Weathering and erosion were important for revealing fossils to early hunters. Anning continued to find exciting fossils throughout her life. Newspapers often reported new finds like Anning's. And scientists were eager to study each big new discovery.

Fossil hunters discovered more and more kinds of fossil animals. People realized that the world's oceans had long ago been full of these huge, seemingly monstrous animals. They also began to understand that many kinds of living things that once lived on Earth are now gone forever. For people in the 1800s, these were completely new and shocking ideas.

Large chunks of rock still fall from the cliffs near Lyme Regis. The area is still a very popular vacation spot. If you go there, you can take fossil-hunting tours. You can even visit a museum of Mary Anning's work. You will also find many people following in Mary Anning's footsteps looking for fossils along the coast. Who among them, perhaps another 12 year old, will discover another ancient sea creature like Anning's *Ichthyosaurus*?

Along the coast of England, large chunks of rock still fall from the cliffs near Lyme Regis. Anning roamed the coast and used hammers to break apart the rocks to find fossils.

How Does Water Change Earth's Surface?

Science Vocabulary

glacier

minerals

sediment

sedimentary rock

Weathering, erosion and deposition are changing Earth's surface all around you. Water is an important cause of these changes. You will learn that water changes Earth's surface in different ways. Some of these changes are easy to observe because they happen quickly. But sometimes these changes happen over millions of years!

NGSS

4-ESS2-1. Make observations and/or measurements to provide evidence of the effects of weathering or the rate of erosion by water, ice, wind, or vegetation.

ESS2.A. Rainfall helps to shape the land and affects the types of living things found in a region. Water, ice, wind, living organisms, and gravity break rocks, soils, and sediments into smaller particles and move them around.

Cause and Effect Cause and effect relationships are routinely identified, tested, and used to explain change.

Planning and Carrying Out Investigations

1. Rainwater Causes Weathering and Erosion

You learned that water can weather rock and erode soil. These processes change Earth's surface and, when a lot of water is flowing, these changes can happen fast.

Think about the last time there was a storm where you live. During a storm, rainwater can erode soil very quickly. You might see splashing rain drops, moving soil on a bare spot of ground. When the rainwater hits the soil, it loosens the soil at the surface. This is the beginning of erosion. The water splashes bits of soil and small rocks and starts to flow downhill. When it rains enough, small streams start to form. Eventually, small streams join together into larger streams and then rivers. The force of this water carries bits of rock and soil along with it. So, within minutes or hours, a heavy storm can cause a lot of erosion.

Rainwater can also weather rock. Think about the stream during a heavy rainstorm again. As the water rushes over the ground, the bits of sand and soil that it carries slowly grind down the rock they flow over. Some of the rainwater also flows down into the soil and rock. Very slowly, the water mixes with some of the *minerals* in the rock and soil. **Minerals** are the chemicals that rock is made out of. Because the minerals are mixed with the water, they are carried away as the water flows. The movement of these minerals changes the structure of the rock. In these ways, rainwater weathers rock.

Rainwater flows downhill after a rainstorm, collecting into ever larger streams and rivers. The force of the water erodes previously weathered material. It also grinds down and weathers the rock it flows over.

2. Rainwater Causes Deposition

Over time, rain weathers rock. It also erodes large amounts of material. What happens to the eroded bits of rock and soil?

The rainwater carrying sand, rock, and soil will eventually stop moving. When the water stops moving, it deposits the sand, rock, or soil in new areas. These small pieces of sand, rock, and soil are now *sediment*. **Sediment** is any eroded material, such as weathered rock, sand, and soil, that is deposited in a new place.

As the rain slows, the rainwater flowing over the ground starts to slow down. Usually, larger pieces of material settle and are deposited first. During a heavy rainstorm, you might see a small layer of rocks on the sidewalk. As the rain turns into a drizzle or stops completely, the water deposits the smaller pieces of material such as sand or soil.

Deposition Makes Layers

Sometimes rainwater deposits sediment in more than one layer. After a storm, you might see a layer of dried mud covering some of the sidewalk or street. This mud is made of many tiny pieces of sediment. If it rains again several days later, a new layer of sediment will be deposited on top of the first layer. The new layer might be made of a different type of sediment. So, you might see different colors or textures from the original layer of mud.

When rainwater slows down or dries, it can deposit a layer of mud that can crack as it dries.

Flooding waters erode weathered material, moving it downhill. The water deposits this material as sediment in new areas, often along the banks of the stream.

3. Deposition Helps Form New Rocks

Suppose you are at the Grand Canyon. You may notice that it is made of many layers of different colored rock. Where did these layers come from?

These layers of rock were formed by deposition. Much of this material was deposited by water at different times. Some of the rocks in the Grand Canyon are 2 billion years old!

Remember how rainwater can deposit layers of sediment along the sidewalk? On some places on Earth, the same thing happens on a much larger scale. Many large rivers deposit huge amounts of sediment where they slow down or reach the sea. After many years, these sediments can add up to form a deep layer. Sometimes the environment changes, and a new kind of sediment starts being deposited. This forms a different layer. New layers always form on top of the older layers.

As more sediment is deposited, the sediment is buried and changes over time. Sediment is heavier than water. The layers on top push down on the layers beneath them, and the pieces of rock and soil get smashed together. Minerals from the water can act like glue to help the pieces stick together. Eventually, the material can become solid rock. Rock that is formed from deposited sediment is called **sedimentary rock**. Many of Earth's surface rocks are sedimentary rocks.

Sedimentary rock forms when layers of sediment are pressed together into one solid piece. Sedimentary rock, like this sandstone, often shows those layers.

Over time, deposited sediment can add up to form deep layers. As these layers are buried, they very slowly turn into a type of stone called sedimentary rock. Many layers of sedimentary rock can be seen in the Grand Canyon.

4. River Water Weathers and Erodes

Weathering, erosion, and deposition can happen very quickly, but it usually takes a long time for them to change a whole landscape. The Grand Canyon was carved by these processes, but it took millions of years.

A *canyon* is a deep valley carved by water in an area of rock. The Grand Canyon is one of the deepest canyons in the world. At the bottom of the Grand Canyon flows the Colorado River. Millions of years ago, this river started flowing and weathering the rock in the area.

Weathering alone cannot carve a canyon. Erosion must also happen. As the Colorado River carried huge amounts of sediment from the canyon to the ocean, the water eroded the rock. Most scientists think it took about 6 million years for the river to weather and erode the whole Grand Canyon. Recently, other scientists found new evidence that the canyon might be over 17 million years old. Scientific explanations can change and improve with new evidence.

Erosion and weathering can make an area look completely different. The Colorado River still runs through the Grand Canyon, deepening it over time.

The Grand Canyon was formed over millions of years. First, sediment was deposited in layers. The layers pushed on each other and formed sedimentary rock with the pressure. Then the Colorado River weathered and eroded the rock to form a canyon.

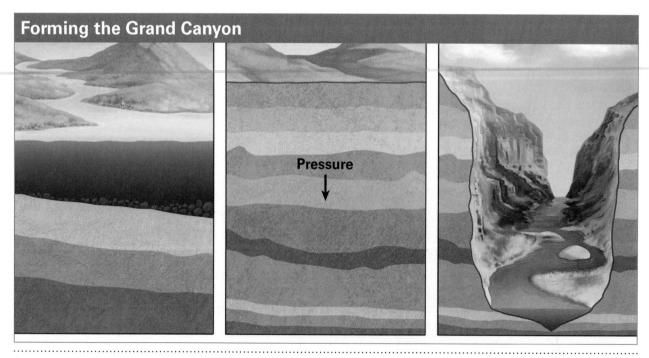

Forming the Grand Canyon

Pressure

5. Ice Causes Weathering and Erosion

You learned how liquid water can cause material on Earth's surface to weather, erode, and be deposited. Frozen water can also cause these changes on Earth's surface.

One way ice can weather rocks is with *ice wedging*. Ice wedging is a process in which cracks in a rock get bigger from water inside them freezing. Ice wedging happens because water takes up more space as it freezes into ice.

First, a rock with a crack in it fills up with liquid water from rain or some other source. Then the temperature drops below freezing. The water starts to freeze and expand. Ice takes up more space than liquid water. The expanding ice pushes against the inside of the crack. It spreads the sides of the rock apart and makes the crack bigger. When the weather warms up, the ice melts. Since the crack is now larger, more water can get in and freeze. This pattern repeats. Each time the water freezes, it expands, and the crack gets bigger.

Erosion also happens with ice wedging. The ice wedging causes bits of rock to break off. These pieces that the ice breaks off do not always stay in the crack. Often the melted ice, rain, or other sources of water carry these bits of rock away from the crack. Gravity can make the pieces fall out too. In these ways, the weathered rock erodes.

Over time, freezing and thawing ice can break apart even very strong rocks, like this one in Antarctica. Liquid water, wind, and gravity help erode the weathered materials.

Glaciers are huge rivers of ice. They move very slowly, slower than you can see. But their force scrapes off huge amounts of rock and moves it to new places.

6. Glaciers Cause Weathering, Erosion, and Deposition

Glaciers are another way ice weathers and erodes rock. They also move weathered rock and deposit it as sediment. This happens in high mountain valleys and in cold places like Antarctica.

Ice from glaciers starts out as snow. A **glacier** is a slowly moving river of ice. Glaciers form where it is so cold that not all of the snow melts in the summer. Over time, so much snow piles up that it gets pressed and sticks together. This forms a glacier.

Very slowly, the glacier flows down the mountain. Glaciers weather and erode rock as they flow down valleys. Glaciers are slow, but they are so large that they create a lot of force. The weight of the ice scraping along the ground grinds off large amounts of rock underneath them. This weathered material moves downhill with the glacier. Large glaciers carve out whole valleys and change the V-shape of river valleys to a U-shape. A U-shaped valley is evidence there once was a glacier flowing through the valley.

Glaciers deposit large amounts of rock, sand, and mud at their bases. The glacier carries its sediment down the valley to lower elevations, where it is warmer. This part of the glacier starts to break off and melt. Here, it deposits the soil and rocks that it carried. This is usually many kilometers from where the glacier started.

Glaciers weather and erode the land where they flow. Over thousands of years, they can create a U-shaped valley like this one. The shape of this valley is evidence that there used to be a glacier here.

How Does Water Change Earth's Surface?

1. Rainwater Causes Weathering and Erosion   A storm can cause erosion quickly. Raindrops loosen and move soil, eroding it. As the rain forms larger streams, the force of the water increases. The sediment in the water flows over rocks, wearing it down.

2. Rainwater Causes Deposition   When flowing water slows down or stops, the soil and sand it carries eventually stop moving. These small pieces of rock are then deposited as sediment. Over time, different layers of this sediment form on top of one another.

3. Deposition Helps Form New Rocks   Where a lot of sediment is deposited, the lower layers are squeezed by the weight of the layers above. Eventually they turn into sedimentary rock. Most of Earth's surface rocks on its continents are sedimentary rocks.

4. River Water Weathers and Erodes   As rivers flow, they weather and erode the rock they move over. Millions of years of this can produce large canyons, like the Grand Canyon in the southwestern United States.

5. Ice Causes Weathering and Erosion   Ice wedging happens when water gets in the cracks of a rock and freezes. The freezing water pushes the sides of the rock apart. Over many cycles of freezing and melting, ice wedging can crack rocks apart.

6. Glaciers Cause Weathering, Erosion, and Deposition   Glaciers are huge rivers of ice. The weight and power of the slow-moving ice scrapes off rock, erodes it, and deposits the pieces as sediment further downhill. This erosion carves U-shaped valleys.

Dripping Water Did That!

Weathering and erosion can create deep canyons and huge caves. Water also causes special kinds of deposition in caves deep underground. These look like delicate works of art. How does water create sculptures out of rock?

Each year, thousands of people visit huge caves. They travel from all over the world for a chance to adventure through maze-like passages. Jewel Cave in South Dakota and Mammoth Cave in Kentucky are two of the longest caves in the world. You could walk for more than a hundred kilometers in each! But people do not visit these underground worlds to see how far they can walk. Believe it or not, they are there to see deposition.

These huge caves and others like them, such as Oregon Caves in Oregon and Carlsbad Cavern in New Mexico, are no where near one another. And they are found in very different climates. Even so, they are all formed of the same material—limestone. Deposition in limestone caves is more than just layers of clay or sand. Cone-shaped rocks stick up from the floor. Some cones hang from the ceiling. There is also stone shaped like curtains, columns, icicles, or drinking straws. All of these forms are created by water, one drop at a time. Visitors of the caves want to learn exactly how dripping water could form such amazing stone shapes. But how did the caves form in the first place?

This room inside Carlsbad Caverns, New Mexico, is called the Chinese Theater.

Some caves form when water flows underground. Water might drip from the ceiling, hang in the air, and form pools and streams.

Water in Caves

Some caves form through weathering and erosion at Earth's surface. Wind and water may carve a cave from the side of a cliff. This kind of cave might be home to animals such as bears.

Other kinds of caves form when water flows underground. It moves through spaces in the soil and down through cracks in solid rock. If this rock is limestone, water mixes with and carries away the rock. Minerals that make up the limestone are completely mixed in with the water that moves over it. The rooms and passages of a limestone cave form as water mixes with the rock and carries it away.

As water continues to drip into the open cave spaces, it carries more minerals with it. The water deposits minerals on the floor or ceiling of the cave. Drip by drip, these minerals build up for thousands of years. This dripping and depositing creates all the different and amazing stone shapes that you find in a cave.

If you ever visit a limestone cave, you will probably feel lots of moisture in the air. You will usually hear water dripping. This means the cave is still forming. As long as there is water in a cave, it will keep shaping the cave and its rock formations. A cave that is still growing and changing is called an *active* cave. In active caves, water can also form cave ponds and streams.

A stalactite and a stalagmite can grow so long that they might meet in the middle of the cave.

Cave Cones

If you want to experience what a cave is like, go to a room and turn off the lights! Without human-made light, a cave is completely dark. You cannot see anything. But with lights, beautiful formations may be revealed.

You might see cones hanging down toward the floor. *Stalactites* are long cave formations that grow down from the ceiling. Stalactites look like icicles. Water seeping into a limestone cave drips from the ceiling. The water leaves minerals that form thin, hollow tubes. These stalactites look like soda straws, which is what they are called. Over time, water can flow along the outer edge of the soda straw, depositing more minerals. These minerals eventually make the icicle shape.

In a cave, you might also see cones reaching up to the cave top. These are called *stalagmites*. They are formed because water dripping from the ceiling of a cave can deposit minerals on the floor. Stalagmites are often found directly beneath a stalactite. Stalagmites can be wide or narrow, tall or short. A stalactite and a stalagmite can grow so long that they meet. When they do, they become one very large structure called a column.

Cave Textures

If you visit a cave, you should not touch any of its surfaces. Some formations can break very easily. So, even just touching others can damage them. This is because the oils in your skin can change the minerals. To satisfy curious visitors and still keep caves safe, guides often have samples that visitors are allowed to feel. If you could touch a cave, you would feel many different textures.

Pieces of rock that fall off the walls and ceiling feel very rough. So do the eroded surfaces of limestone. Another cave formation occurs where water splashes and leaves behind minerals. It is called cave popcorn. Just like the food, cave popcorn has a very bumpy and rough surface.

Other surfaces in a limestone cave are very smooth. Flow stone looks likes a liquid and is often described as a frozen waterfall. Other surfaces called "curtains" look like soft, folded fabric. Curtains with brown and tan stripes are called "cave bacon."

With ceilings hung with bacon and floors covered in popcorn, it is a wonder tour guides can keep visitors from tasting cave formations! Of course, if they did, all they would get is a mouthful of rocks.

A cave can have smooth and rough textures. "Cave bacon" curtains hang from the ceiling of this cave.

How Does Wind Change Earth's Surface?

Science Vocabulary

dust storm

windbreak

Wind is a powerful force that changes Earth's surface through weathering, erosion, and deposition. These three processes can create beautiful landscapes and interesting shapes in rock. But wind can also cause damage to plants and houses. People can design ways to prevent some of this damage.

NGSS

4-ESS2-1. Make observations and/or measurements to provide evidence of the effects of weathering or the rate of erosion by water, ice, wind, or vegetation.

ESS2.A. Rainfall helps to shape the land and affects the types of living things found in a region. Water, ice, wind, living organisms, and gravity break rocks, soils, and sediments into smaller particles and move them around. **ESS2.E.** Living things affect the physical characteristics of their regions.

Cause and Effect Cause and effect relationships are routinely identified, tested, and used to explain change.

Planning and Carrying Out Investigations

1. Wind Causes Weathering and Erosion

You learned how water changes Earth's surface through weathering, erosion, and deposition. Wind also causes these processes. This is especially true in dry, open areas where strong winds are common and a lot of rock is exposed.

Think about visiting a dry desert. You observe the landscape and see miles of sand all around you. Where did it come from? Sand is made up of small bits of weathered rocks that are all about the same size. In deserts, wind often causes weathering by blowing sand and other material against cliffs and large rocks. This wears them down and creates more bits of sand and dust. Over time, the rock is scraped and polished away.

Wind also has the ability to erode. This is especially true where there are not many plants to protect the ground. When a gust of wind blows, it picks up sand and other bits of material. It carries these bits with it. Wind can carry pieces the size of sand only for short distances at a time. But over time it can move them several kilometers. Tiny pieces like dust can blow thousands of kilometers away.

Wind erosion leads to more weathering. The material that the wind carries helps to weather rock that it hits, creating more loose material. In this way, erosion causes more weathering. And weathering causes more erosion.

This is the surface of a sand dune in Death Valley National Park, California. In dry areas, wind is a powerful cause of weathering and erosion. Here the wind is eroding sand between the plants.

Arches National Park has rock in many shapes. Weathering and erosion from wind and gravity helped carve these pillars from solid rock.

2. Wind Weathers Rock into Natural Structures

Grains of sand in a desert are small pieces of evidence of weathering and erosion. Some evidence is much larger, like the Delicate Arch in Utah. It is a large sandstone arch that is 14 meters (almost 46 feet) tall. That is higher than a four-story building! It is shaped like a giant, upside-down U. How did rock become shaped like this?

The Delicate Arch and other natural arches were formed because of the dry, windy climate. Later, over long periods of time, strong winds weathered and eroded the rock that was left. When sand is carried by a strong wind, it can weather rocks. On its own, wind cannot cause a lot of damage to rock. But the wind picks up sand and other material. The sand hits against the rock and breaks off tiny pieces. Gravity causes these pieces to fall off, especially when they have been weakened by wind. It takes a lot of time, but the sand in the wind can carve large rocks into interesting shapes. It helped to carve arches out of solid rock!

Wind continues to carve new arches. It also keeps carving old ones. The same process that created the arches is slowly working to destroy them. As wind and sand remove more material, each arch keeps getting thinner. Eventually, weathering will remove so much of their support that gravity will make these arches fall.

In windy areas, you might see large structures carved from the rock. This one in Arches National Park is called the Delicate Arch.

When wind deposits a lot of sand in one place, it creates hills called sand dunes. Wind continues to move sand dunes even after they are formed. It also creates patterns in sand, like these ripples and waves, that are constantly changing.

3. Wind Deposits Material in New Places

You learned that material eroded by water is eventually deposited in new places. This happens when the water slows down. The wind eventually slows down too. Sand and dust that are eroded by wind also get deposited in new places.

Think about the sandy desert again. Wind eventually deposits sand after blowing it to new places. The sand that you see in the desert was deposited and built up over time. Often, an object such as a rock, plant, or building slows down the wind that runs into it. This contributes to deposition.

The size of the pieces of eroded material affects their erosion and deposition. Large pieces such as large grains of sand are too heavy to be lifted high. Most winds can only carry them across the ground for a few centimeters or so at a time. Where the sand is carried and dropped by the wind, it can build up into hills called *sand dunes*. Some dunes are 400 meters (about 1,300 feet) tall!

As long as the wind blows, it carries sand over the ridges of the dunes and deposits it on the other side, where the wind is weaker. In this way, the wind causes sand dunes to move one grain at a time. Some dunes can move about 25 meters (82 feet) every year. Over time, these hills of sand can move many kilometers.

Wind blows large amounts of dust from dry areas, like the Sahara in Africa. Dust storms are sometimes so large they can be seen from space and transport dust to other continents.

4. Wind Can Transport Material Long Distances

In rivers, the force of water sometimes transports large rocks and even boulders. Wind cannot move pieces that are nearly this large. But wind can move some material much farther than any stream or river. The wind lifts small pieces of dust high into the atmosphere. Some dust blows all the way around the world before it settles!

You learned that wind carries sand by bouncing it across the ground a little bit at a time. Sand grains are too heavy to be carried higher. But the wind erodes lighter pieces of material differently. Dust is made up of very small pieces of rock, much smaller than pieces of sand, so it is very light. Wind carries dust high into the sky.

Think back to the desert. As wind blew across the ground near Delicate Arch, it eroded the weathered bits of rock. The distance that these bits went depended on their sizes. Larger, heavier pieces of sand were deposited in the same general area, in sand dunes. Other, tiny bits of dust blew high up into the sky.

Often, these tiny pieces of dust are deposited very far away by *dust storms*. A **dust storm** occurs when a strong wind like a weather front blows dust from a dry region. When dust storms pass through, they can deposit a layer of dust over everything. They also move large amounts of material. Sometimes the dust is blown thousands of kilometers.

Sometimes there is so much wind erosion that it creates large dust storms. It can be almost impossible for people and animals inside of the dust storm to see.

During the Dust Bowl years, wind deposition caused a lot of damage on the Great Plains. Here, a house is partly buried beneath a giant heap of deposited sand.

5. Wind Erosion Can Cause Damage

Weathering and erosion caused by wind can create beautiful landscapes like patterns in sand and interesting arches. But sometimes these processes can cause damage.

Wind erosion damages plants because bits of flying sand cut their stems and dust covers their leaves. When wind blows away soil, that soil is no longer there for plants to grow in. So, farms and gardens can be severely damaged by wind erosion. Buildings can also be damaged when sand blows against them.

Wind can cause even more damage in an area that does not have enough plants. During a drought, many plants die due to lack of water, and the soil is left bare. When wind begins to blow, it can erode away the top layer of soil. This happened in the Great Plains of the United States during the 1930s. For thousands of years, native grasses there protected the soil. They kept it in place. But farmers tilled up the grasses to plant wheat. When a drought came, their crops died and exposed the soil to the wind. The erosion was so bad during that time it was called the *Dust Bowl*.

During the Dust Bowl years, wind eroded so much dry soil it created large dust clouds. Sometimes, these clouds were so thick they blocked out the sun. Sand was deposited in large heaps that buried houses and farming equipment. Millions of people chose to leave their homes.

People can prevent much of the damage caused by wind erosion by planting windbreaks in open areas. Windbreaks slow down the wind and prevent flying sand and dust from hitting plants as hard. They can help protect houses as well.

6. Controlling Damage from Wind Erosion

Wind erosion can cause serious damage to farms, houses and the environment. The wind blows no matter what. But people can prevent some of the damage it causes.

People can learn lessons from events of the past, like the Dust Bowl. It is important not to remove too many native plants in areas that have long droughts. People can choose better places to farm. And they can plant crops in ways that hold onto the valuable topsoil.

People can protect farms and houses from wind by making windbreaks along the edges of fields. A **windbreak** is a row of plants that is grown in an open area to help slow down the wind and reduce its harmful effects. The plants can be trees, bushes, or tall grasses planted in a row. Some windbreaks are planted in an L-shape around a field or home on the sides that face the wind. This creates a wall of protection.

Even thin windbreaks slow down the wind that goes through. By slowing the wind, they protect plants from drying out as much. And they catch some of the flying sand. Thicker windbreaks slow the wind down even more. They stop it completely in the area right behind them.

You can see how wind changes landscapes. Wind weathers rock into smaller pieces, moves it and deposits it in new areas. Sometimes wind causes damage, but with good planning most of this can be prevented.

How Does Wind Change Earth's Surface?

1. Wind Causes Weathering and Erosion   Wind causes weathering by blowing bits of material against cliffs and large rocks. This wears and breaks the rock down into sand and dust. Wind also erodes sand and dust.

2. Wind Weathers Rock into Natural Structures   Wind can form natural arches and other landforms in windy climates. The sand in the wind can carve large rocks into interesting shapes. Gravity helps shape the rocks too.

3. Wind Deposits Material in New Places   The sand eroded by wind is eventually deposited in new places. Sand dunes build up where wind deposits large amounts of sand. The wind keeps moving dunes to new places.

4. Wind Can Transport Material Long Distances   Bits of eroded material can travel far and wide. Wind can carry tiny bits of dust high into the sky. Dust storms can move large amounts of dust thousands of kilometers away.

5. Wind Erosion Can Cause Damage   Sand carried by wind can cause damage to plants and buildings. Without plants to hold soil in place, wind erodes it. During the Dust Bowl, wind carried sand that ruined homes and farms.

6. Controlling Damage from Wind Erosion   People can prevent damage caused by wind erosion by making windbreaks. A windbreak is a row of plants grown to slow down the wind and reduce its harmful effects.

It's a Dust Storm!

The tiniest bits of dirt can be one of the greatest dangers in nature, if you have enough of them. When lifted into the air by wind, they can form dust storms. These sometimes deadly storms are a dramatic example of wind erosion in action.

Suppose you are traveling in the desert while listening to the radio. Suddenly, an announcer is warning of an approaching storm. She gives instructions telling listeners what to do when the storm hits. But you do not think you will need them. You see clouds, but they seem too far away to be a problem. Fifteen minutes later, the wind is now very strong. An enormous cloud of dirt and debris is rushing toward you. How did the danger build up so quickly?

Dust storms can develop quickly. During a dust storm, extremely strong winds carry huge amounts of sand and dust. You might see clear skies one moment. Then you notice the sky growing dark quickly as a huge wall of dust approaches. The wall of dust can be up to one kilometer (about 3,300 feet) high and several kilometers across. These storms can also last several hours or even days!

People cannot do much to prevent dust storms. But they can predict them and prepare for them. To predict dust storms, first scientists need to know where and when they occur.

A summer dust storm approaches Highway 60 in Phoenix, Arizona.

Two things are needed to create a dust storm: wind and dirt. Windstorms can occur in many places. However, dust storms usually happen only in or near deserts. A desert gets very little rain. Without moisture in the ground, surface dirt is loose and dry. Also, fewer plants grow in deserts. As a result, deserts have little plant cover. So, when winds blow through a desert, they can easily sweep up the exposed, dry surface material.

Dust storms can occur in any desert region. Most of the world's deserts are in North Africa, central Asia, Australia, and southwestern United States. In North Africa, dust storms occur during summer at the southern edges of the Sahara deserts. These huge African dust storms can last for several days and have even been seen by astronauts in space!

Shorter, stronger types of dust storms usually occur in spring and summer. For example, in the United States, you may encounter a sudden dust storm while driving into the city of Phoenix, Arizona. Phoenix is located in the southwestern U.S. desert region.

People living in a city like Phoenix listen to the radio or television for storm alerts. They cannot stop a storm from coming. But they can be aware of dust storm predictions and prepare themselves for them.

In places where dust storms occur often, you may hear storm warnings announced on the radio. You may see warning signs along the roads.

Keeping Safe in Dust Storms

Scientists know when and where dust storms normally occur. They also know what kinds of weather create dust storms. When all of the conditions for a dust storm happen at once, officials send out warnings.

So, how can you keep safe during a dust storm? Of course the best thing to do when you hear a storm alert is to take shelter. But dust storms can hit with little warning. People may have to act quickly. They have to know what to do to stay safe if they are away from home.

Dust and dirt whirling in the air make breathing and seeing difficult. You should cover your eyes, nose, and mouth immediately. Wrapping a bandanna, your shirt, or other piece of cloth around your nose and mouth will help keep dirt out. Moisten the cloth a bit if you have water. You should protect your eyes during dust storms, too. Cover your face with your arm. Wrap a piece of cloth tightly around your head to protect your ears. Knowing these few safety tips can help you when a storm suddenly hits.

Dust storms can also clog up machinery. So, all air travel stops during dust storms. Car drivers should not enter the storm if they can avoid it. If they are caught in a dust storm, drivers should pull off the road and stop.

During a dust storm, dust and dirt fill the air. Dirt clogs machinery, so traveling by car or plane is unsafe.

Living with Dust Storms

People cannot prevent dust storms entirely. But they can prevent *desertification*. Desertification is what happens when human activities cause land to become more desert-like. This process can cause dust storms in places they do not normally occur. The Dust Bowl of the 1930s is a famous example of desertification. Human activity had removed plant cover from large areas of land. Then little rain fell for many years. These events together led to dust storms and great amounts of soil erosion.

Dust storms have a long-term effect that can be quite beautiful. Dust storms may occur regularly, along with sand storms, for an extremely long time in one region. Layers of sand and dirt build up where the storms deposit them. When these layers are buried for millions of years, they become new rock. Now, imagine wind and water erosion working again. They uncover the rock that ancient dust storms helped create. Wind carves the rock into stunning new shapes, such as the arches in Arches National Park in Utah.

If you are ever caught in a dust storm, make sure to take cover until it passes. And, while you safely take shelter there, think about how you are witnessing Earth reshape itself!

The layers of rock in Arches National Park were first formed by dust storms and sand storms. Then, wind and water eroded the rock to create the arches.

How Do Living Things Change Earth's Surface?

Science Vocabulary

dam

till

Plants and animals cause weathering, erosion, and deposition. Like water and wind, living things can change Earth's surface with these processes. Sometimes living things also slow down or prevent the processes from happening. In this lesson, you will discover some of these changes caused by plants and animals, including humans.

NGSS | **4-ESS2-1.** Make observations and/or measurements to provide evidence of the effects of weathering or the rate of erosion by water, ice, wind, or vegetation.

ESS2.A. Rainfall helps to shape the land and affects the types of living things found in a region. Water, ice, wind, living organisms, and gravity break rocks, soils, and sediments into smaller particles and move them around. **ESS2.E.** Living things affect the physical characteristics of their regions.

Cause and Effect Cause and effect relationships are routinely identified, tested, and used to explain change.

 **Planning and Carrying Out Investigations**

1. Plants Cause Erosion and Weathering

One reason why Earth is special is that it is covered in plant life. Plants can be big, like a tree, or so small you need a microscope to see them. Each plant helps change Earth's surface.

Plants change Earth's surface through weathering and erosion. Suppose you are hiking in a rocky area without many plants. It is hard for plants to grow where there isn't any soil. Small plants like moss grow on the rock first. They take minerals from the rock. This is a type of weathering, and it weakens the rock. Eventually the surface of the rock starts to break down and become soil.

It is hard to observe soil forming because it takes a long time, but other changes are easier to see. As larger plants like trees start to grow in a rocky area, their roots grow into the small cracks in the rock. Slowly, as the tree grows, its roots break the rock apart. This forms more soil and makes it easier for other plants to grow there as well.

Plants affect erosion too. You learned that plants help make soil, and often this soil remains in place. Eventually though, some of this soil erodes away. The rock that plants have weathered can then be more easily eroded.

The roots of a tree can grow into cracks in rocks, forcing them apart. The weathered pieces can then be eroded more easily by water and wind.

Beach grass catches grains of sand that are moving in the wind. It causes a lot of deposition in sandy areas where the grass lives. This builds up and slows down sand dunes.

2. Plants Prevent Erosion and Weathering

You just learned that plants can cause weathering that leads to erosion. But plants can also prevent or slow down weathering and especially erosion.

Plants' roots affect weathering and erosion. Again, picture the roots of the trees in a rocky area. Although these roots can crack rock, they can also slow down and trap pieces of rock and soil. The roots hold on to this material. They keep water and wind from carrying it away. The soil then helps prevent the rock underneath it from quickly weathering away.

Sometimes roots also cause deposition. Water that is carrying sediment can be slowed down by roots. Some of the sediment in the water gets deposited and builds up. The roots continue to grow and catch more sediment. Eventually the deposited material becomes packed. This makes it harder to erode, and the soil is now deeper than before.

Plants in dry, sandy areas slow down weathering and erosion, and they cause deposition. The leaves of small plants catch and deposit sand that is being blown over the ground by the wind. This slows down the process of wind erosion. The sand continues to build up, catching and depositing more sand. Over time, small hills of sand can form. Eventually, shifting dunes can turn into grasslands.

Tree roots can trap rock and soil. This helps prevent erosion in the area around them.

When a prairie dog burrows, it scrapes away the top layer of soil and pushes deeper soil to the surface. This loosens the soil. Wind and water can now erode it more easily.

3. Animals Cause Erosion and Weathering

Plants are not the only living things that can cause weathering and erosion. Animals, including humans, change Earth's surface with these processes too.

Animals can cause weathering. For example, you might see snails along rocky ocean shorelines. Some of these snails eat algae that grow just under the surface of the rock. They use their hard mouthparts to scrape away the surface of the rock to eat the algae. This constant scraping of many thousands of snails weathers and erodes the rock over time.

Animals that *burrow*, or dig holes for shelter, change Earth's surface. On the American prairie, you might see many mounds with holes in them. These are the homes of prairie dogs, a type of burrowing animal. The holes protect the prairie dogs from weather and predators. To make a burrow, a prairie dog scrapes away the top layer of soil. This breaks up the hard surface. The prairie dog continues to dig deep into the ground and push soil up to the surface. This movement of soil is erosion. The soil is now loosened and more exposed. Wind and water might carry it away.

Animals cause erosion in other ways too. When too many animals live in one place, they tend to eat and trample all the plants. Without the plants to protect the soil, it is much more likely to be eroded by wind and water.

Animals cause weathering and erosion on rocky shorelines. Snails and other animals scrape rock as they feed on algae, repeatedly removing the top layer.

A beaver dam causes a flowing river to slow down. The river then deposits much of its soil and mud in the beaver pond behind the dam.

4. Animals Cause Deposition

Animals like sea snails and prairie dogs change Earth's surface with weathering and erosion. Can animals change Earth's surface with deposition?

A beaver is one animal that changes Earth's surface by depositing material. Beavers build *dams*. A **dam** is a wall of material that blocks the flow of a stream or river. Beavers use dams to get food and to protect themselves. The dams also allow them to access their homes. Beavers build their dams on a stream or river using rocks, mud, and pieces of trees. The dam stops water from flowing. Water builds up behind the dam, which causes a pond to form. Some of these ponds are larger than a football field!

The water flowing into the pond deposits sediment. Upstream of the dam, the river erodes rock and soil as it flows. It carries sediment along in the current. But once a dam is in place, the water no longer can flow easily. When it reaches the dam, the river slows down. The sediment that it is carrying slows down too. Much of the rock and soil is deposited at the bottom of the pond.

The sediment builds up over many years. It is now deposited on the bottom of the beaver pond, instead of flowing in the water. So, the water flowing out of the dam has less sediment and is clearer than it was. A large dam that exists for many years can cause a lot of deposition.

5. Humans Cause Erosion

Like other animals, humans change Earth's surface. As you know, many natural processes cause erosion. But humans often make this process happen much faster than is natural.

Humans sometimes cause erosion without trying. Suppose you and your friends walk through a field to get to school. Where you walk, some of the grass is worn down. If the ground is wet you might leave footprints.

When people walk over the same area often, they can wear a path where plants no longer grow. Since the soil is exposed, it might be eroded by water or wind. Paths are not always bad because they keep all of the damage in one place. But if they are in the wrong place, like somewhere steep, it can be a problem.

Construction projects can cause a lot of erosion. When people clear land to make room for new buildings, they scrape away the plants that used to live in the area. While they are building, a lot of the soil is left uncovered. This lets water and wind erode the soil.

Sometimes, humans speed up soil erosion by having pets or raising animals. Usually, plants eaten by wild animals grow back quickly. But if there are too many animals in an area, they can eat the plants faster than they grow back. This uncovers soil and rock so that it erodes faster.

Paths are formed by walking in the same area many times, which erodes material. In the right places though, paths help prevent erosion.

Construction is a human activity that causes erosion. By scraping away the plants that used to live here, the soil is no longer protected from water and wind.

Since erosion can cause damage, humans design solutions to prevent it. Sometimes people build terraces, like this one. By making many sections of flat land, terraces help prevent erosion.

6. Humans Can Reduce Erosion

Like other organisms, humans can also prevent weathering and erosion. Since erosion can cause damage, humans take measures to prevent this from happening.

You have learned how soil forms and collects. This takes a long time. Soil erosion can happen much faster than the soil forms and valuable soil can be lost. The soil that is eroded can damage buildings or pollute the water.

One cause of soil erosion is planting crops on steep slopes or in dry areas. Before they plant their crops, farmers *till* the soil. To **till** the ground is to break it up or turn it over to prepare the soil for planting crops. Before the crop plants come up or after they die, erosion increases.

One way to prevent soil erosion is by only planting crops in the right places. Wind erosion is a risk where it is very dry. Water erosion is a problem in steep, wet areas. People usually should not till the land in very steep and dry places.

In some parts of the world, people make *terraces* on hillsides. Each terrace is flat like the step of a staircase. Rainwater stays on each terrace for a long time so the plants can use the water for growing. This prevents soil erosion and lets people farm where the land is steep.

You can see how living things, including humans, change Earth's surface. Living things weather, erode and deposit material. They move this material to new places.

How Do Living Things Change Earth's Surface?

1. Plants Cause Weathering and Erosion Plants weather and erode Earth's surface. Plant roots in particular can weather rock down in many ways. Plants like moss take minerals from rocks and break the rocks down. By weathering rock, plants help form new soil.

2. Plants Prevent Erosion and Weathering Plant roots can also prevent erosion by holding onto soil and rocks. They slow down the rate of erosion, and sometimes even cause deposition. Plants help keep the soil in place.

3. Animals Cause Erosion and Weathering Some animals weather rocks by scraping them as they feed. Other animals change Earth's surface by burrowing into it and moving material. Too many animals in one place can destroy most of the plants, leading to faster erosion.

4. Animals Cause Deposition Some animals, like beavers, cause deposition. Beavers build dams across streams and rivers. When the water behind the dam slows down, it deposits the sediment it was carrying.

5. Humans Cause Erosion Humans have greatly increased the amount of erosion on Earth. This is often caused by humans removing the wild plants that protect the soil. Activities like construction projects and farming can all increase erosion.

6. Humans Can Reduce Erosion People should farm and build in ways that do not cause too much erosion. Crops should normally not be planted in steep or dry areas. People have designed solutions like terraces to let them farm in these areas responsibly.

Saving Soil

Humans change Earth's surface more than any other species. The history of the Great Plains of North America serves as just one example of how people have reshaped the planet.

People first came to the Great Plains about 12,000 years ago. For food, they mostly hunted animals and gathered wild plants. Then they started farming in small areas near rivers, avoiding the grassy soils that covered most of the Plains. In the mid-1800s, European settlers began to move from the east to the west. As they did, they completely changed the surface of the Great Plains. The change began when they dug into the grass.

People built this home from blocks of sod in the prairie.

The climate of the Great Plains includes cold winters, hot summers, a lot of wind, and little rain. The plants native to the region are mostly tall grasses. The deep roots and lower stems of the grasses keep loose earth in place. This forms a special layer in the ground called *sod*. Sod traps any rain that falls. This process allows very deep, rich soil to develop through the years.

Settlers from the East realized that the rich soils of the Great Plains would be perfect for farming. They wanted to use it to grow crops, so they cleared fields by digging up sod. In some places the sod was so thick that the settlers used chunks of it to build homes. But removing this sod would eventually lead to devastating changes in the landscape.

In tilling, plows are used to clear the ground before and after growing crops.

Soil Is Formed ... and Lost

Grasslands have covered the Great Plains for thousands of years. As some soil eroded, more soil would form. Insects, grasses, and tiny living things made new soil from rock and dirt. Grasses held the rich, loose soil in place. Animals such as bison ate the grasses without disturbing the soil much. And enough rain fell to maintain this soil and the living things it supports. Life, soil, and erosion were each balanced with one another.

Most trees and shrubs on the Plains naturally grew only near creeks and rivers. These wet areas were often far apart. At one time, people could look for long distances in any direction and see only grass. This is why many describe the Plains as a sea of grass. But the Plains also get little rain. So, even with all that grass, people also call it the Great American Desert. In such a dry place, even small changes can upset the balance between life, soil, and erosion.

Settlers began to farm on the Plains by clearing the grasses with plows. A plow is made of blades that are like huge knives for cutting into the ground. Farmers use plows to till the soil before planting seeds. Plows also bury weeds and dead crop plants. With tilling, soil is left without plant cover for a many months. In a windy place like the Plains, tilling tips the balance from soil formation toward soil erosion.

A Big Bowl of Dust

At first, people farmed in the Great Plains without many problems. But several changes caused farmers to till more of the soil. Starting in the late 1800s, inventors made many new machines. New plows let farmers till more land easily and quickly. Then during the 1910s and 1920s, it rained more than normal. The extra rain let farmers grow more plants. A demand for wheat caused wheat prices to be high. The government pushed people to replace great amounts of grassland with wheat farms. People around the country began to depend on the wheat. Meanwhile, a large amount of the Great Plains lost its natural grass cover.

During the early 1930s, almost no rain fell for several years. This is called a *drought*. Crops could not grow, so people left the farms. The powerful spring windstorms of the Great Plains came as usual. Only this time, soil that had taken so many years to form was easily carried away. Scientists estimate that 850 million tons of soil was lost. This era of severe dust storms throughout the Great Plains is called the Dust Bowl.

Periods of soil erosion have happened many times in history. Droughts still happen as part of natural changes in climate. The Dust Bowl is one example of how human changes to land can act with natural changes to create disasters.

A dust storm approaches buildings in Stratford, Texas, in 1935.

A blanket of snow gets trapped in the remains of old crop plants. This keeps the soil warmer through winter and means more water for the soil the rest of the year.

One Possible Solution

The good news is that people have learned a lot from events like the Dust Bowl. Scientists who study soil problems all over the world look for solutions. Where farming methods cause problems, people try other ways to grow food. One method is *no-till farming*. As the name suggests, no-till farming does not rely on usual tilling methods. Its goal is to disturb the soil as little as possible.

In normal tilling, farmers plow a field many times each season. In no-till farming, plows disturb the soil only when it is time to plant seeds. This has several advantages. One is that soil gets packed down less because machines drive over the field less. Loose soil is good for crops because air, water, and nutrients can move more easily to the plants. Using less equipment also means using less fuel.

Tilling removes weeds and stubble from fields. Stubble is the remains of old crop plants. No-till farming leaves stubble on the fields. Stubble helps to trap snow in winter, which means more water for the soil later. Stubble and snow also act like a blanket over the soil. They keep it warmer through winter and hold the soil in place the rest of the year. Stubble also protects new seeds in the spring.

With no-till farming, soil erosion occurs at about the same speed as soil formation. And this may be the key to bringing life, soil, and erosion back into balance in places like the Great Plains.

How Do Fossils Form and What Do They Show?

How can you know what the world was like before any humans were around to see it? That may seem like an impossible question to answer. But there is evidence of ancient life all around the world. Scientists study fossils of ancient plants and animals to learn how life on Earth has changed. They can even learn about the climates and environments of long ago.

NGSS

4-ESS1-1. Identify evidence from patterns in rock formations and fossils in rock layers to support an explanation for changes in a landscape over time.
4-ESS2-1. Make observations and/or measurements to provide evidence of the effects of weathering or the rate of erosion by water, ice, wind, or vegetation.

ESS1.C. Local, regional, and global patterns of rock formations reveal changes over time due to earth forces, such as earthquakes. The presence and location of certain fossil types indicate the order in which rock layers were formed.
ESS2.A. Rainfall helps to shape the land and affects the types of living things found in a region. Water, ice, wind, living organisms, and gravity break rocks, soils, and sediments into smaller particles and move them around.

Patterns Patterns can be used as evidence to support an explanation.
Cause and Effect Cause and effect relationships are routinely identified, tested, and used to explain change.

Planning and Carrying Out Investigations

Constructing Explanations and Designing Solutions

1. Fossils Are the Remains of Ancient Life

If you go to a science museum, you might see skeletons of giant dinosaurs like a *Tyrannosaurus rex*. You might also see rocks with shapes of insects, plants, and fish pressed into them. These are all examples of *fossils*.

A **fossil** is evidence of an animal or plant that lived a long time ago. For a fossil to form, material has to cover the remains of the organism to help keep its shape and preserve it. There are many kinds of fossils. Fossils are evidence of what Earth was like thousands, millions, or billions of years ago.

Some fossils are traces of an organism and not the remains of the organism itself. Fossilized dinosaur footprints, bird nests, and burrows that animals made in the ground are examples. They are called *trace fossils*.

Some fossils form from whole organisms, especially small ones like insects. Some of these fossils formed when an insect got stuck in a tree substance called resin and died. The resin hardened into a clear substance called *amber* with the insect trapped inside. This preserved the insect as a *whole body fossil*.

Most of the time, only part of an organism is fossilized. Fossils of bones and shells are the most common ones found. That is because these parts of the animal are hard. They are preserved better than soft parts.

There are many different types of fossils. These insects in amber are whole body fossils.

These preserved teeth of a *Tyrannosaurus rex* are examples of fossils. A fossil is the remains of a plant or animal that lived long ago.

Many of the best-preserved fossils come from areas that used to be shallow seas. A large amount of sediment is deposited here, covering animals when they die.

2. How Fossils Are Made

Did you ever wonder where the dinosaur skeletons in museums came from? Different kinds of fossils form in different ways.

What Becomes a Fossil

Most fossils form when plants and animals get buried under the surface of the Earth. Special conditions have to be present for a plant or animal to fossilize. Usually, material like soil has to cover an organism soon after it dies. If the plant or animal is not buried right away, its body breaks apart quickly. It never becomes a fossil. So, most animals never leave behind fossils.

Where Fossils Form

Many fossils that people find are from things that lived in shallow water, like coral and fish. This is because most deposition happens in low areas like shallow seas. Rivers carry sediment downhill. At the river's mouth, sediment is deposited. This sediment then covers some of the dead creatures here, eventually preserving them as fossils. As the layers of sediment accumulate and turn to sedimentary rock, the fossils are trapped and protected inside of them. Almost all fossils are found in sedimentary rocks.

Scientists use fossils like these to reconstruct skeletons of dinosaurs and other creatures that lived long ago. Fossils give scientists information about what these creatures looked like and how they behaved.

How Bones Become Fossils

When conditions are right, an animal's bones, or sometimes the whole body, are buried before they rot. The soft parts of the animal often still rot away, but the bones are much harder. They last long enough to fossilize.

As the animal's remains are buried deeper and deeper underground, changes take place. Rainwater that flows down through the sediment becomes *groundwater*. It picks up minerals from the rock and sediments. This mineral-rich water moves over and through the bones. Some of the minerals are deposited and crystallize inside the bone. At the same time, the water dissolves the minerals that used to be in the bone. In this way, the bone's original materials are slowly replaced with rock!

Have you ever had the chance to hold a dinosaur bone? If you did, you would probably notice that it is very heavy. Fossilized bones still look about the same because their shape has been preserved. But they are much heavier because most of the material has been replaced by rock. This process happens slowly. It takes thousands or millions of years, and the details of the bone are preserved. When many of an animal's bones fossilize in one area, scientists can reconstruct the animal's entire skeleton. Then you can see what the animal looked like!

When bones become fossils, most of the bone material is replaced by rock. This process can take thousands or millions of years.

How Bones Become Fossils

Organism dies. Sediment covers the organism's remains.

Water carries away bone minerals. Water and rock minerals enter bones.

Exposed fossil is rock in the shape of bones.

3. Fossils Are Revealed and Studied

You learned that sedimentary rock forms in layers. Some rock can be several kilometers thick and made up of hundreds of layers. Many fossils are often set deep inside these layers. It is very hard to see the fossils that are deep underground, far from the surface.

Weathering and erosion expose some of these fossils. People dig other fossils out of the ground and rock. There are still many more fossils that are deep underground. You might never see the fossils that are in some layers because they are too deep inside of the rock.

Many fossils are deep inside layers of sedimentary rock. The fossil record is the history of how life on Earth has changed.

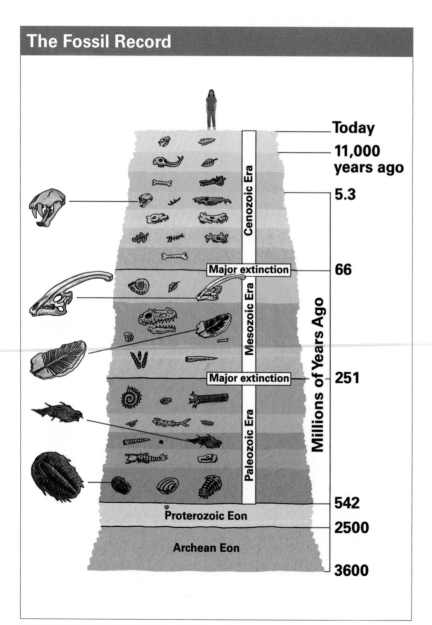

The Fossil Record

Today
11,000 years ago
5.3
Cenozoic Era
Major extinction — 66
Mesozoic Era
Major extinction — 251
Paleozoic Era
542
Proterozoic Eon
2500
Archean Eon
3600

Millions of Years Ago

The Fossil Record

When fossils are revealed, scientists can study them. They use what they find to understand what Earth used to be like and to learn about the creatures that were alive then. This is called the **fossil record**. It is the history of how life on Earth has changed.

Do you remember how sedimentary rock forms? The younger layers are laid down on top of older layers. If the layers have not been moved, the top ones are younger. The deeper layers are older. This means the deeper rocks contain fossils of creatures that lived longer ago. The shallow fossils are of animals that lived more recently.

The fossil record is evidence of animals and plants that lived long ago. Some looked very different than organisms living on Earth today.

Clues About the Ancient Earth

How do scientists know what Earth used to be like? Earth has been around for much longer than people have. No one was around to record what the surface looked like or what creatures lived there. Instead of observing these things directly, scientists must look at the evidence they find in rocks. The fossil record is the best evidence we have to learn about the ancient Earth.

Many fossils are exposed in places like the Grand Canyon by weathering and erosion. Recall that the Grand Canyon is made of layers of sedimentary rock. A river cut deep through the rock layers, which exposed many fossils. In some layers, scientists have found fossils of animals that once lived in an ocean. But the Grand Canyon is now in a dry desert. So, these fossils are evidence that the environment there has changed. They show us what Earth in that area used to be like.

Fossils near the surface are sometimes revealed naturally by weathering and erosion. People dig out other fossils.

Finding Patterns

There are patterns in the types of fossils in different layers. Toward the top, the plants and animals look more like the plants and animals that are alive today. In deeper, older rocks, people find fossils of many things that do not live on Earth anymore. Many look very strange. This is evidence of how life on Earth has changed over time.

Fossils like this trilobite can be found on many mountains, even though trilobites only lived underwater. Clearly, the environment has changed since they were alive.

4. Fossils Give Clues About Ancient Environments

Fossils are evidence about many things. They help people understand how types of living things have changed over time. They also give information about the climates and the environments where they once lived.

Suppose you find a fossil of a *trilobite* during a hike in the mountains. A trilobite was a small animal that lived in the ocean long ago. So, how is it possible to find a trilobite in the mountains? When the trilobite was alive, the rocks in this area were sediment at the bottom of a shallow sea. Over millions of years, the elevation changed. Fossils provide evidence about Earth's ancient environments and how they have changed.

Millions of years ago, Earth did not look like it does today. The land and oceans have moved and changed. Mountains formed where the land once was flat or covered with water. Other mountains eroded away. The climate has changed, too. When the dinosaurs were alive most places on Earth were warmer than today. Later an ice age occurred. Earth has warmed back up since then.

Fossils show how Earth's climates have changed. The Petrified Forest National Park in Arizona is famous for its many fossilized trees. But the area is now a desert with very little rain. Trees do not grow there. The fossil trees are evidence that this area once had more rain.

This petrified tree is a fossil from Petrified Forest National Park. Trees cannot grow here today. This is evidence that many thousands of years ago, there was far more rain in this Arizona desert.

How Do Fossils Form and What Do They Show?

1. Fossils Are the Remains of Ancient Life Fossils are left behind by animals and plants from long ago. A fossil can give information about organisms that died and the ancient world. There are many different kinds of fossils. Most only preserve the remains of a part of the organism. But some, such as insects trapped in amber, preserve a whole body.

2. How Fossils Are Made An organism usually has to be buried shortly after it dies to form a fossil. Most of the time an animal is eaten or it rots away before this happens. Areas with deposition can form fossils. The deposited material around the bones slowly turns to sedimentary rock. While underground, the bones themselves slowly turn to stone too.

3. Fossils Are Revealed and Studied Weathering, erosion, and people reveal fossils. The fossil record gives evidence about the creatures and environments of long, long ago. Fossils of animals and plants in the top layers look like plants and animals that are alive today. Deeper, older rocks contain fossils of many creatures that do not live on Earth anymore.

4. Fossils Give Clues About Ancient Environments Fossils are evidence of how Earth's environments and climates have changed. Many fossils are found in places where those creatures could not live today. Fossils can show that mountains and oceans have moved and changed. They can show that an area got much cooler, warmer, drier or wetter over time.

Dinosaur Puzzles

Dinosaur fossils remain hidden in sedimentary rocks for millions of years until the day a lucky fossil hunter spots them. A jumble of bones—what a find! But, once people find a fossil, how do they put the pieces together to rebuild the dinosaur?

Many dinosaur fossils are found in rock. When scientists find a fossil, they must carefully remove the rock from around it.

Can you imagine a fast moving dinosaur that hunts in packs and attacks with a "terrible claw?" It sounds like something out of a movie. But in 1964, John Ostrom was exploring on a slope in Montana. He saw large and sharp claws reaching out of an eroded mound. He did further digging, research, and studies. The fossil belonged to a dinosaur that lived 125 million years ago. He gave this dinosaur the name *Deinonychus*, meaning "terrible claw." To make this discovery even more exciting, the dinosaur had many characteristics of birds. This find helped support the theory that today's birds are modern day dinosaurs.

John Ostrom was a *paleontologist*. Paleontologists are scientists that use fossils to learn about dinosaurs and other ancient living things. Ostrom was not just lucky in his find. He had to know where to look for fossils.

Fossil hunters look in areas where sedimentary rock has been weathered, such as cliffs and hillsides. There, at least part of a fossil may be peaking out of the rock. Scientists even hunt for fossils from space using satellites. Like many fossil hunters, Ostrom searched in a place where he had found fossils before. Chances are the conditions in that place millions of years ago were just right for forming fossils.

Building with Bones

Once a fossil is found, the search begins to uncover as much of the animal as possible. Like a puzzle, it helps to have all of the pieces. But this rarely happens. Sometimes a tooth or a leg bone may be the only part of the dinosaur that fossilized. When scientists do not have all the pieces of the animal they are studying, mistakes can happen.

You may have heard of the *Brontosaurus*, a long-necked dinosaur that ate plants. But there has never been such an animal! In the late 1800s, O.C. Marsh was in a rush to identify as many new dinosaurs as possible. He wanted to be the most famous fossil hunter of the time. Marsh found part of the skeleton of a dinosaur with a long tail and a long neck. But he could not find the head. He was in a hurry to put the pieces of the skeleton together. By mistake, he used another dinosaur head to complete the puzzle. He named the dinosaur the *Apatosaurus*.

Several years later, he found the fossil remains of a similar dinosaur. He named this *Brontosaurus*. This skeleton was more complete and included a head. Scientists compared the skeletons. They realized a mistake had been made. The *Brontosaurus* was really the *Apatosaurus* with the correct head. It's a rule: when the same dinosaur is accidentally named twice, the first name sticks. So, these kinds of dinosaurs are really called *Apatosaurus*.

The correct name of the *Brontosaurus* is the *Apatosaurus*. It was a huge dinosaur with a long neck, a long tail, and a small head.

This fossil shows that the dinosaur had feathers. Recently, scientists have discovered other fossils of dinosaurs that have feathers, but are not birds.

Finding Feathers

Piecing together the skeleton from fossilized bones shows the size and shape of the dinosaur. The bones can even give paleontologists clues about the muscles of the dinosaur. Even though muscles do not become fossils, they leave marks on the bones that scientists can study to learn what the muscles were like. But there is one big question that bones cannot help answer: what was a dinosaur's skin like?

This turns out to be a tougher question to answer than you might think. Dinosaurs in pictures and movies are usually covered in scaly skin. And scientists used to think that all dinosaurs did have bumpy skin, like the skin that covers chicken feet. But they only have a few fossils that show the bumpy skin. Like muscles, skin usually decays before it can form a fossil. Very special conditions are needed to form a fossil of skin.

Recently, paleontologists have started rethinking their ideas about dinosaur coats. They have found fossils that show feathers. One of the first feathered fossils was found more than 150 years ago. It was a bird with teeth and a tail like a dinosaur. Today, paleontologists are finding other fossils of feathered dinosaurs. And these dinosaurs were not birds. Most scientists now think that many dinosaurs were covered in small feathers.

Colorful Clues

There is another piece of the puzzle scientists need to help them rebuild images of dinosaurs. They use bone fossils to find out a dinosaur's size and shape. Sometimes they can tell whether the dinosaur was covered in bumpy skin or feathers. But how can they figure out the colors of the skin or feathers?

The colors you have seen in pictures or models are probably not the dinosaurs' real colors. The artists who paint dinosaurs for museums are careful. They work with scientists to make pictures and models as accurate as they can. The artists may use the colors of modern lizards for inspiration. But they have no way of knowing the real colors of the dinosaur. This is starting to change.

Paleontologists are using tools to study rare dinosaur skin and feather fossils. In these fossils they look for signs of *pigments*. Pigments are substances that give most animals their colors. The pigments break down after an animal dies. But they leave traces behind. Scientists study the size and shape of these traces to find clues of the skin and feather colors. So far, one dinosaur has been painted with the white, black, and rust colored feathers it may have had. It is possible that someday fossil finds will lead to a complete—and colorful—picture of many dinosaurs.

Scientists are now hunting for clues about dinosaurs' colors in fossils. Someday, artists may be able to paint the accurate colors of a dinosaur instead of just using their best guess.

Where on Earth Are Earthquakes, Volcanoes, and Mountains Found?

Science Vocabulary

earthquake
elevation
lava
magma
physical map
volcano

When a volcano erupts, it can seem like a random event. People used to think so. But there is actually order and patterns in the features and events at Earth's surface. Scientists go about explaining the world by finding these patterns. They use patterns as evidence to explain what causes volcano eruptions, earthquakes, and other natural events. Maps are one of the best tools for finding these patterns.

 NGSS

4-ESS2-2. Analyze and interpret data from maps to describe patterns of Earth's features.

ESS2.B. The locations of mountain ranges, deep ocean trenches, ocean floor structures, earthquakes, and volcanoes occur in patterns. Most earthquakes and volcanoes occur in bands that are often along the boundaries between continents and oceans. Major mountain chains form inside continents or near their edges. Maps can help locate the different land and water features areas of Earth.

Patterns Patterns can be used as evidence to support an explanation.

 **Analyzing and Interpreting Data**

1. Maps Show Patterns on Earth's Surface

Think about the last time you visited a new place. To get there, you may have used a map or GPS unit that gave you directions. People have been making maps for a long time. Some of the earliest known maps were made on clay tablets over 4,000 years ago. As people learned more about Earth's surface, maps improved. People still use many kinds of maps today.

Maps use symbols, colors and patterns to show locations. They can show different kinds of information. Some show what kinds of plants grow in an area or how many people live there. Maps usually have a *key* that shows what the different colors and symbols represent.

There are many kinds of maps, but all fall into two basic categories. *Political maps* show political boundaries, like those between countries. **Physical maps** show the physical features of an area, like its climate or *elevation*. **Elevation** is the height of an area above sea level. Physical maps can also show where bodies of water and deserts are. Some help you see patterns like how the ground slopes in an area.

Scientists create and study many kinds of maps to find patterns. The patterns that maps reveal can give clues about what causes earthquakes, what makes volcanoes, and how mountains form.

A physical map, like this one of the continental United States, shows an area's physical features. This map shows the elevation of the land using symbols and colors.

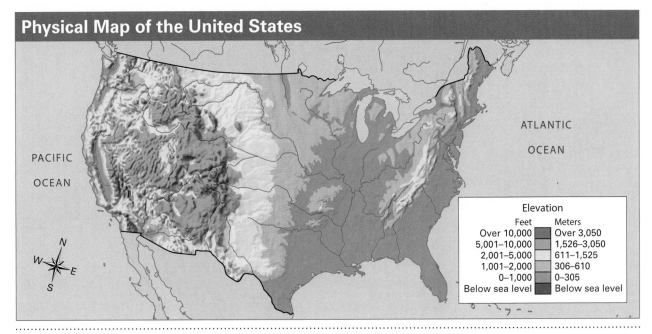

Physical Map of the United States

PACIFIC OCEAN

ATLANTIC OCEAN

N
W   E
S

Elevation

Feet		Meters
Over 10,000		Over 3,050
5,001–10,000		1,526–3,050
2,001–5,000		611–1,525
1,001–2,000		306–610
0–1,000		0–305
Below sea level		Below sea level

2. Earthquakes Occur in Patterns

Suppose that you are in class when, suddenly, the floor sways and shakes. Your teacher tells you to crawl under the desk for protection. Everyone is safe, but what caused the ground to shake? It was a small *earthquake*.

An **earthquake** is a shaking of the ground caused by the sudden movement of rock underground. An earthquake's movement is similar to that of a rubber band. Picture a rubber band stretched between two pegs that you pull on and then let go. When the rubber band slips, it vibrates. Similarly, rock underground moves. Vibrations move out through the ground from where the rock moved. This is an earthquake. On average, an earthquake happens on Earth about once every 10 minutes. Most of these are small and do not cause any damage. Many are not even large enough to feel.

If you mark places where earthquakes have occurred on a map, you will notice patterns. Some parts of the world almost never get earthquakes while other parts of the world have them often. About 4 out of every 5 of the strongest earthquakes happen in an area around the edge of the Pacific Ocean. One region between the Mediterranean and Asia also has many earthquakes.

An earthquake occurs when rock underground suddenly moves. If you study a map that shows where earthquakes occur, you will notice patterns. Most of the world's earthquakes happen in an area around the Pacific Ocean.

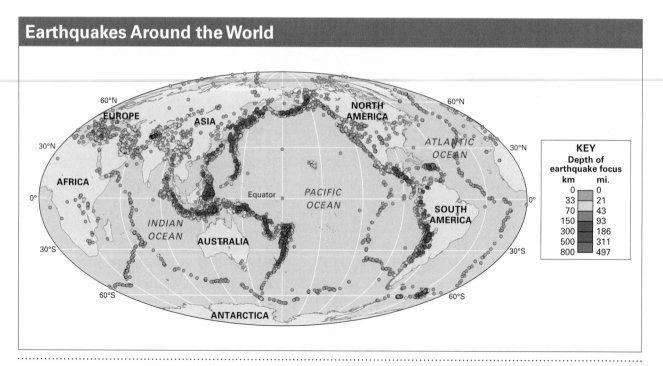

Earthquakes Around the World

3. Volcanoes Occur in Patterns

Many of the areas that have earthquakes are also areas with *volcanoes*. A **volcano** is a place where melted rock and other material erupts from deep inside Earth.

If you dig a hole, you will find that the ground is cool. But if you kept digging, after about 100 m (330 ft) you would notice the warmth of Earth underground. It gets hotter the deeper you go. Deep underground, it is so hot that some rock melts. The heat makes the melted rock move and churn. Melted rock under Earth's surface is called **magma**. In some places, this magma rises to the surface and breaks through during volcanic eruptions. Once magma reaches the surface, it is called **lava**.

There are many kinds of volcanoes. Some have steep slopes, while others have gentle slopes. As magma comes toward the surface, gases come out. Sometimes, the gases build up pressure and cause an explosion.

If you look at the map, you can see that there is a pattern of where volcanoes are. Most volcanoes are along the edges of the Pacific Ocean. There are so many volcanoes here that it is called the *Ring of Fire*. A map can show that volcanoes and earthquakes happen in many of the same areas. This is because they both occur at places where there are cracks in the Earth's crust.

It is so hot deep inside the Earth that the rock is a liquid called magma. This picture shows the surface of a volcano at night. Once the glowing liquid rock reaches the surface, it is called lava.

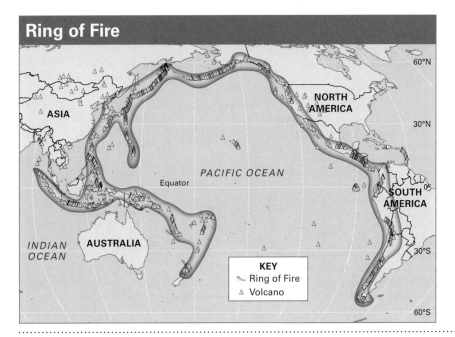

Ring of Fire

60°N
NORTH AMERICA
30°N
ASIA
PACIFIC OCEAN
Equator
SOUTH AMERICA
0°
INDIAN OCEAN
AUSTRALIA
30°S

KEY
Ring of Fire
△ Volcano

60°S

Like earthquakes, volcanoes also occur in patterns. Both are found along the edges of the Pacific Ocean. This area is called the Ring of Fire because there are so many volcanoes.

A mountain is an area with high elevation rising abruptly to a peak. Some mountains are volcanoes, but many are not. Like volcanoes, mountains are formed from movements inside the Earth.

4. Mountain Ranges Occur in Patterns

You might notice different colors, shapes, and lines on a physical map. Some areas might look like small bumps sticking out. They represent *mountains*.

A *mountain* is an area of land with high elevation that rises to a sharp peak. Some are very tall. The tallest is Mount Everest, which is almost 9 km (5.5 mi) above sea level. Mountainous areas have many steep slopes. A group of many mountains is called a *mountain range*.

Some mountains are volcanoes or old volcanoes that do not erupt anymore. In other places, the solid rocks at Earth's surface are pushing up against each other. Very, very slowly, the rocks fold and pile up into mountains.

One type of physical map that shows where mountains are is a *topographic map*. Topographic maps use symbols called *contour lines* to show the elevation of an area. Each line represents a certain elevation. When the lines are far apart, the land is not very steep. The closer together the lines are, the steeper the land.

Like volcanoes and earthquakes, mountains are found in patterns. Most are along the Ring of Fire or in a line between Asia and the Mediterranean Sea. Before people made detailed maps, no one understood the patterns of earthquakes, volcanoes, and mountains. Maps helped scientists discover these patterns.

The Earth's surface shows a lot of variation, like mountains and valleys. These differences in elevation can be shown using a topographic map, like this one. The contour lines each follow a certain elevation, showing patterns of steepness.

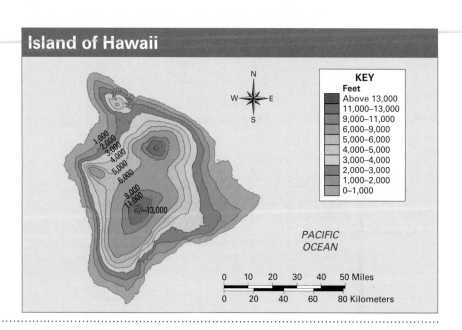

Island of Hawaii

KEY
Feet
Above 13,000
11,000–13,000
9,000–11,000
6,000–9,000
5,000–6,000
4,000–5,000
3,000–4,000
2,000–3,000
1,000–2,000
0–1,000

PACIFIC OCEAN

0   10   20   30   40   50 Miles
0   20   40   60   80 Kilometers

Where on Earth Are Earthquakes, Volcanoes, and Mountains Found?

1. Maps Show Patterns on Earth's Surface   Maps have been important to people for a long time. There are two main kinds of maps. One kind is a physical map, which shows the features and elevation of an area. Scientists study maps to look for patterns.

2. Earthquakes Occur in Patterns   An earthquake is the shaking of the ground that happens when underground rocks move suddenly. Some maps show where earthquakes occur. These maps reveal that earthquakes happen in patterns. Most are in a ring around the Pacific Ocean or in an area between Asia and the Mediterranean.

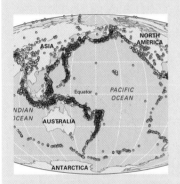

3. Volcanoes Occur in Patterns   Deep under Earth's surface, it is so hot that the rock there is liquid magma. A volcano is a place where lava erupts from deep inside of Earth. If you study a map, you will see that volcanoes also occur in patterns. They are mostly along the edges of the Pacific Ocean in the Ring of Fire.

4. Mountain Ranges Occur in Patterns   Mountains are areas with high elevation. They also form from movements inside Earth and occur in patterns. Many are found in the same areas as earthquakes and volcanoes. Topographic maps show an area's elevation and how quickly it changes. They show mountains and other surface features.

Watching Vesuvius

Because they can erupt at any moment, active volcanoes can be dangerous. Mount Vesuvius is one found along the coast of Italy. It has been a long time since Vesuvius has caused any harm. But, almost two thousand years ago, its eruption buried cities.

People have lived all around the base of Mount Vesuvius for thousands of years.

In 79 CE, between 10,000 and 20,000 people lived in or near the city of Pompeii in Italy. At the time, many may have believed that volcanoes were active only in the distant past. They knew the story of the hero Heracles. In the story, he traveled along the coast of Italy. He came to a "plain of fire" and saw a hill that "vomited out fire." This hill was known in Pompeii as Mount Vesuvius.

In 79 CE, Mount Vesuvius had been quiet for hundreds of years. That August, several strong earthquakes shook Pompeii and the nearby city of Herculaneum. But the people did not think this meant anything unusual. Small earthquakes were common in the area. Also, both cities had survived a larger earthquake just seventeen years before. Scientists know now that earthquakes can be signs of volcanic activity.

Mount Vesuvius began to erupt on the morning of August 24. People could see a large cloud rising from the mountain. The cloud had a strange color and shape. Few had likely seen anything like it before. And many would not survive to tell about it.

This is how the view of Mount Vesuvius erupting may have looked to Pliny the Younger.

A young man named Pliny the Younger later wrote about that fateful morning in the cities surrounding the giant volcano. Pliny lived in a town near Mount Vesuvius. In letters, he wrote what it was like in the days after the volcano started erupting. Pliny's uncle was a commander of Roman ships. Soon after the ash clouds appeared, he learned of people trapped in villages near the volcano. He organized ships to rescue them by boat.

Vesuvius spat so much hot ash, gases, rocks, and lava into the sky that the day was as dark as night. Meanwhile, Pliny saw "broad sheets of fire and leaping flames" from the volcano. The strong earthquakes continued. Buildings shook so hard that people left the cities if they could.

Most people from Pliny's town went to the shore. They saw the sea sucked away and creatures stranded on the beach. As ash continued to fall, people had to stand up from time to time to shake it off and avoid being buried. Finally, Vesuvius quieted and people headed home. Pliny thought the land looked like it was covered in snow.

Many people closer to Vesuvius did not survive. Pliny's uncle and others died during the rescue effort. Pompeii was buried by about 9 m (30 ft) of ash and rock. Herculaneum was buried by mudflows caused by the volcano. And at least 2,000 people were dead.

Scientists have uncovered much of the city of Pompeii. You can see Mount Vesuvius in the distance.

Finding Whole Cities

Pompeii and Herculaneum stayed buried and untouched for nearly 1,700 years. People had not forgotten the cities, but they no longer knew exactly where they were. This changed in 1709, when people digging a well discovered the remains of Herculaneum. They found a wall, which was part of the city's theater. An organized digging of Herculaneum began in 1738. Work at Pompeii began five years later.

Since the 1700s, researchers have uncovered and studied other ancient cities and towns near Vesuvius. Because these places were so deeply buried, they were protected from weathering and erosion. Also, no one could dig into the ruins to steal or break things. This has created a unique opportunity to learn how people lived so long ago.

Under the volcanic materials, Pompeii and Herculaneum were preserved nearly exactly as they had been in August of the year 79. Scientists have learned about the arts and culture from recovered statues, wall paintings, and tiled floors. The ruins have also told much about the people's daily lives. Scientists have mapped and studied streets, public gathering places, and homes in the cities. They have even found the remains of bread in ovens.

Watching a Volcano

While some scientists study the people of Pompeii and nearby cities, others study Mount Vesuvius itself. This deadly volcano has not stayed quiet. It is still active from time to time. A major eruption in 1631 killed 3,000 people. The most recent major event took place in 1944. And, while no eruptions since 79 have been so violent, you might wonder why people continue to live near a dangerous volcano.

One reason people still live in the area is that volcanic materials produce very rich soil. Many crops grow on and around the sloping sides of the mountain. Aside from the rich soil, the coast and surrounding areas are also very beautiful and have pleasant weather.

The population near Vesuvius has continued to grow over time. In the late 1700s, people recognized the need to learn more about Vesuvius. Local governments decided to build an observatory on the mountain. It was completed in 1845, and has been in use ever since. Scientists from around the world come to Vesuvius to study volcanoes.

Today, about 3 million people live within the area that Vesuvius could affect. So, it is now more important than ever to keep an eye on the volcano. A network of scientists and machines watch all of the volcanoes along Italy's southwest coast. They expect to be a lot more prepared than the people of long-ago Pompeii and Herculaneum.

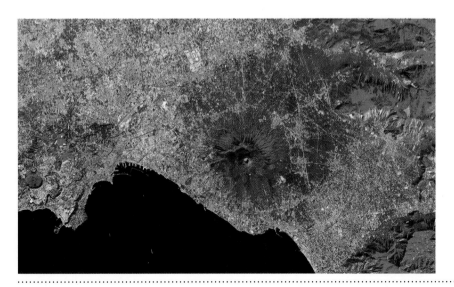

This false-color image of Mount Vesuvius was taken from space. The cities surrounding Vesuvius are colored aqua in the image and may be affected when Vesuvius erupts again.

What Can People Do About Natural Hazards?

Science Vocabulary

natural hazard

seismic hazard map

tsunami

Earthquakes, volcanoes, and tsunamis—like the 2011 Japanese tsunami seen above—are all natural hazards. Most natural hazards cannot be prevented, but the destruction they cause can be reduced. Scientists study natural hazards so that people can prepare and protect themselves.

NGSS

4-ESS3-2. Generate and compare multiple solutions to reduce the impacts of natural Earth processes on humans.

ESS3.B. A variety of hazards result from natural processes (e.g., earthquakes, tsunamis, volcanic eruptions). Humans cannot eliminate the hazards but can take steps to reduce their impacts.
ETS1.B. Testing a solution involves investigating how well it performs under a range of likely conditions.

Cause and Effect Cause and effect relationships are routinely identified, tested, and used to explain change.

Constructing Explanations and Designing Solutions

1. Most Natural Hazards Cannot Be Prevented

You have learned that Earth's surface is always changing. Earthquakes shake the ground and volcanoes erupt. Some mountains rise higher even while weathering and erosion break mountains down. Luckily, most of these changes do not have effects that you notice right away.

Every once in a while, a big change happens suddenly, and people can be hurt. Their homes might be damaged or destroyed, and people may be injured or killed. Changes like this are called natural hazards. A **natural hazard** is a danger caused by changes on Earth's surface or by weather. Examples of natural hazards caused by changes on Earth's surface are earthquakes and volcanic eruptions. Dust storms and hurricanes are caused by changes in weather.

It is impossible to stop most natural hazards. An earthquake cannot be stopped from shaking the ground. A volcano cannot be stopped from erupting. People have tried to stop many kinds of natural hazards, but have had little success. As you have learned, there are some natural hazards that people can reduce, like dangerous erosion and dust storms. But most hazards are just too powerful.

One thing people can do is to try to understand which natural hazards are likely to occur and where. With this information, you and others can prepare for them. If people plan for natural hazards, they will be much safer.

Some natural hazards are caused by changes on Earth's surface. Others are caused by changes in weather. Some, like this dust storm, are the result of both.

⚙ *Engineering Design*

2. Hazards from Earthquakes Can Be Reduced

There are many ways in which earthquakes cause damage. They make the ground move very quickly. It rises up and down and from side to side. Earthquakes can cause landslides and make some kinds of soil suddenly act like quicksand. Earthquakes can even lead to fires.

Earthquakes Can Damage Cities

Most of the damage that earthquakes cause is to buildings and structures. When people are killed or injured in an earthquake, it is usually from walls and ceilings that crumble and fall on them. The shaking caused by an earthquake can make bridges fall. It can bend and break pipelines, train tracks, and even break riverbanks. When these objects move, destruction can result. Most of the damage from an earthquake in San Francisco in 1906 was not caused by the earthquake directly. It was caused by gas pipes breaking, which led to fires. Since the earthquake broke the water pipes, too, people could not stop the fires.

The ground a city is built on affects how much damage earthquakes cause there. Some cities are built on mostly solid rock. Others are built on loose sediment. Which do you think is more dangerous? Vibrations from earthquakes are not as strong in solid rock as in loose soil. Cities built on loose soil shake a lot. Imagine a shaking bowl of gelatin. Shaking can cause much damage to cities built on loose soil.

Earthquakes are a natural hazard that can cause a lot of damage. The shaking caused by earthquakes can make buildings and even roads collapse. Some cities are more prepared for this than others.

Buildings Can Be Made to Handle Earthquakes

One way that cities can prepare for an earthquake is by making buildings strong. Engineers have to design buildings that do not cave in during strong earthquakes. To do this, engineers first come up with a design. Then, they test the design by creating models of buildings and placing them on shaking machines. The engineers observe how well the models hold up and make changes to their design until they come up with a stable one.

Maps Show Where Earthquakes Happen

Maps help protect people from earthquakes. **Seismic hazard maps** show where earthquakes have occurred. This is where they are most likely to happen again. Other maps show what materials are underground and help predict which areas will shake the most. Cities can make rules, called *building codes*, based on these maps. Building codes tell people how strong to make buildings in a certain place.

Another kind of map uses sensors to help save lives after an earthquake. When a strong earthquake occurs, lives can be saved if rescue workers arrive quickly. So, some cities have sensors hooked up to a computer. After an earthquake, the sensors send information about where the shaking was strongest. This is usually where there is the most damage. Rescue workers use that information and go as fast as possible to help people in those areas.

Even though people cannot prevent earthquakes, they can prepare for them. A seismic hazard map, like this one, shows the patterns of earthquakes that have already occurred. Cities can use maps like this to make building codes that help protect people.

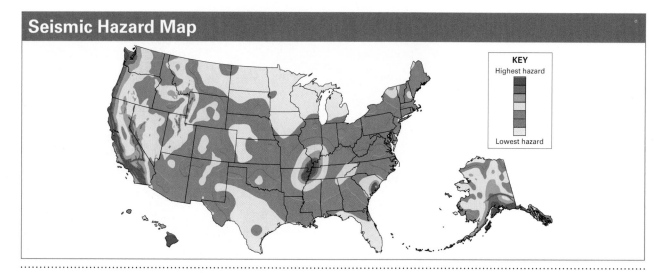

Seismic Hazard Map

KEY
Highest hazard

Lowest hazard

3. Hazards from Volcanoes Can Be Reduced

Living near a volcano has many benefits. Areas around volcanoes often have rich soil for growing crops, and the mountain slopes are beautiful. So, many people like to live near volcanoes. But volcanic eruptions are very dangerous.

Lava and Ash Can Cause Damage

Different volcanoes behave in different ways. Some types of lava flow out as a smooth liquid. It pours out like a red glowing river. Lava flows are very hot. They burn everything in their path, like houses, roads, and plants. Other kinds of magma are stickier and have a lot of gas under pressure. The gas explodes during the eruption, launching lava and pieces of rock. They fly through the air as ash and larger chunks, called *tephra*. Ash and tephra can break rooftops. They can cover plants and kill them.

Gas and Ash Flows Can Cause Damage

Gases like carbon dioxide and water vapor come out of volcanoes. Sometimes they build up around a volcano, pushing away the oxygen. Since animals—including humans—need oxygen, a cloud of volcanic gas can cause many deaths when it comes out of a volcano. Sometimes very hot gases mix with ash. They flow down the volcano as an *ash flow*. Ash flows can move faster than any car, and are hotter than most kitchen ovens can get. So, the ash flows leave a path of destruction behind them.

When magma is under pressure, it can explode out of a volcano. Ash and tephra, like the piece shown above, fly though the air. They can damage houses, plants, people, and wildlife.

Like most other natural hazards, volcanic eruptions cannot be prevented. When a volcano erupts, it releases hot, glowing lava that burns anything it touches.

A Volcano Can Cause Landslides and Mudflows

Eruptions can cause deadly *landslides* when they break off parts of a volcano. Eruptions add material to volcanoes, forming steep slopes. Later eruptions can loosen this material. Ash and rock slide down the slopes causing damage.

Volcanoes can also cause mudflows. Snow and ice build up on top of tall volcanoes between eruptions. The heat from eruptions can quickly melt the snow and ice. This water flows quickly down the steep slopes, mixing with soil and rocks. Mudflows from volcanoes can cover valleys. Sometimes they bury towns many kilometers away.

Evacuation Plans Can Save Lives

The biggest danger from a volcano is not noticing the signs of an eruption. Usually a volcano is quiet. It seems harmless. But before a volcano erupts, it causes many small earthquakes. It also releases gas. Scientists study volcanoes to learn when eruptions will happen. They look for the signs and changes that occur before an eruption. Then they try to warn people to leave the area before an eruption.

Even with these signs, it is very hard to predict an eruption. Sometimes a volcano makes signs of an eruption and then it does not erupt. So, scientists are careful about warning people to evacuate. But it is still important to be prepared. People can test different evacuation routes to find the ones that work the best.

When some volcanoes erupt, ash flows, landslides, and mudslides travel downhill to places far away from the volcano. They can be very destructive, burying people alive and damaging property. This house has been hit by a volcanic mudslide.

A tsunami is a type of fast-moving ocean wave that strikes land like a huge rising tide. When tsunamis reach land, they can cause much damage.

⚙️ *Engineering Design*

4. Hazards from Tsunamis Can Be Reduced

Imagine you are visiting the beach when suddenly the water starts moving out to sea. Where water once was, there now is only sand. Some people run to gather shells from the exposed ocean bottom. Then someone shouts, "A *tsunami* might be coming!" What would you do?

A **tsunami** is a damaging type of fast-moving wave often caused by underwater earthquakes or landslides. They used to be called tidal waves, but they are not caused by tides. Tsunamis can start in deep water when an earthquake or landslide pushes a large amount of water. In the deep ocean, a tsunami is not dangerous and may only be 1 m (about 3 ft) tall. As the tsunami reaches shallow water, it slows down and gets taller. Some tsunamis grow to over 30 m (about 100 ft). That is tall enough to cover a large building!

Often, the water on the beach flows out before the tsunami comes. So, if you are ever at the beach and the water moves out to sea, run away! Go as fast as possible to high ground. A tsunami will come in a few minutes.

Tsunamis Can Damage Coastlines

Tsunamis move very fast, as fast as a jet airplane! Sometimes they reach land after only a few minutes. They can also travel across whole oceans. Tsunamis land like a quickly rising tide. They can damage coastal towns and cities. A tsunami in 2004 that started off the coast of Indonesia killed hundreds of thousands of people.

Warning Systems Help People Prepare

The 2004 tsunami in Indonesia was deadly because people were not prepared. They did not think a tsunami would happen there, so they did not have a system to warn others. A warning system in the Indian Ocean could have helped people know to evacuate. They might have had time to go to safety. Thousands of people could have survived.

People can prepare for a tsunami if they know that one is coming. They can have time to leave the beaches and go to higher ground. Some countries with coastlines on the ocean work together to make tsunami warning systems.

The Pacific Tsunami Warning System is one such system. Engineers designed this system to watch for possible tsunamis around the Pacific Ocean. They tested this system many times to make sure that it worked. The system uses sensors on the ocean floor. If an earthquake happens in deep water, the sensors send data to stations. They predict where the tsunami might go and when it will reach land. Then they send out warnings to these places.

Leaders in different places make evacuation plans. They install signs to show people in low-lying areas where to go if a tsunami is coming. You can see how it is important to have a plan for natural hazards like tsunamis. How can you prepare for natural hazards?

Signs help show people the quickest path to safety if a tsunami is coming.

To help prepare for tsunamis in the Pacific Ocean, engineers designed the Pacific Tsunami Warning System. This system uses sensors, like the ones in this picture. The sensors detect earthquakes so that scientists can warn people.

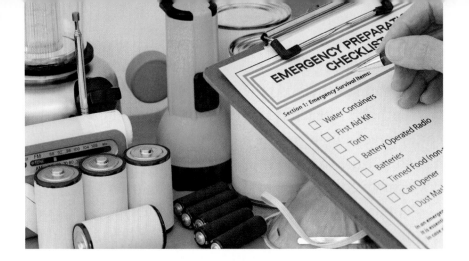

Having an emergency supply kit is one way to prepare for a natural disaster. You should include food, water, and other items in your supply kit.

5. People Should Prepare For Emergencies

You have probably heard someone say, "It's better to be safe than sorry." When it comes to natural disasters, the saying is true. Just about every place has natural hazards of some type. Some areas like the Great Plains do not have many earthquakes, volcanoes, or tsunamis. But they have *tornadoes* and *blizzards*. It is important to find out what types of disasters are most likely to happen where you live.

Your family should have an emergency supply kit in case there is a natural disaster. The kit should include enough food and water to last several days. What if there is no electricity for a few days? The kit should include flashlights and batteries. You also need to plan how to stay warm with clothing, blankets, or sleeping bags.

Plans are very important too. What if a disaster happens when you are away from your family? You will need to have plans for whom to call. Everyone in your family should plan to call the same person, such as a relative who lives out of town. What if there is a fire in your house? Your family can agree on a place to meet outside. This way your family will know that everyone is safe.

It is also important to test plans. You can test different ways to leave your house in case of a fire or try different sleeping bags to see which are the warmest. Testing these things will help prepare you for natural disasters.

What Can People Do About Natural Hazards?

1. Most Natural Hazards Cannot Be Prevented Weather and changes to the Earth's surface cause natural hazards. People cannot stop most of these disasters. But they can study natural hazards and where they are likely to occur. This information helps people stay safe from natural hazards.

2. Hazards from Earthquakes Can Be Reduced Most of the damage caused by earthquakes affects buildings and structures. Earthquake risk is not the same everywhere. Maps and sensors help people predict where earthquakes might happen. Engineers can design safer buildings.

3. Hazards from Volcanoes Can Be Reduced Volcanoes produce many hazards, like lava, ash, mudslides, and poisonous gases. Scientists try to predict when volcanoes will erupt. For people who live near volcanoes, it is very important to be prepared with an evacuation plan.

4. Hazards from Tsunamis Can Be Reduced Fast-moving ocean waves called tsunamis can cause damage to shorelines and kill many people. Warning systems help people prepare for tsunamis and save lives. But people who live near ocean coastlines have to be aware of tsunamis and prepare for them.

5. People Should Prepare for Emergencies Natural hazards exist just about everywhere. People should be aware of the natural hazards that are likely where they live. It is important to have an emergency plan for these events and test it. Emergency supply kits can help you after a disaster happens.

A Burning Curiosity

Imagine watching a volcano erupt—from the top of the volcano! Most people would probably rather watch from further away. A volcanologist may do both.

This volcanologist stands on the rim of a volcano in Russia. The hammer she might use to collect rock samples sits at her feet.

A volcanologist is a scientist who studies volcanoes, lava, magma, and other related Earth activity. Most people find active volcanoes very interesting. After all, if you live or travel anywhere near one, you always want to know what it is up to! Volcanologists do too. But unlike most people, they are more likely to run *toward* an erupting volcano than away from it.

Being a volcanologist requires having a thirst for adventure. More importantly, working around volcanoes can be very dangerous. Some volcanologists have even died while studying eruptions. So, why do they do this work? They are like artists, musicians, and many other kinds of scientists. They cannot imagine doing anything else.

Despite their common desire to see an eruption up close, volcanologists mostly do much quieter work. Many volcanoes are not active. This means they have not erupted in thousands of years. So, volcanologists spend a lot of time outdoors, hiking around inactive volcanoes. They look at how lava, volcanic rock, tephra, and ash change the landscape. They collect materials and analyze them in the laboratory.

Volcanologists use special tools to study volcanoes. These scientists are measuring the gases at the crater of a volcano in Africa.

Studying Volcanoes

Long ago, people who studied the world thought great winds inside Earth caused volcanoes. It was not until the 1800s that scientists began to study volcanoes with organized scientific methods. As part of these methods, scientists would find evidence to support their explanations. They began to understand and show that heat inside Earth, and not wind, causes volcanoes to form and erupt.

To become a volcanologist now, you must study geology in college. Most volcanologists focus their research in a special area. Some study patterns of where volcanoes occur. They research the substances that make up Earth and use maps to study the different kinds of eruptions and volcanic materials. Others study the connections between volcanoes, earthquakes, and the shape of Earth's surface. Volcanologists may spend time studying Earth directly. They go outdoors, walk around, and observe volcanic formations. This method is called field geology.

Volcanologists use special tools to study volcanoes. A *seismograph* has sensors to detect earthquakes caused by volcanoes. To study the gases given off by volcanoes, scientists may use balloons with sensors or special machines that read gas levels in the air. They also use computer systems and satellites to study changes in the shape of Earth's surface.

Images taken by Haroun Tazieff inspired others to learn about volcanoes. This photo shows the center of a volcano in Africa.

What Volcanologists Can Do for You

A volcanologist's most important job is predicting eruptions. Millions of people around the world live near volcanoes. Volcanoes can throw so much ash and material into the air that they can also affect people very far away. For example, in 2010 a volcano in Iceland erupted. Ash from it affected airline travel all over Europe for weeks.

Volcanologists know that changes in earthquake patterns near a volcano mean an eruption is more likely. Changes in the air near a volcano are often another clue. The eruption of Mount Saint Helens, in Washington, was correctly predicted in 1981. The 1991 eruption of Mount Pinatubo in the Philippines and the 2010 event in Iceland were also predicted. In each case, many lives were saved.

Some volcanologists work with the public. One famous volcanologist in France was Haroun Tazieff. His interest in and knowledge of volcanoes inspired other people to learn about them. He took photos looking down into volcanoes. Books he wrote about his adventures were very popular. And he filmed streams of flowing lava and created dramatic movies for television. Millions of people became familiar with volcanoes by watching his shows. Tazieff later worked for the French government, leading a department that works to prevent natural disasters.

Volcanoes in Space

People have been interested in Earth's volcanoes for hundreds of years. Because most eruptions are dangerous, volcanologists use tools to study them from far away. The tools fly near erupting volcanoes in airplanes or helicopters. They use telescopes and satellites to take pictures of them.

Scientists also use this technology to find out if volcanoes occur on other planets and moons. In the early 1600s, the scientist Galileo was the first person to use a telescope to study other planets. Scientists have been improving telescopes ever since, making them more powerful. They also use robots loaded with cameras and radios to explore space.

Scientists have in fact discovered that there are volcanoes on other planets and moons. We now know that long ago, lava flowed over large areas of Earth's moon. Scientists discovered volcanoes on the planets Venus and Mars. The largest known volcano is Olympus Mons on Mars. This volcano is more than 500 km (340 mi) across!

Far from Earth, there are even volcanoes that erupt ice instead of rock and ash. These ice volcanoes occur on moons around Jupiter, Saturn, and Neptune. Pictures have been taken by spacecraft. Someday, maybe adventurous volcanologists will get to travel millions of miles to see ice volcanoes erupt in person!

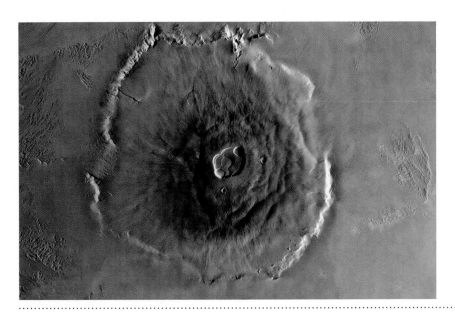

Volcanoes are on other planets. Olympus Mons on Mars is the largest known volcano ever discovered.

Waves and Information

If you visit the ocean, pay close attention to the way the water moves. You may notice that it rises and falls in a repeating pattern before it reaches the shore. This is a wave! There are many different types of waves. In this unit, you will learn about the different types of waves and how they affect you.

Unit Contents

Unit 4 Overview

Graphic Organizer: This unit is structured to first teach how to model many kinds of **waves** with the same properties and then introduce the concept of **sending information** using waves and other patterns.

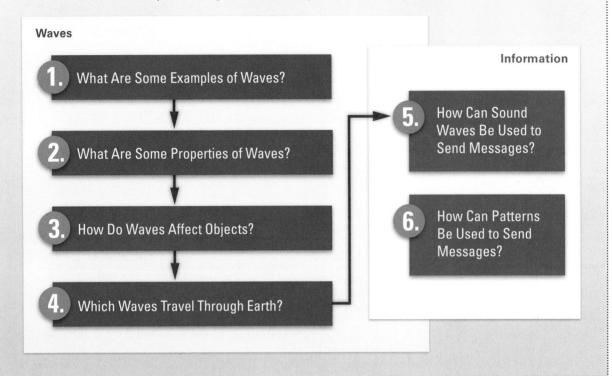

Waves

1. What Are Some Examples of Waves?

2. What Are Some Properties of Waves?

3. How Do Waves Affect Objects?

4. Which Waves Travel Through Earth?

Information

5. How Can Sound Waves Be Used to Send Messages?

6. How Can Patterns Be Used to Send Messages?

NGSS Next Generation Science Standards

Performance Expectations

4-PS4-1. Develop a model of waves to describe patterns in terms of amplitude and wavelength and that waves can cause objects to move.

4-PS4-3. Generate and compare multiple solutions that use patterns to transfer information.

Disciplinary Core Ideas

PS4.A: Wave Properties

- Waves, which are regular patterns of motion, can be made in water by disturbing the surface. When waves move across the surface of deep water, the water goes up and down in place; there is no net motion in the direction of the wave except when the water meets a beach.

- Waves of the same type can differ in amplitude (height of the wave) and wavelength (spacing between the wave peaks).

PS4.C: Information Technologies and Instrumentation

- Digitized information can be transmitted over long distances without significant degradation. High-tech devices, such as computers or cell

phones, can receive and decode information—convert it from digitized form to voice—and vice versa.

ETS1.C: Optimizing the Design Solution

- Different solutions need to be tested in order to determine which of them best solves the problem, given the criteria and the constraints.

Crosscutting Concepts

Patterns

- Similarities and differences in patterns can be used to sort and classify natural phenomena.

- Similarities and differences in patterns can be used to sort and classify designed products.

Developing and Using Models

Constructing Explanations and Designing Solutions

Have you ever wondered...

If you go to the ocean, you can see water waves. But, waves are all around you, not just in the ocean! This unit will help you answer these questions and many others you may ask.

How do your ears work to hear different sounds?

Why do waves near the shore splash?

What makes some sounds higher-pitched than other sounds?

What Are Some Examples of Waves?

A wave is a repeating pattern of high and low points like you see in this image. A wave moves along matter. In this instance, a wave is moving along sea water. But the matter does not move long distances with the wave. You will learn about three examples of waves. Matter in each example moves in its own pattern. So, you can group a wave by how its matter moves.

NGSS 4-PS4-1. Develop a model of waves to describe patterns in terms of amplitude and wavelength and that waves can cause objects to move.

PS4.A. Waves, which are regular patterns of motion, can be made in water by disturbing the surface. When waves move across the surface of deep water, the water goes up and down in place; there is no net motion in the direction of the wave except when the water meets a beach.

Patterns Similarities and differences in patterns can be used to sort and classify natural phenomena.

Developing and Using Models

1. Water Waves

Have you ever thrown a pebble into a puddle of water? When you do, water splashes, and ripples of water spread out from where the pebble landed. These ripples form a *wave*.

These ripples form a water wave.

Water Waves Move in Repeating Patterns

A wave moves along **matter**, or anything that takes up space. A **wave** is a repeating pattern of moving matter. A wave has crests and troughs. A **crest** is the highest point of a wave. A **trough** is the lowest point of a wave. Crests and troughs form around a **rest position**, or the position that matter is in before a wave travels through it. For example, before you threw the pebble in the puddle, the water was still. So, the water was at its rest position.

One example of a wave is a water wave, which is a wave that moves along the surface of water. The water moves in small circles when a wave travels along it. When you throw a pebble into the water, a wave forms that moves along the water's surface. When you throw a pebble into a puddle, the highest point of the ripple is the crest. The lowest point of the ripple is the trough. One crest and trough is often followed by many other crests and troughs. The wave spreads and forms the pattern that you see.

Water waves in the ocean are like those in a puddle but bigger. The wind pushes the ocean water, and the water forms a pattern of crests and troughs.

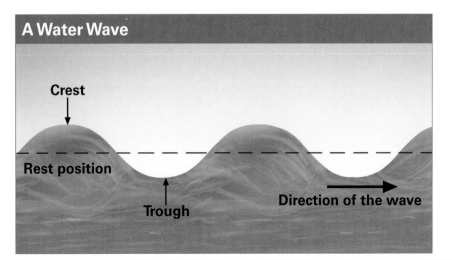

A Water Wave

Crest

Rest position

Trough

Direction of the wave

A water wave is a wave that moves along the surface of water. Like all waves, water waves move in a repeating pattern of crests and troughs.

Matter in Water Waves Moves in Circles

You now know how the crests and troughs of water waves move. But how does the matter that the wave moves along move?

In a water wave, the matter moves in circles. The water that the wave travels through is the wave's matter. The matter does not travel with the crests and troughs, so it does not travel far from where the wave started.

If you watch a duck bob on a wave, you might notice that it moves in small circles. The duck moves in circles because the water moves in circles. The circles are small since the water does not move far from where the wave started. So, the duck does not travel far either.

The matter of a wave in a puddle moves in the same way. Picture a wave in a puddle with a leaf floating on it. When the wave moves under the leaf, the leaf moves in a small circle. It moves up as a crest moves under it and then moves down as a trough moves under it. Like the leaf, the water moves in small circles.

Have you ever seen waves near an ocean shore? The water in these waves falls forward instead of moving in circles. These waves are called *breaking waves*. The water of these waves gets taller near the shore and then falls forward onto the shore. Then it moves backward into the ocean. Instead of moving in small circles, the water moves on and off the beach.

Like all objects on a water wave, this cork moves with the wave's matter. It moves up as the crest of the wave moves under it. It then moves down as the trough moves under it.

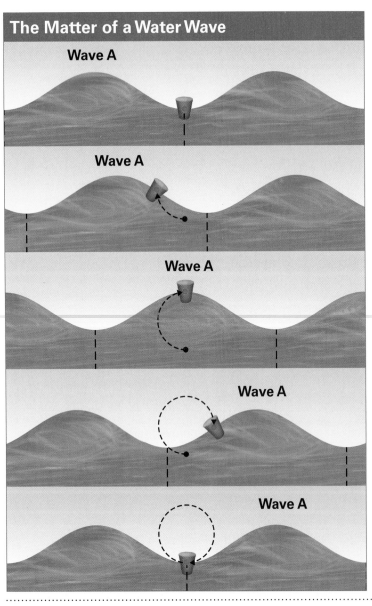

The Matter of a Water Wave

Wave A

Wave A

Wave A

Wave A

Wave A

2. Waves on a String

You just learned about a wave that moves along water. Can you think of another example of a wave?

Waves on a String Move in Repeating Patterns

Another example of a wave is a wave that travels along a string. A wave on a string also has a pattern of crests and troughs. To make a wave on a string, take a string and lay it on the ground. Have a friend hold one end in place while you hold the other end and shake it back and forth to the left and right. This movement creates a pattern of crests and troughs. The crests and troughs move down the string, away from your hand. Your hand makes new crests and troughs behind them. So, there is a repeating pattern of crests and troughs moving along the string. Since the crests and troughs move along the string, the wave moves along the string, too.

There are many other examples of waves on a string. For instance, waves on a string are common in many musical instruments. When someone plays a guitar or violin, waves travel along the strings of the instrument. Together, they make the vibrations you see in the string.

When you shake one end of a string, a wave travels along the string away from you. The wave is made of a repeating pattern of crests and troughs.

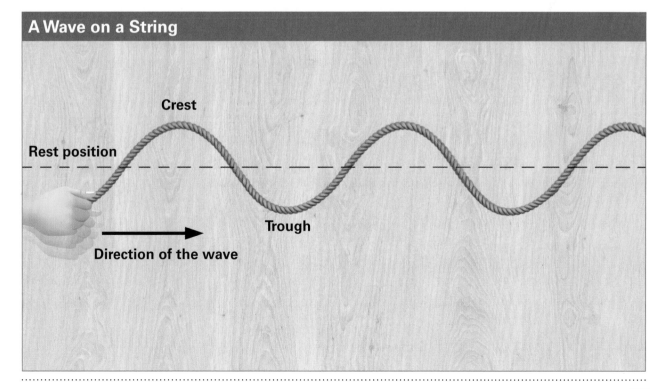

A Wave on a String

Crest

Rest position

Trough

Direction of the wave

Matter in Waves on a String Moves Side to Side

In a wave on a string, the matter is the string. The matter does not travel with the wave, just like in a water wave. To understand how the matter moves, think about shaking a piece of string side to side. The wave travels along the string away from you, but the string does not also move away from you. Instead, the string stays in your hand.

You can also see that the matter does not travel with a wave by tying a piece of yarn to the string. When you shake the string side to side, the yarn also moves side to side, but it does not travel along the string. It stays in the same place that you tied it. You could tie the yarn near your hand, and the yarn would move side to side but stay near your hand. You could tie it in the middle of the string, and it would still stay in the middle of the string.

You could also tie many pieces of yarn to the string. You would see that each piece of yarn moves side to side, but that they do not move closer together or further apart. They do not move along the string either. Just like the yarn, the matter of a wave on a string moves side to side but stays in the same place.

In a wave on a string that has a piece of yarn in the middle, the piece of yarn does not travel with the wave. It only moves side to side. The matter of a wave moves in the same way.

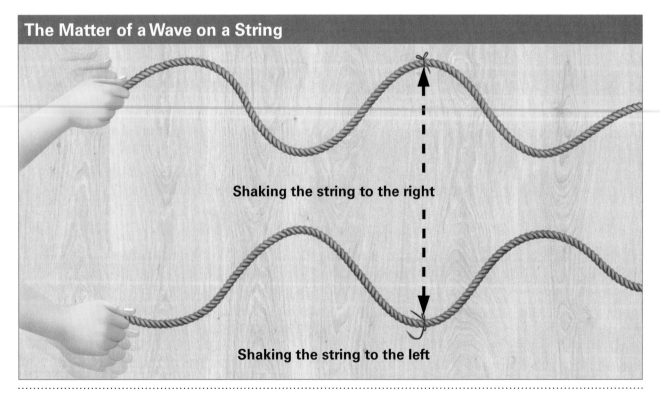

The Matter of a Wave on a String

Shaking the string to the right

Shaking the string to the left

3. Sound Waves

You are listening to your favorite band's new song. "What a great sound!" you say. But what is sound?

Sound Waves Move in Repeating Patterns

You might not realize it, but sound is another example of a wave. A sound wave is also made of a pattern of crests and troughs. But the crests and troughs in sound waves are different from the crests and troughs in other examples of waves.

You can see this difference if you make a model of a sound wave with a coiled spring toy, just like in the diagram. You can push one end of the coil back and forth toward the other end. The coils will then push closely together in one area and spread apart in the area next to it. You can see the areas where the coils come together and spread apart. The place where the coils push closely together represents where the crest of a sound wave is. The place where the coils spread apart is the trough of a sound wave.

The crests and troughs of a sound wave can move through the air. Air is made of matter. Unlike the other examples of waves that you learned about, a sound wave's crests and troughs are matter that is pushed together and spread apart. The matter pushes closely together into a crest and spreads apart into a trough.

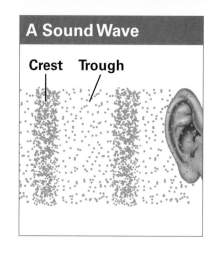

A Sound Wave

Crest   Trough

Sound waves are made of repeating patterns of crests and troughs. The crests are where the air pushes together, and the troughs are where the air spreads apart.

This coiled spring toy models the crests and troughs of sound wave. The places where the coils are pushed together are crests. The places where they are spread apart are troughs.

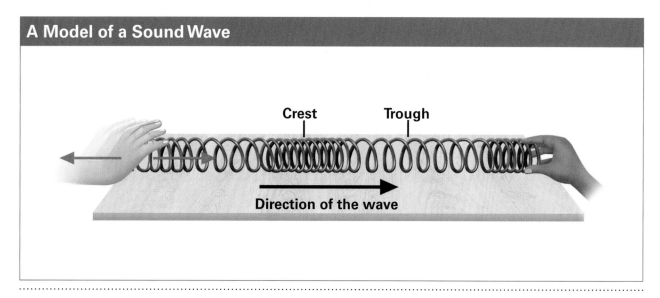

A Model of a Sound Wave

Crest   Trough

Direction of the wave

Matter in Sound Waves Moves Forward and Backward

As in the other examples of waves, the matter in sound waves does not move long distances along the crests and troughs or far from where the wave started. But the matter does not move in circles or side to side. Instead, it moves forward and backward in the direction of the wave.

Think about the model of a sound wave in a coiled spring toy. The wave moved along the spring from one end to the other. But how did the matter move? Recall that the coils of the spring are the matter. When you moved your hand forward and backward to make the wave, the coils you held in your hand moved forward and backward, too. They did not move *through* the spring like the crests and troughs of the wave did.

You can also see how matter moves in a sound wave by tying a piece of yarn to a coil in the middle of the spring toy. When you make a wave in the spring, the yarn moves forward and backward. But it does not move to the end of the spring. It also does not move back toward your hand. It stays in the middle of the spring, moving forward and backward in the same place. The matter of a sound wave moves in the same way as this yarn. When sound waves move through air, the matter moves forward and backward without traveling a long distance.

Like the yarn on this spring toy, the matter of a sound wave does not move with the wave. It moves forward and backward. It does not travel far through the air.

The Matter of a Sound Wave

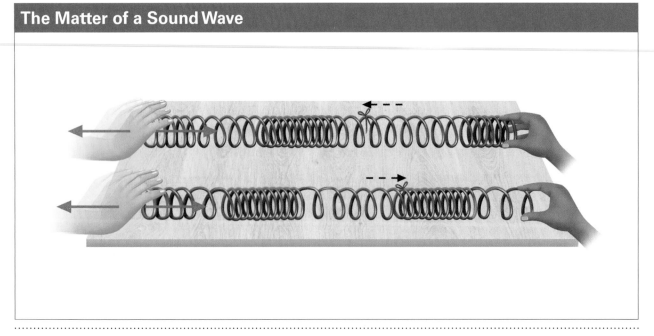

4. How Waves Are Similar and Different

You have learned about three different examples of waves. These three waves have three main similarities.

Waves Have Similarities

The first similarity is that each example of a wave has a repeating pattern of crests and troughs. In water waves and waves on a string, the crests and troughs are the highest and lowest points in the wave. In sound waves, the crest is where the matter is most pushed together, and the trough is where it is most spread apart.

The second similarity is that in each example, the crests and troughs move through matter. In water waves, the crests and troughs move along the surface of the water. In waves on a string, they move along the string. In sound waves, they move through the air.

Another similarity is that in each example, the waves spread out in all directions that they can. Think about dropping a pebble in water. The wave spreads out from the pebble. But the wave does not move in only one direction. It spreads out in all directions and forms a ring around where the pebble fell.

All three examples of waves are made up of a pattern of crests and troughs. What similarities and differences do you notice between the crests and troughs of these waves?

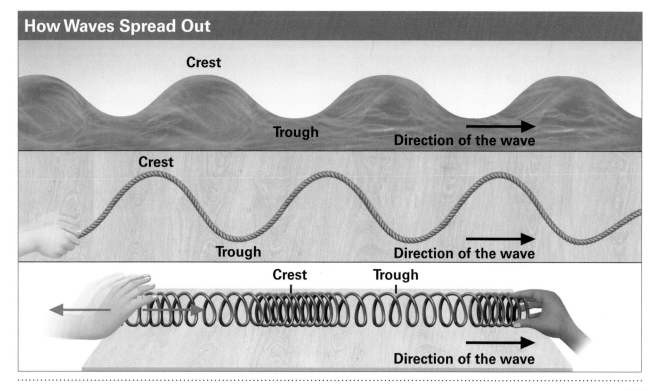

How Waves Spread Out

Crest

Trough

Direction of the wave

Crest

Trough

Direction of the wave

Crest Trough

Direction of the wave

Waves on a string also spread out in all directions. Think about holding a long piece of string in the middle with a friend on each side of you. Now suppose you shake the middle of the string back and forth to make a wave. Does the wave move toward just one of your friends? No. The waves move in both directions along the string toward both of your friends. The waves spread out in all directions along the string.

Sound waves also spread out in all directions. Think about clapping your hands, which causes a sound wave. Can people in front of you hear you clap? Can people behind you hear you clap? Can people on your left and to your right? People in all directions can hear you clap because the sound wave spreads out in all directions.

Waves Have Differences

Along with these similarities, all three examples have different patterns as well. The way that matter moves in each example is different. Because of this difference, scientists classify waves by how their matter moves. If the matter moves in small circles, it is similar to a water wave. If the matter moves side to side, it is similar to a wave on a string. If the matter moves forward and backward, it is similar to a sound wave.

This wave on a string began in the center. Notice that the wave spreads out on both directions along the rope. This happens because all waves spread out in all directions that they can.

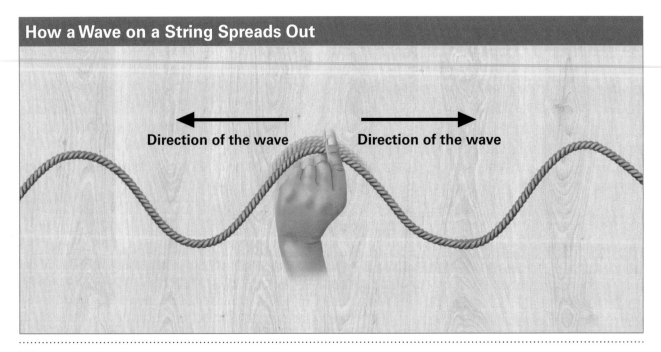

How a Wave on a String Spreads Out

Direction of the wave   Direction of the wave

What Are Some Examples of Waves?

1. Water Waves   A wave is a repeating pattern of moving matter. A wave has crests and troughs. Before a wave travels through matter, the matter is at its rest position. A water wave is one example of a wave. It has a pattern of crests and troughs that move along the surface of water. But the matter in the water moves in small circles.

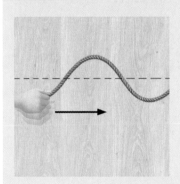

2. Waves on a String   A wave on a string is another example of a wave. The string is the matter. The crests and troughs of this wave move along a string. But the matter in the string does not travel with the wave. The matter stays in the same place while moving side to side. The matter does not move closer together or further apart on the string.

3. Sound Waves   A sound wave is also an example of wave. The crests and troughs of a sound wave are places where matter is pushed together and spread apart. The crests and troughs can move through the air, but the matter in the air moves forward and backward.

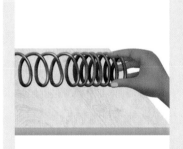

4. How Waves Are Similar and Different   Each example of a wave is made up of crests and troughs. Each example also moves through the matter. But how the matter in each example of a wave moves is different, so scientists classify a wave by how its matter moves.

Walls of Water

For hundreds of years sailors told stories of huge ocean waves that came out of nowhere. These walls of water that battered ships became known as *rogue waves*. But do these waves really exist and, if so, how do they form?

"Don't let nobody on deck!" barked the radio call from the *Edmund Fitzgerald*, a ship traveling on Lake Superior. The *Fitzgerald* and the ship that they were radioing were caught in a storm on November 9, 1975. The radio warning was one of the last things ever heard from the *Fitzgerald*. At some point after the call, the ship sunk. Everyone on board was lost.

No one knows for certain what happened on that November night. But some people think that the *Fitzgerald* was hit by one or more rogue waves. A rogue wave is a wave that is at least twice as tall as other waves in the area. Rogue waves often come from a different direction from the way the wind is blowing.

Throughout history, ships have reported being hit by rogue waves. The *RMS Queen Mary* supposedly was almost flipped over by a rogue wave in 1942. But people who heard the story questioned whether rogue waves were real. Maybe the sailors on board were exaggerating what they saw.

A rogue wave is a wave at least twice as tall as the other waves in the area.

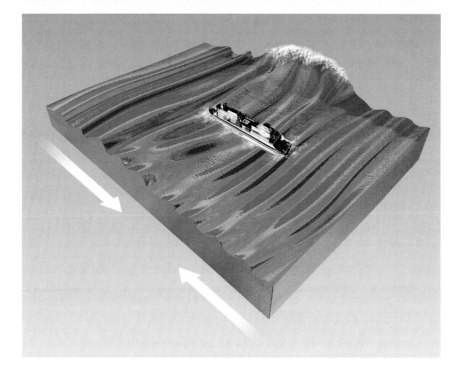

According to one hypothesis, rogue waves form when waves moving in different directions meet and combine.

Understanding Rogues

On New Year's Day, 1995, people finally had proof that rogue waves actually exist. On that day, waves were beating against an oilrig in the North Sea near Norway. The oilrig had a tool that measured the height of the waves that hit it. All of them were around 5–8 meters (16–26 feet) tall. But suddenly, the tool measured a 26-meter (85-foot) tall wave. It was a rogue wave—the first to be measured by a reliable tool.

Since then, scientists have been studying rogue waves even more. They want to know how they form. And they want to know if there is a way to predict them. Scientists use computer models to find out what weather and water conditions can produce a rogue wave. Then, when someone reports a rogue wave, they compare their models to the conditions that produced the wave.

Scientists have different ideas as to how rogue waves form. One idea says that they form when the wind is blowing in the opposite direction as the current is moving. Another says that rogue waves form when waves coming from different directions meet and combine.

Not so Freaky

However they form, these giant walls of water did not get the name *rogue waves* for being ordinary. People used to think they were very rare. After all, the first proof of rogue waves did not show up until 1995! But, scientists have since learned that these monster waves are much more common than they thought.

In 2000, scientists decided to count the number of rogue waves they could find in a certain amount of time. They used two satellites to take images of the oceans for three weeks. In that short length of time, they found ten rogue waves. Each was more than 25 meters (82 feet) tall. The scientists discovered that, basically, rogue waves were happening all the time!

The scientists saw that the so-called freak waves were not so freaky after all. They collected over a million images of the oceans for two years. They analyzed the images looking for rogue waves. Then, they used this data to make a map. The map showed where rogue waves were most likely to happen. In 2007, they shared their map with the world. Their plan is to use the map along with weather reports to predict where and when rogue waves may form.

A rogue wave that hit this ship completely covered its deck with water. The wave was about 18 meters (60 feet) tall.

Rogue waves can cause a lot of damage to ships. Scientists are working to predict rogue waves. Engineers are designing ships that can survive rogue waves.

Rogue Proofing

Rogue waves can happen at any moment. Even giant cruise ships that carry land-lovers are at risk. In 2005, a cruise ship called the *Norwegian Dawn* was hit by a rogue wave. It was so tall, it broke windows on the ship's 10th deck!

Rogue waves have hit all kinds and sizes of boats. They have hit cruise ships, oil tankers, and ships that carry goods across the water. The waves have caused a lot of damage to the ships. And, they have killed many people. Could science prevent this kind of loss?

Scientists and sailors know that, even with the help of data maps and computer models, people cannot always predict rogue waves. There will always be ships that must face them. So, engineers are working on designing ships that can survive rogue waves. One idea is to make the outside of the ship stronger. Another idea is to give ships stronger windows and doors. The stronger windows and doors would help keep water from flowing in and causing the ship to sink.

So, if you are ever on the high seas and your ship comes upon a rogue wave, don't go on deck to see for yourself. Go inside. Shut the doors tight. A rogue wave is no joking matter!

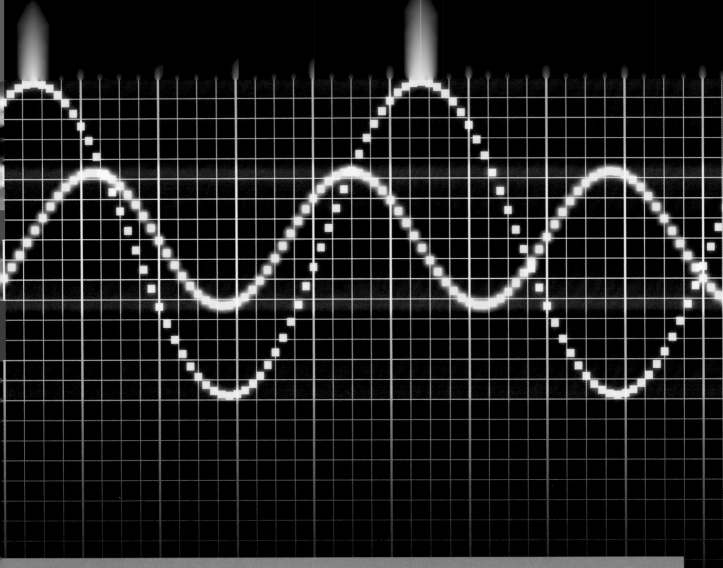

What Are Some Properties of Waves?

Science Vocabulary

amplitude
dependent
frequency
independent
wavelength

This image represents the crests and troughs of a wave. You will learn about three properties of waves that are related to a wave's crests and troughs. Each of these three properties tells you something different about a wave. Recognizing patterns in these properties helps you describe and compare waves.

NGSS | **4-PS4-1.** Develop a model of waves to describe patterns in terms of amplitude and wavelength and that waves can cause objects to move. | **PS4.A.** Waves of the same type can differ in amplitude (height of the wave) and wavelength (spacing between wave peaks). | **Patterns** Similarities and differences in patterns can be used to sort and classify natural phenomena. |  **Developing and Using Models**

1. The Properties of Water Waves

Think about being in a swimming pool on a warm summer day. The water is cold, so you step into it slowly. Your friend has a different idea. He jumps into the pool. SPLASH! The waves that you make are small. But the waves that your friend makes are much larger.

The Amplitude of Water Waves

The water waves that you and your friend made are both water waves, but different. One of the ways you can tell these waves apart is by their *amplitude*. A wave's amplitude describes how big the wave is.

Amplitude is the largest distance that matter moves from its rest position. In water waves, the rest position is midway between the crest of the wave and the trough of the wave. The amplitude of a water wave is the distance from its rest position to its crest. The distance from the rest position to the trough is also the amplitude of the wave. Matter returns to its rest position after a wave has passed through it.

When you and your friend jumped into the pool, the waves you caused had different patterns. When you stepped in, the waves had a small amplitude. When your friend jumped in, the waves had a large amplitude.

Amplitude is the largest distance that matter in a wave moves from its rest position. A wave's amplitude describes its height.

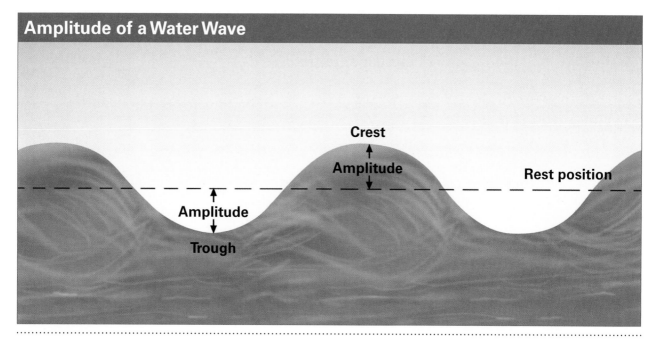

Amplitude of a Water Wave

Crest
Amplitude
Rest position
Amplitude
Trough

The Wavelength of Water Waves

The crests and troughs of a water wave can also be used to measure another property called *wavelength*. **Wavelength** is how stretched out a wave looks. It is the distance between one crest and the next crest in a wave. The distance between a trough and the next trough in a wave is also wavelength. These distances are the same. If the crests of a water wave are close together, the wave has a short wavelength. If the crests are far apart, the wave has a long wavelength.

Water waves can have very different wavelengths. The wavelength of a wave in a pool might be one meter long. In a sink, the wavelength might only be a few centimeters long. The crests are farther apart in the wave in the pool than the wave in a sink. The water wave in the pool has a longer wavelength and the water wave in the sink has a shorter wavelength.

The Frequency of Water Waves

Water waves have a third property called *frequency*. **Frequency** is how often a crest passes a certain point in a certain amount of time. The frequency of a wave depends on its wavelength and on how fast the wave moves. You can count crests to measure the frequency. For example, you could count how many crests pass you in one minute while you stand in the shallow part of a pool. If 12 crests pass you, then the frequency would be 12 crests per minute.

Wavelength describes how long a wave is. If a wave's crests or troughs are close together, the wave has a short wavelength. If they are far apart, the wave has a long wavelength.

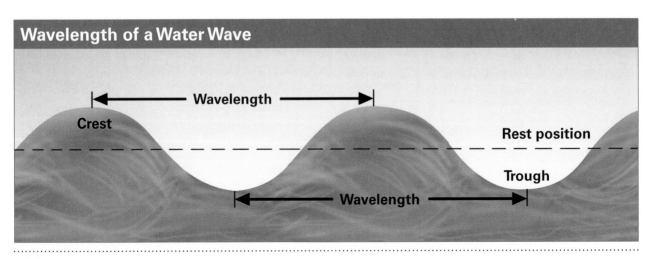

Wavelength of a Water Wave

Wavelength

Crest

Rest position

Trough

Wavelength

2. The Properties of Waves on a String

As you have learned, waves on a string are repeating patterns of crests and troughs, just like water waves. So, the properties of waves on a string are very similar to the properties of water waves.

Amplitude of Waves on a String

Just like a water wave, the amplitude of a wave on a string describes the size of the wave. Picture a jump rope lying on the ground in a straight line. It is at its rest position. You can draw a line with chalk along the rope to see where the rest position is. Then you take one end of the rope and shake it side to side, creating a wave. The amplitude of the wave is the distance from the wave's rest position to its crest. The amplitude is also the distance from its rest position to its trough because these two distances are the same.

You can shake the rope using your whole arm by swinging your arm side to side as far as you can. You reach as far as you can to the left, then as far as you can to the right. You make very big waves that have a large amplitude.

You can also shake the rope using just your wrist. You keep your whole arm still and shake only your hand side to side. You make very small waves. These waves have a small amplitude.

To measure the amplitude of a wave on a string, measure the distance from one crest or trough to the wave's rest position. This distance is the wave's amplitude.

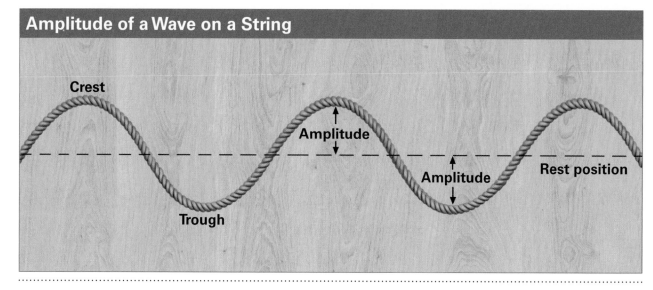

Amplitude of a Wave on a String

Crest

Amplitude

Amplitude

Rest position

Trough

Wavelength of Waves on a String

In a water wave, the wavelength is the distance between the crests of the wave. In a wave on a string, the wavelength is also the distance between the crests of the wave. The distance between the troughs of the wave is also the wavelength.

You can make waves of different wavelengths in a jump rope. You can shake your hand very quickly side to side. The crests and troughs are close together, so the wave has a short wavelength. You can shake your hand side to side very slowly. The crests and troughs are far apart, so the wave has a long wavelength.

For all waves, wavelength and amplitude are *independent* of each other. Two things are **independent** if they do not affect each other. So, a wave with a large amplitude can have a short or a long wavelength. A wave with a small amplitude can also have a short or long wavelength.

Frequency of Waves on a String

Waves on a string also have frequency. Think about shaking a jump rope. You could draw a mark on the sidewalk that is next to the middle of the jump rope. Then you could shake the rope and count how many crests pass the mark in a minute. That number per minute is the frequency of the wave.

The distance between a wave's crests or troughs is the wavelength. These distances are the same.

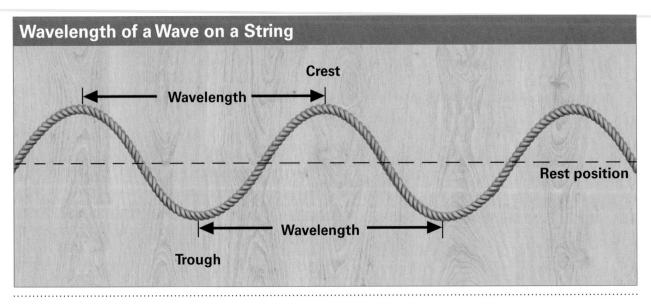

Wavelength of a Wave on a String

Crest

Wavelength

Rest position

Wavelength

Trough

This student is playing a trumpet loudly. Do you think that the amplitude of the sound waves from the trumpet is large or small?

3. The Properties of Sound Waves

You have learned that water waves and waves on a string both have amplitude, wavelength, and frequency. Sound waves also have these three properties.

Amplitude of Sound Waves

Like the other types of waves, the amplitude of sound waves is the size of the waves. But crests and troughs in sound waves are different from those in the other types of waves. Recall that the crests and troughs in sound waves are the areas where the matter pushes together and spreads out. The amplitude of sound waves is how much the matter pushes together at the crests and how much it spreads out at the troughs. If the matter pushes together a lot, the waves have a large amplitude. If the matter does not push together much, the waves have a small amplitude.

Sound waves move through air. They are hard to see since you cannot see air. But you can hear sound waves! So, you measure the properties of sound waves by how they sound.

Sound waves with large amplitudes are loud. The sound waves you make when you yell have large amplitudes. The matter pushes together a lot, so the sound is loud. Sound waves with small amplitudes are quiet. The sound waves you make when you whisper have small amplitudes. The matter does not push together much, so the sound is quiet.

Wavelength of Sound Waves

Sound waves also have wavelength. Like the other examples of waves, the wavelength of sound waves is the distance between two crests that are next to each other. You listen to find the wavelength of a sound wave. A high-pitched sound has a short wavelength. A low-pitched sound has a long wavelength.

Wavelength and amplitude are independent. A police siren is high pitched and loud. A bird chirping is also high pitched but soft. Thunder is low pitched and loud. A frog croaking is also low pitched but soft.

Frequency of Sound Waves

Sound waves also have a frequency, which is how many crests pass a specific point in a certain amount of time. Many people measure the frequency of sound waves as how many crests enter your ear in a second.

In all waves, frequency and wavelength are *dependent* on each other. Two things are **dependent** when they affect each other. The wavelength of a wave affects its frequency. More waves will pass a given point in a certain amount of time if a wave has a short wavelength. So, a wave with a shorter wavelength will have a greater frequency. A wave with a longer wavelength will have a smaller frequency. High-pitched sounds have a high frequency. Low-pitched sounds have a low frequency.

The frequency of a sound wave is how many crests pass a specific point in a certain amount of time. If you had the right tools, you could measure the frequency of a sound wave by counting how many waves entered your ear in a certain amount of time.

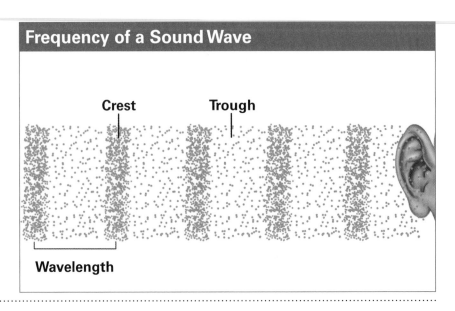

Frequency of a Sound Wave

Crest   Trough

Wavelength

What Are Some Properties of Waves?

1. The Properties of Water Waves   Amplitude, wavelength, and frequency are properties that describe water waves. Amplitude is the height of the water wave. Wavelength is the distance between the crests of a water wave. It is also the distance between the troughs of a water wave because these distances are the same. Frequency is the number of crests that pass a specific point in a certain amount of time.

2. The Properties of Waves on a String   Waves on a string have the same three properties that water waves do. Amplitude is the height of the waves on strings. Wavelength is the distance between the crests of waves on strings. Wavelength and amplitude are independent of each other. Frequency is the number of waves that pass a certain point in a certain amount of time.

3. The Properties of Sound Waves   Sound waves have the same properties as water waves and waves on strings. Amplitude is how loud a sound wave is. Wavelength is the pitch of the sound wave. Frequency also affects the pitch of a sound because wavelength and frequency are dependent. This is true of water waves and waves on a string, too.

Doing the Wave

If you have ever been to a sporting event, you may have done "The Wave." What does The Wave have in common with waves that travel through water or strings?

On August 23, 2008, people cheered as they watched a world record being set at Bristol Motor Speedway in Bristol, Tennessee. But it was not a racecar setting a record. It was the fans in the crowd. The 157,574 fans were doing the stadium wave, also known as The Wave. Once the wave traveled around the entire stadium, the people there had set the record for the largest stadium wave.

The wave in Bristol was not only the world's largest stadium wave. It was also a very fast one. The stadium is 0.8 km (0.5 mi) around, and the wave swept around it in just 58 seconds. So the Bristol Wave traveled at a swift 48 kilometers per hour (30 miles per hour)!

To make a stadium wave, you need a group of people. Each person stands up, raises his or her hands, and sits back down. Each person stands up just after the person next to them does. How long has the stadium wave been used at sporting events? Who invented this crowd pleaser?

Sports fans use The Wave to cheer on their team. A person stands, raises her arm, and then sits back down. Each person stands right after the person next to them does.

Krazy George led the first Wave seen on television in 1981.

The Origin of the Stadium Wave

Not everyone agrees on when The Wave was first done in a stadium. But professional cheerleader "Krazy" George Henderson claims to have invented the stadium wave. During a 1981 baseball game, Henderson decided to try something new. He told three sections of people to stand up, one after another. He hoped to trigger a wave that would go around the whole stadium.

The first two tries did not work. The wave stopped part way. But soon the fans realized what Henderson wanted. So, on the third try, the wave circled the entire stadium. By the fourth try, the fans had mastered The Wave. "The place was going nuts," Henderson said.

Since then, the stadium wave has spread all over the world. It became particularly popular after soccer fans did The Wave during the 1986 World Cup in Mexico. Today, fans of many sports do The Wave, which has become a symbol of sport enthusiasm.

Other people say that they did The Wave before Henderson did. But the wave that Henderson led in 1981 was the one seen on television. For that reason, Henderson is usually given credit as its inventor.

These days, the stadium wave is performed in at all different kinds of sporting events. Here, fans perform the wave at a soccer game.

Properties of Stadium Waves

Waves such as water waves, string waves, and sound waves all have properties. Some of these properties are amplitude, frequency, and wavelength.

Amplitude looks at how much matter moves from its rest position. Does a stadium wave have amplitude? Sure it does. The amplitude of a stadium wave is the number of people standing at once compared to the rest position, where everybody is sitting. The more people who stand, the larger the amplitude of the stadium wave is.

Stadium waves also have frequency. Frequency is how often a wave passes a certain point. To measure the frequency of a stadium wave, you could measure the time needed for the wave to return to its starting point. Suppose that a stadium starts behind home plate. The wave circles the field and returns to home plate in 1 minute. So, the frequency of the stadium wave is 1 wave per minute.

Stadium waves also have wavelength. Wavelength is how long a wave is. If only one wave travels around a stadium at a time, its wavelength is the distance around the stadium. The stadium in Bristol is 0.8 km (0.5 mi) around. So the wavelength of the world's largest wave was 0.8 km!

A stadium wave has the same properties as other waves. If a wave goes all the way around a stadium, the wavelength is the distance around the stadium.

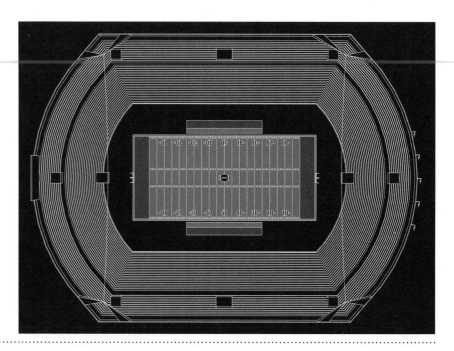

Scientists and Stadium Waves

You may think that stadium waves have nothing to do with science. But, in 2002, a team of scientists from Hungary thought that they could learn something from stadium waves.

The scientists used several methods to study stadium waves. First, they analyzed videos of stadium waves to build a model. They decided that a person could be in one of three states while doing a stadium wave. A person could be sitting, standing, or sitting back down. Then, the team built a computer model of a stadium wave. They tested and observed it many times, and discovered many things.

The team discovered that as few as 30 people are needed to start a stadium wave. So, if enough of your friends are at a game, you could work together to start a wave. Another discovery was that a stadium wave is more likely to happen when the game is boring. So, don't try to start a wave when something exciting is happening.

The stadium wave is more than just a sports tradition. It is a wave that has the properties of other waves. The next time you do The Wave, observe the details. Science is everywhere—even at the big game!

Like a water wave, a stadium wave starts in one spot and spreads outward. Unlike a water wave, a stadium wave spreads out on only one side.

How Do Waves Affect Objects?

Science Vocabulary

vibrate

Moving matter creates waves by causing a pattern of crest and troughs. You will discover how water waves, waves on a string, and sound waves affect objects in two ways. You are able to hear because these three examples of waves affect parts inside of your ear and other objects.

 NGSS **4-PS4-1.** Develop a model of waves to describe patterns in terms of amplitude and wavelength and that waves can cause objects to move.

PS4.A. Waves, which are regular patterns of motion, can be made in water by disturbing the surface. When waves move across the surface of deep water, the water goes up and down in place; there is no net motion in the direction of the wave except when the water meets a beach.

Patterns Similarities and differences in patterns can be used to sort and classify natural phenomena.

 **Developing and Using Models**

Nature of Science

1. Water Waves Affect Objects' Shape and Position

Suppose that it is a summer day, and you are at your neighborhood pool. You sit in an inflatable chair on top of the water. You notice little waves pass by you as you bob up and down in the water. Why do you move in the water?

Water Waves Can Be Formed

All waves are caused by moving matter. Many water waves are caused by wind, or moving air. First, the wind pushes a piece of the water forward. But the water does not have space to move forward since more water is in front of it! So, the water moves upward instead, forming the crest of a wave. The weight of the crest pushes the water in front of it forward, which also gets pushed upward into a crest. Then, as the new crest forms, the first crest sinks back down and becomes a trough.

The crests move smoothly in this pattern over the surface of the water. Each part of the water gets pushed up into a crest and then sinks back down into a trough. This pattern repeats and spreads out, which forms water waves.

All waves are caused by moving matter. In this illustration, steps A, B, and C show how air creates a water wave.

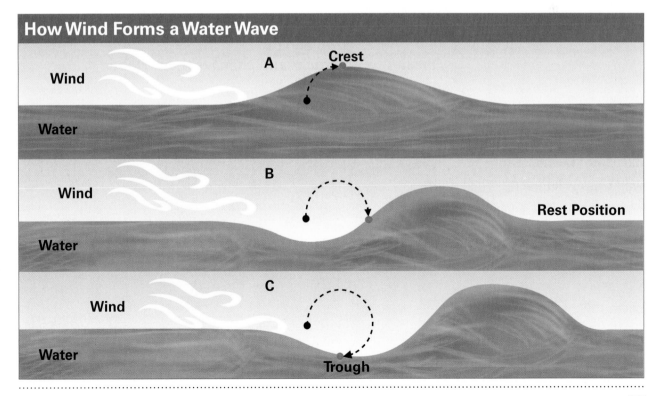

How Wind Forms a Water Wave

Wind — Water — A — **Crest**

Wind — Water — B — **Rest Position**

Wind — Water — C — **Trough**

The motion of a wave can cause an object to change. It can cause an object to change in two different ways.

Water Waves Change an Object's Position

The first way that a water wave affects an object is by changing its position. Water waves push on objects floating on the water. Recall that water moves in circles when a wave travels through it. So, an object floating on water also moves in circles when a wave passes. As the water moves upward and backward, the object is pushed upward and backward. As the water moves forward and downward, it is pushed forward and downward. Consider the chair floating on the pool. It moves in circles because of the wave's motion.

Water Waves Change an Object's Shape

The second way that a water wave can affect an object is by changing the object's shape. For example, the motion of a water wave can change the shape of rocks near the ocean because waves that hit large rocks push on them and can break off pieces. When the pieces break off, the rock is a different shape. This change is called *weathering*. Weathering sometimes makes rocks smooth. But it can also create rock formations like cliffs and caves. Weathering happens because the waves' motion pushes on the rocks and changes their shape.

This natural cliff was carved out by breaking waves hitting the rocks. The motion of water waves hit the rocks and broke pieces off, making them change shape.

2. Waves on a String Affect Objects' Shape and Position

You have learned that waves on a string move in the same way as water waves. You also have learned that shaking your hand back and forth makes a wave on a string. Why does moving your hand create a wave?

Waves on a String Can Be Formed

Like water waves, waves on a string are caused by moving matter. When you shake a string, your hand moves side to side, which pulls the end of the string you are holding side to side. The motion of the end of the string then pulls the part of the string next to it, which makes this part of the string form a crest and a trough. This pattern repeats and spreads out down the entire string, forming a wave.

Can you think of something else that creates a wave on a string? A waving flag is one example because a flag is made up of small pieces of string that are woven together into fabric. Wind is moving matter that can cause a wave on a flag. When wind blows on the flag, it moves a small piece of the fabric. That piece pulls on surrounding fabric, making it move. The fabric is pushed by the wind in a repeating pattern. This movement causes the flag to flap back and forth as a wave.

Waves on a string are caused by a moving object. When one piece of fabric is moved by wind, it pulls on the fabric around it in a repeating pattern, creating a wave.

Jumping on a trampoline forms a wave on a string.

The motion of a wave can make objects move. For example, shaking a string causes a wave to travel along the string. When the wave reaches the yarn, the yarn also moves.

Waves on a String Change an Object's Position

When a wave on a string touches an object, it can affect it in the same two ways that a water wave can. The motion of a wave on a string can change an object's position. Recall that if you tie a piece of yarn to the middle of a string and make a wave, the yarn does not travel along the string with the wave. But the wave does move the yarn side to side. When a wave travels along a string, it makes the string to move side to side. The string's motion then pulls the yarn side to side.

Waves on a String Change an Object's Shape

The motion of a wave on a string can also change an object's shape. Think about a trampoline. The surface of a trampoline is stretchy material that is held to a base with springs. When nothing is on the trampoline, it is at its rest position. When you jump on the trampoline, the surface of the trampoline moves up and down from its rest position, creating a wave. This motion makes the springs stretch. When you get off of the trampoline, its surface is back in its rest position and the springs are no longer stretched. So, the waves that cause the motion of the trampoline's surface stretch the springs and make them change shape.

A Wave on a String Affects Objects

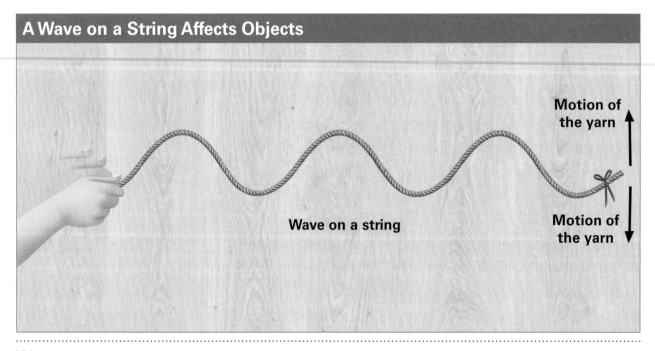

Motion of the yarn

Wave on a string

Motion of the yarn

3. Sound Waves Affect Objects' Shape and Position

It is easy to see how water waves and waves on a string move objects. Even though you cannot see sound waves, you can see how they affect objects, too.

Moving matter causes a sound wave. Here, the motion of the drum sticks moves the drum head, which pushes on the air and creates a sound wave.

Sound Waves Can Be Formed

A sound wave is caused by moving matter. When you beat on the head of a drum, you push the head down. The air near the head of the drum spreads out, making the trough of a sound wave. Then the head of the drum springs back up, higher than its rest position. It pushes the air above it together, making a crest of a sound wave. The head of the drum vibrates up and down very quickly, making a repeating pattern of crests and troughs in the air. To **vibrate** means to quickly move back and forth repeatedly. So the vibrating motion of the head of the drum makes sound waves.

Sound Waves Change an Object's Position

Even though you cannot see sound waves, they push on objects and make them change positions. You cannot see sound waves in the air because you cannot see air. But if you go to a party or any place where music is played very loudly, you may feel the vibrations in your feet as you stand on the floor. You feel this because sound waves travel through the floor in addition to moving through air. This motion then pushes on your feet and makes them move.

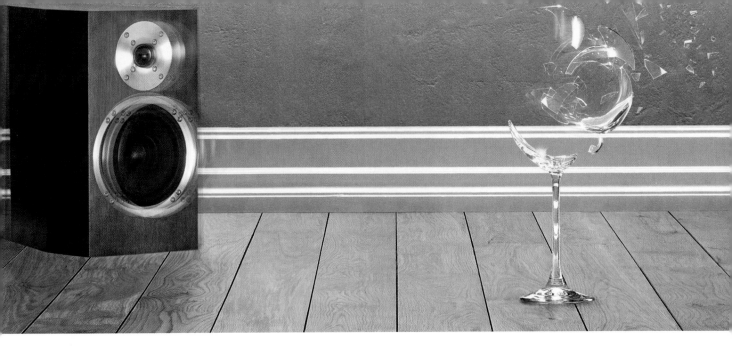

The motion of sound waves can change objects. In this image, the object on the left is a speaker that produces sound waves. Here, the sound waves change the shape of the glass by making it break.

Sometimes you can see a sound wave moving an object even though you cannot see the sound wave. Picture two guitars next to each other. If you play one guitar loudly enough, you can see the strings of the other guitar vibrate. The sound waves from the first guitar travel through the air to the strings of the other guitar. The matter that the waves are moving along pushes on the strings and makes them move.

Sound Waves Change an Object's Shape

Sound waves can also change an object's shape. For example, the motion caused by sound waves can sometimes break glass! A loud note of the right pitch can make the sides of a drinking glass vibrate. If it vibrates enough, the glass can crack and break.

Another way to see that sound waves change an object's shape is by placing a glass of water in front of a speaker and then playing music. The sound waves that come out of the speaker move through the glass, making it vibrate. The vibrating glass pushes on the water, which cause waves in the water. These small water waves mean that the water is a different shape from when it was at its rest position.

4. You Use All Three Types of Waves to Hear a Guitar

Suppose that you are at a park listening to a mariachi band playing. The musicians are playing guitars as they sing festive songs, and you bob your head to the music. As you listen to the mariachi band, you are using all three types of waves.

Waves on a String Can Cause Sound Waves

As you have learned, when you play a stringed instrument, like a guitar, you make a wave on the string. If you strum a guitar, the motion of your hand pulls the strings up and down. You pull the strings into a pattern of crests and troughs that repeats and spreads out. So when you play a guitar, your hand is moving matter that causes waves on a string.

The movement of these waves on the guitar string produces sound waves. The waves travel through the guitar strings and pull them back and forth. They continue to move up and down after you have removed your hand. When the strings move up and down, they push on the air around them. They push the air together into crests and spread it apart into troughs. The pattern of crests and troughs repeats in the air. In other words, the motion of the strings causes sound waves in the air. Like all waves, the sound waves spread out in all directions.

When a musician plays a guitar, such as in a mariachi band, waves are formed on the strings of the guitar. These waves then push on the air and create sound waves.

Waves Move Objects Inside of Your Ear

To detect sound, sound waves have to travel into your ears. Some of the sound waves of a guitar move through the air and reach your ear. You hear the guitar when the waves push on parts inside of your ear and cause them to move. Here's how it works.

The sound waves are funneled into your ear. Inside your ear is the *eardrum*. Sound waves hit the eardrum and make it vibrate. The vibrating eardrum pushes on three tiny bones behind it that vibrate one after another.

The vibration of the three bones causes water waves. The last of the three bones is attached to a circular structure in the ear that is filled with liquid. The vibration of the last bone makes water waves in the liquid. These waves push on tiny hairs in the ear and make them move. The motion of the hairs causes nerves to send electrical signals to the brain that your brain interprets as sound.

In other words, to hear a guitar, each part of your ear makes another part move. First, the guitar makes sound waves that travel to your ear. The waves cause your eardrum to vibrate, which makes three tiny bones vibrate. The bones vibrating make waves in a liquid. These waves push on small hairs, making them move.

You use waves on a string, sound waves, and water waves to hear a guitar. The waves on the guitar strings make sound waves that enter your ear. The sound waves move parts inside of your ear, which send electrical signals to your brain.

How You Hear Sound Waves

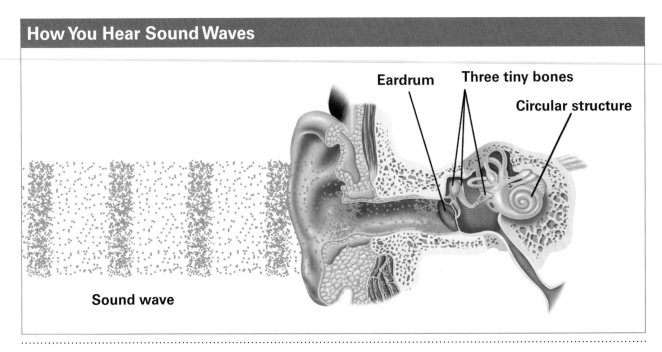

Eardrum

Three tiny bones

Circular structure

Sound wave

How Do Waves Affect Objects?

1. Water Waves Affect Objects' Shape and Position

Water waves are caused by moving matter such as air. Water waves can move objects in two different ways. Water waves can change an object's position. They can push on an object, like an object floating on the wave. They can change the shape of an object, too.

2. Waves on a String Affect Objects' Shape and Position

Waves on a string are caused by moving matter. When you shake a rope to make a wave, the motion of your hand makes a wave. Waves on a string can move an object in two different ways. They can pull on an object and change its position. They can also change the shape of an object.

3. Sound Waves Affect Objects' Shape and Position

Sound waves are caused by moving matter. Even though you cannot see sound waves, they can move an object in two different ways. They can push on an object, like when sound waves push on the ground and make it vibrate. They can change an object's position and the the shape of an object. Sound waves can even change the shape of glass by breaking it!

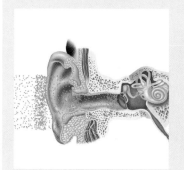

4. You Use All Three Types of Waves to Hear a Guitar

When you listen to guitar music, you are using all three types of waves. The guitar strings are examples of waves on a string. They push on the air around them and create sound waves that travel into your ear. The sound waves move different parts inside of your ear, such as a tiny bone that creates water waves.

Boom!

A sonic boom is a loud sound caused by something that is going faster than the speed of sound. How is a sonic boom similar to other sounds, and when might you hear a sonic boom?

Suppose that your family is at an air show. You enjoy looking at different planes on the ground. But the most fun is when planes are flying overhead. You hear the show's announcer say, "Ladies and gentlemen! An F-18 is approaching and will break the sound barrier!" You watch as it zooms by. A strange cloud seems to form around the airplane. It's already gone past you when—BOOM!—you hear a sonic boom.

You heard a sonic boom because the plane was moving faster than the speed of sound. The speed of sound in air is 1,238 kilometers per hour (about 770 miles per hour). That's fast! The cloud also formed because of the plane's swift speed. When an object is moving very fast, the air around it spreads out and cools down. The water vapor in the cooler air sometimes comes together to form a cloud around the plane.

Many people think that a sonic boom is the sound of something "breaking" the sound barrier. But the sound barrier is not really an object that breaks. A sonic boom is what you hear when a shock wave reaches your ear. What is a shock wave? Read on to find out.

A cone-shaped cloud sometimes forms when a plane travels near the speed of sound. The cloud forms because the air around the plane cools down.

What a Shock!

To understand what a shock wave is, think about a boat going through water. As the boat moves, it pushes the water in front of it. The water cannot move out of the way fast enough, so it piles up in front of the boat. The boat pushes through the piled up water, and the water forms a V-shaped wave behind the boat. This V-shaped wave is called the wake of the boat.

A similar thing happens with airplanes. When a plane moves through the air, it makes sound waves. Those waves move away from the plane in all directions at the speed of sound. When the plane moves close to the speed of sound, the sound waves "pile up" in front of the plane. This is similar to the way water piles up in front of a boat. When the plane moves at or faster than the speed of sound, the piled up sound waves form a shock wave. The shock wave is similar to the wake of a boat. But instead of being a V-shaped wave, a shock wave is cone-shaped.

What does a shock wave have to do with a sonic boom? A shock wave is made up of lot of sound waves that have piled up together and combined to make one big sound wave. When a sound wave reaches your ear, you hear a sound. When a shock wave reaches your ear, you hear a very *loud* sound. That very loud sound is a sonic boom.

As a boat moves through water, it makes a V-shaped wave, which is called the boat's wake.

As a plane moves through the air at the speed of sound, it makes a cone-shaped wave, which is called a shock wave.

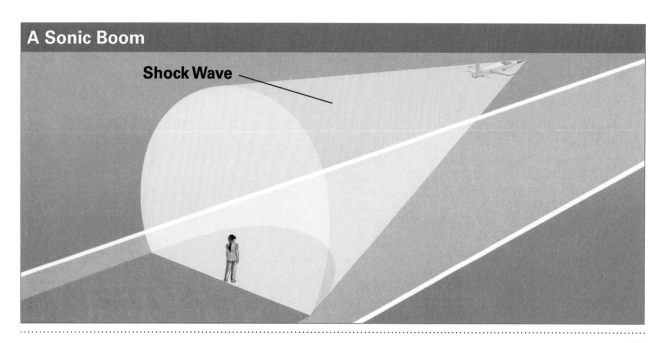

A Sonic Boom

Shock Wave

Lighting makes a shock wave by heating up the air around it. You hear the sonic boom of thunder when the shock wave reaches your ear.

I've Heard That Before

You do not have to go to an air show to hear a sonic boom. Sonic booms are actually more common than many people know. In fact, you have probably already heard many of them—maybe even today!

The crashes and rumbles of thunder that you hear during storms are sonic booms. They happen because when lighting flashes, it heats up the air around it very quickly. The heated air expands, or gets bigger, and pushes outward away from the lightning. The air pushes out so fast that it forms a shock wave. When the shock wave reaches you ear, you hear the sonic boom of thunder.

Sonic booms are not always so loud and dramatic. The crack of a whip is a mini sonic boom. If you flick a whip just right, parts of the whip move faster than the speed of sound. The whip makes a shock wave, which makes the cracking or snapping sound that you hear. You could call it a "sonic snap."

Anything that moves faster than the speed of sound can make a shock wave and cause a sonic boom. Rockets move faster than sound when they are launched. So, rockets can make shock waves. Normally, you cannot see a shock wave. But, on February 11, 2010, the weather was just right for people to see the shock wave made by a rocket. It looked like ripples in the sky.

The bright spot near the center of the photo is a rocket being launched. The circular ripples around the rocket are the shock wave that the rocket made.

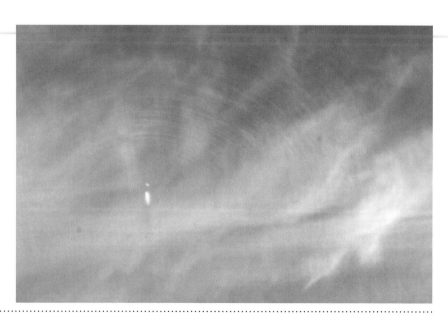

It Came from Outer Space

On February 15, 2013, people in Chelyabinsk, Russia watched in awe as a huge space rock streaked across the sky. It glowed brighter than the sun. People were still staring up at the sky several seconds later when disaster hit in the form of a powerful sonic boom.

The space rock was so big and moved so quickly that it made a huge shock wave. When that shock wave reached the ground, the sonic boom it made was very loud. The boom was so loud that it did more than just hurt people's ears. A sonic boom, like all sound waves, is made up of matter that moves back and forth. So much matter was pushed by the Russian sonic boom that it broke the windows of thousands of buildings. The force was even strong enough to blow the roof off a building!

The Russian sonic boom was an extreme example of a sonic boom. But even booms that are not as loud can cause damage. Sometimes the booms from planes can break windows. But don't worry. Most planes cannot go faster than sound. And those that can? Well, you'll have to go to an air show to see them!

This photo shows the trail of the Russian meteor after it streaked through the sky.

Which Waves Travel Through Earth?

During an earthquake, the ground shakes and moves objects. If it's strong enough, an earthquake can knock down buildings, shatter windows, and cause cracks in the road. You will discover that earthquakes create three types of waves. Each of these waves is similar to the examples of waves that you have already learned about.

NGSS

4-PS4-1. Develop a model of waves to describe patterns in terms of amplitude and wavelength and that waves can cause objects to move.

PS4.A. Waves, which are regular patterns of motion, can be made in water by disturbing the surface. When waves move across the surface of deep water, the water goes up and down in place; there is no net motion in the direction of the wave except when the water meets a beach.

Patterns Similarities and differences in patterns can be used to sort and classify natural phenomena.

Developing and Using Models

1. Seismic Waves Move the Earth

In the afternoon of March 11, 2011, the people in Japan were surprised by a sudden shaking of the ground. Buildings swayed. Things fell off shelves. They knew it was an earthquake. But they may not have known that, at the time, it was the strongest earthquake to ever hit Japan.

An **earthquake** is a shaking of the ground. Earthquakes happen when part of Earth's crust moves suddenly. The *crust* is the outside layer of Earth's surface. You learned that moving objects form waves by causing matter to move in repeating patterns. Similarly, when part of Earth's crust moves, it pushes on nearby parts of the crust and creates waves. These waves are called **seismic waves**.

Seismic waves travel along Earth's crust and through Earth's other layers. The waves make the ground move and cause the shaking that people feel. Earthquakes also cause objects on Earth's surface, such as buildings and people, to move.

There are three different kinds of seismic waves: P-waves, S-waves, and surface waves. Each of these waves is similar to the three different examples of waves that you already learned about. Every earthquake has all three kinds of seismic waves.

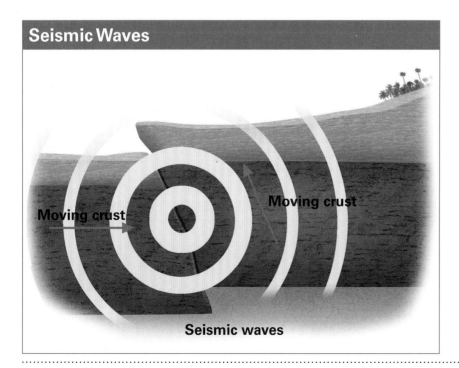

Seismic Waves

Moving crust

Moving crust

Seismic waves

Earthquakes occur when part of Earth's crust moves suddenly. Earthquakes create seismic waves that travel through Earth's crust.

2. P-waves Are Similar to Sound Waves

You usually cannot feel P-waves. But before you feel an earthquake, dogs might start barking. They can sense an earthquake because they can sense P-waves.

P-waves are similar to sound waves because they move in the same way. When a P-wave travels through the ground, it pushes together and pulls apart rocks and other matter in the earth, forming crests and troughs.

P-waves Are the Fastest Seismic Waves

P-wave is short for *primary wave*. Primary means to come first. P-waves are called this because they are the fastest seismic waves. So, P-waves are the first seismic waves to arrive during an earthquake. They arrive before S-waves and surface waves.

Tools called *seismographs* measure earthquakes. When a seismograph detects any kind of seismic waves, it prints jagged lines. If the wave's amplitude is large, the seismograph will print longer lines, and if the wave's amplitude is small, it will print shorter lines. When it does not detect waves, it prints a straight line.

Scientists observe a pattern when measuring an earthquake. They know that P-waves are the fastest seismic waves, so seismographs detect them first. They see that the first waves detected have the smallest amplitude. They conclude that P-waves have the smallest amplitude of the three types of seismic waves.

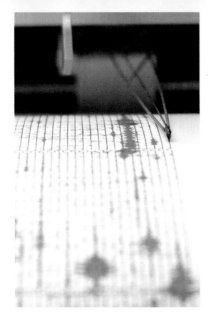

Seismographs measure the amplitude of seismic waves.

A P-wave pushes together in some areas, and spreads apart in other areas. So, a P-wave moves in the same way as a sound wave.

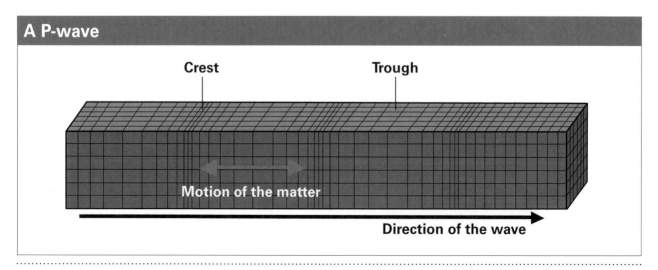

A P-wave

Crest

Trough

Motion of the matter

Direction of the wave

P-waves Move Through All Kinds of Matter

As you have learned, earthquakes occur when a piece of Earth's crust moves. This movement creates seismic waves that cause shaking. The waves travel away from the part of the crust that moved.

P-waves can move through all different kinds of matter. For example, they can move through Earth's crust, which is solid rock. They can move through the ocean and through lakes, which are liquid. They can also move through the hot, liquid inner layers of Earth. P-waves can even move through air.

P-waves Spread out in All Directions

Like all waves, seismic waves spread out in any direction that they can. Because P-waves can move through any kind of matter, they spread out in all directions. When a P-wave travels, it spreads upward toward Earth's surface and downward through Earth's inner layers. It also spreads out in a circle, traveling in all directions away from the part of the crust that caused the earthquake. Even though P-waves do not have a large amplitude, some can travel all the way through Earth. These P-waves can be detected by seismographs that are all the way on the other side of Earth!

Because P-waves are similar to sound waves, they spread out in the same way. P-waves spread out in all directions since they can move through all kinds of matter.

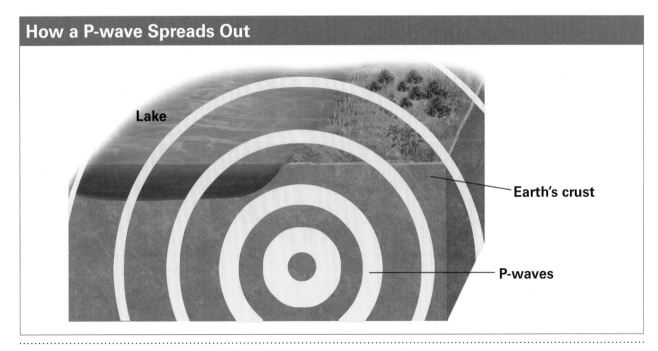

How a P-wave Spreads Out

Lake

Earth's crust

P-waves

3. S-waves Are Similar to Waves on a String

The second kind of seismic waves are called S-waves. S-waves are similar to waves on a string because they move in the same way. When S-waves travel through matter, they move the matter side to side. Rocks and the earth move side to side as the crests and troughs of the S-waves move through them.

S-waves Are Slower than P-waves

S-wave is short for *secondary wave*. They are called secondary waves because they are the second seismic waves to arrive when an earthquake happens. They move slower than P-waves.

Another pattern scientists notice about their data is that seismographs detect S-waves several seconds after they can detect P-waves. Recall that seismographs print jagged lines when they detect seismic waves. The jagged lines printed for the S-waves will usually be larger than the jagged ones printed for the P-waves. Scientists learn from this pattern that S-waves usually have a larger amplitude than P-waves. Because S-waves have a larger amplitude, they cause more damage than P-waves. But S-waves are still small enough that they do not cause very much damage.

S-waves travel through matter side to side. Because of this movement, they are examples of waves on a string.

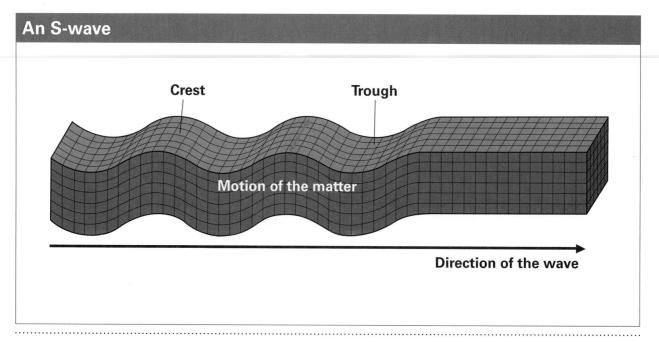

An S-wave

Crest

Trough

Motion of the matter

Direction of the wave

S-waves Only Move Through Solid Rock

Like P-waves, S-waves move through the inside of Earth. They move rocks and other matter side to side. S-waves can only move through solids, such as Earth's crust. They cannot move through the ocean or through the air. They also cannot move through the hot, liquid inner layers of Earth.

S-waves Spread Out in All Directions

S-waves spread out in all directions that they can. They travel in straight lines away from where the earthquake started. They travel until they reach liquid, molten rock, or air since they cannot pass through these kinds of matter. Like all waves, they get weaker as they spread. Weaker waves have smaller amplitude.

To understand why waves get weaker, think about spreading a spoonful of peanut butter onto bread. If you have a small piece of bread, you can have a thick layer of peanut butter, even with just a spoonful. But if you have a large piece of bread, the peanut butter gets spread out much more, and the layer gets very thin. In the same way, the strength of the waves is not spread out very much near the center of the earthquake. But as the waves move away from the center, they are spread thinly over more area, so the waves are weaker.

S-waves spread out as they travel away from the center of an earthquake and get weaker as they spread. So, the further away from the center of an earthquake an S-wave is, the weaker it is.

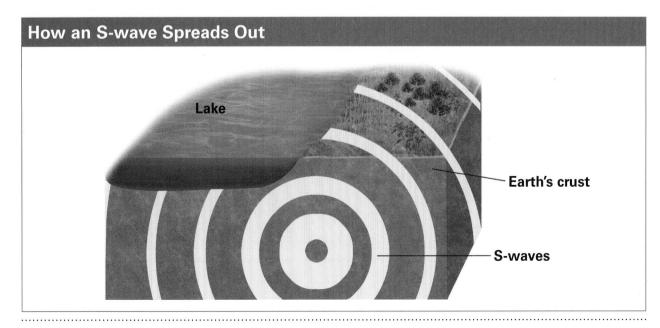

How an S-wave Spreads Out

Lake

Earth's crust

S-waves

4. Surface Waves Are Similar to Water Waves

The last kind of seismic waves are called surface waves. Surface waves are similar to water waves.

Surface Waves Are the Slowest Seismic Waves

You learned about P-waves and S-waves, the first and second seismic waves to arrive during an earthquake. The last seismic waves to arrive during an earthquake are surface waves. Surface waves move in the same way as water waves. They make the ground roll in small circles, just like the surface of water does when waves move through it.

Surface waves have much larger amplitudes than the other kinds of seismic waves. If you look at a seismograph during an earthquake, you will see small jagged lines when the P-waves pass and slightly larger lines when the S-waves pass. You will see much larger lines when surface waves pass. Based on this pattern, scientists conclude that most of the shaking you feel during an earthquake is caused by surface waves. Since surface waves have the largest amplitude of the different seismic waves, they cause the most damage during an earthquake. Surface waves make objects shake. In very strong earthquakes, they can even make buildings collapse.

Surface waves are like water waves. They travel along Earth's surface and move the matter in small circles.

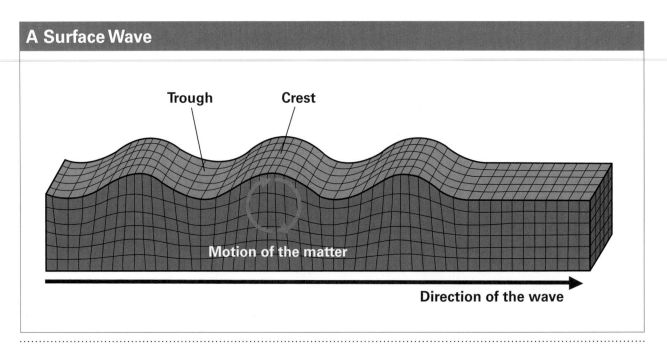

A Surface Wave

Trough Crest

Motion of the matter

Direction of the wave

Surface Waves Only Move on Earth's Surface

Surface waves travel differently from P-waves and S-waves. Surface waves can only move along Earth's surface. They cannot move down through the inner layers of Earth. Instead, they roll along on the top of Earth's crust, or its surface.

Surface Waves Spread out over Earth's Surface

Surface waves spread out in every direction along Earth's surface, traveling away from where the earthquake started. They form a circle around the center of the earthquake. This is another way they are similar to the water waves caused when a rock drops in a puddle. As the waves move further from the center, the circle grows bigger. The bigger the circle is, the more spread out the waves are.

All seismic waves get weaker as they spread out. Their amplitude gets smaller, so they cause less damage when they are spread out. If you are very close to the center of an earthquake, the amplitude of the surface waves will be largest, and they will cause the most damage. If you are far enough away, you will not feel any shaking at all.

Seismic waves create earthquakes, which can cause a lot of damage like this one.

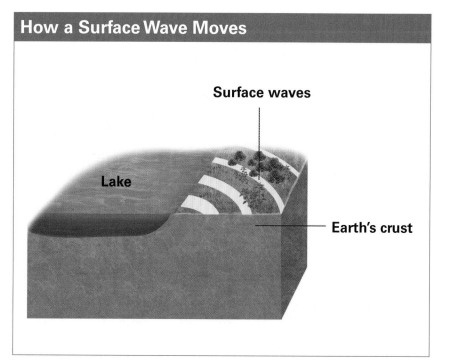

How a Surface Wave Moves

Surface waves

Lake

Earth's crust

Surface waves are seismic waves that travel along Earth's surface. They spread out in a circle and get weaker as they travel away from the start of an earthquake.

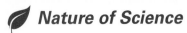

5. Scientists and Engineers Study Earthquakes

You have learned about many patterns that happen during earthquakes. You learned that earthquakes cause three types of seismic waves. You also learned that P-waves are the fastest seismic waves. Scientists look at data from seismographs to find these patterns.

Scientists look for patterns like these to learn about the world. They could look at data from one earthquake and see that the P-waves were faster than the S-waves. But it would not show a pattern in all earthquakes. To see this, they need to look at data from many earthquakes. When they do, they see that all earthquakes have the same pattern.

Finding these patterns is important for engineers. It helps engineers design solutions that keep people safe during earthquakes. For example, engineers used the pattern that P-waves are the fastest seismic wave to design the Earthquake Early Warning system. The Earthquake Early Warning system tells people that an earthquake is about to happen several seconds before the shaking starts. The warning gives people time to get to a safe place, such as under a sturdy table.

Scientists look at data from different earthquakes to find patterns. They collect data using seismographs. These patterns help engineers design solutions that keep people safe during earthquakes.

Which Waves Travel Through Earth?

1. Seismic Waves Move the Earth   Earthquakes happen when Earth's crust suddenly moves. This movement causes seismic waves. There are three kinds of seismic waves. Each kind is an example of one the different types of waves you learned about earlier.

2. P-waves Are Similar to Sound Waves   P-waves are the first seismic waves to arrive during an earthquake. They are an example of sound waves because they move in the same way. P-waves can move through any kind of matter. So, they also spread out in all directions.

3. S-waves Are Similar to Waves on a String   S-waves are the second seismic waves to arrive during an earthquake. They are an example of waves on a string because they move in the same way. They move matter side to side. S-waves can only travel through solid matter.

4. Surface Waves Are Similar to Water Waves   The last seismic waves to arrive are surface waves. They move in the same way as water waves. They can only move along Earth's surface and spread out in all directions. They form a circle around the center of an earthquake. Surface waves cause the most damage in an earthquake.

5. Scientists and Engineers Study Earthquakes   Scientists collect data from earthquakes using seismographs. They look at data from many different earthquakes to find patterns. These patterns then help engineers design solutions that keep people safe during earthquakes.

Protecting People from Tsunamis

When part of Earth's crust moves, it can create seismic waves. But, if the part of the crust that moves is underwater, the motion can also create a kind of wave called a *tsunami*. How is a tsunami different from other water waves?

The sudden upward motion of the crust causes seismic waves that travel through Earth. It also causes a tsunami that travels through water.

Suppose that you are using the Internet, when suddenly you see a breaking news alert. An earthquake has hit California! You click to a news website and start watching its live video. The reporter is at the beach talking to someone. But behind the reporter you notice the ocean is rising up in a big wave. "Run! It's a tsunami!" you hear someone yell.

A tsunami is an ocean wave that is different from regular water waves. Regular ocean waves are made by wind blowing over water. Tsunamis form when a part of Earth's crust that is underwater moves suddenly. For example, when the crust moves upward, it pushes up on the water above it. The water forms a big crest that moves outward and away from where it started.

The sudden motion of Earth's crust is called an earthquake. When an earthquake happens underwater, Earth's crust moves and pushes on the water above it. This can cause a tsunami. The source of the earthquake that hit Japan on March 11, 2011, was underwater. The motion also made a tsunami that turned out to be more damaging than the earthquake.

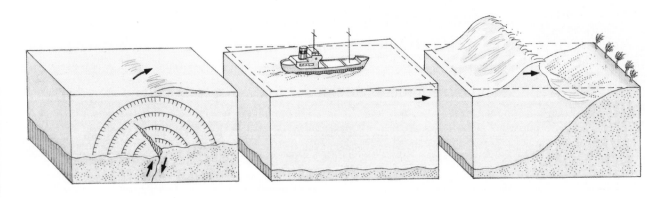

Mud and junk left behind by the tsunami in Japan covered huge areas of land.

Monster Wave

Tsunamis also differ from other ocean waves in the way that the water moves. In regular waves, only the water at the ocean's surface moves in circles as the wave moves forward. So the water washes part way up the shore and then goes back into the ocean. But a tsunami involves more than just the water at the surface. The deeper water is also moved by the wave. Much more water tends to move inland and flood the area.

The tsunami that hit Japan in 2011 was enormous. In some places it was as tall as 18 m (60 ft). That's taller than a three-story building! The tsunami moved quickly inland flooding large areas along the coast. In one area, the waters traveled more than 9.6 km (6 mi) inland.

As the tsunami washed ashore, it swept up cars, trees, buildings, and, sadly, people. When the water cleared, the objects carried by the tsunami were piled up everywhere. Whole cities were destroyed.

Disaster crews found the bodies of some of the people who were killed by the tsunami. But others were washed into the ocean. In the end, over 15,500 lives were lost, most from drowning in the tsunami. Together, the earthquake and tsunami made up one of the worst natural disasters in Japanese history.

Tsunamis can flood large areas in a short amount of time. Knowing the warning signs of a tsunami can help keep people safe.

Watching for Waves

Tsunamis can be very dangerous and can move very quickly. So people who live near the ocean should know the warning signs of a tsunami. People who go on trips to the seashore should also know the signs.

The most easily noticed sign of a possible tsunami is a strong earthquake. An earthquake that is strong enough to knock people down or that lasts for 20 seconds or more may happen before a tsunami hits.

Another thing that often happens before a tsunami is that the water along the shore "drains" back into the ocean. The water moves away from the shore so quickly that people sometimes go to look at it. But that is not a good idea! A tsunami might be coming.

Finally, people often hear a loud noise before a tsunami hits. The noise sounds like a train or a plane coming from the ocean.

Many people in Japan noticed these signs and moved away from the water as quickly as possible. They took shelter at the top of tall buildings far away from the ocean. They warned other people that a tsunami was coming.

Forecasting Tsunamis

The March 2011 tsunami hit Japan soon after the earthquake did because the source of both was close to Japan. But that tsunami did not affect just Japan. It traveled all the way across the ocean. It even reached the United States and Antarctica! However, the tsunami was not as large in those places. And it reached those places several hours after the earthquake in Japan.

Tsunamis can travel very far. So, scientists and engineers are working on a way to forecast these devastating waves. They want to be able to tell people when a tsunami is coming and how big it will be.

To detect tsunamis, engineers have built special buoys and placed them in the ocean. A buoy is a floating object that is attached to the ocean floor so that it does not move. The tsunami buoys have tools that measure a tsunami as it goes by. The buoy then sends the information to tsunami warning centers. Scientists at the centers read the information and send out warnings to areas that might be in the tsunami's path.

Tsunamis can cause a lot of damage. But luckily, big tsunamis do not happen often. And, thanks to scientists and engineers, a person could have hours to prepare for a tsunami before it hits land nearby.

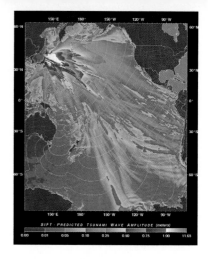

Scientists made this map in March 2011 to warn people around the Pacific ocean of the approaching tsunami. The thin white lines tell when the tsunami will hit, and the colors tell how tall the tsunami will be.

Engineers have built buoys like this one to detect tsunamis. Scientists read the information collected from the buoys and warn people of possible tsunamis.

How Can Sound Waves Be Used to Send Messages?

In real life, you cannot see sound waves, like the ones coming from this saxophone. But you can hear them, so sound waves can be used to send information. When you talk, you are sending information with sound waves. You will learn how sounds, and other things, are coded or grouped to make them easier to write and communicate.

NGSS **4-PS4-3.** Generate and compare multiple solutions that use patterns to transfer information.

PS4.C. Digitized information can be transmitted over long distances without significant degradation. High-tech devices, such as computers or cell phones, can receive and decode information—convert it from digitized form to voice—and vice versa.

Patterns Similarities and differences in patterns can be used to sort and classify designed products.

Constructing Explanations and Designing Solutions

1. Using Sound Waves to Send Information

Suppose you are playing baseball in a playground. You hit a foul ball. It pops up and goes sailing toward a nearby group of kids. "Look out!" you yell to the kids.

Sound waves, like all waves, can travel from place to place. So, sound waves can be used to send information. When you yelled to the kids, you were using sound waves to send information. You were warning the kids of danger from the falling ball. Whenever you talk to someone, you are sending information with sound waves. What are some other ways to send information using sound waves?

In some parts of Africa, sound waves from drums are used to send information over distances of up to 32 km (20 mi). Some African languages are made up of mostly high- and low-pitched sounds. So, two drums—one high-pitched and one low-pitched—can be used to imitate speech. Each word is made up of a pattern of high and low pitches. For example, the word "hello" might be made up of one high-pitched sound followed by two low-pitched sounds. So, you could hit two drums in a high-low-low pattern every time you wanted to greet someone. These drums are called *talking drums* because drummers who are far apart can use them to talk to each other.

Sound waves can be used to send information. These Yoruba talking drums use patterns of high and low pitches to imitate spoken languages. So, people can communicate words using only talking drums.

2. Digitizing Sound Waves

You can press down on the strings of a violin at different places on its neck to make different-pitched sounds. Each place on the neck creates a different pitch. So, a violin can make many different sounds.

Think about playing a violin in a concert. You know which sound to play on your violin by reading a sheet of paper with musical notes on it. It helps you play in harmony with the other instruments.

When you play an instrument, you can make many sounds with different pitches. To play a violin, you press down on its strings at different points on the violin's neck. You can move your finger a little bit up the neck, and the pitch gets higher. You can move it a little bit down the neck, and the pitch gets lower.

Each sound you make on an instrument is called a note. Each musical note is represented by a letter. An instrument can make many different pitches. But there are only 12 notes because, in music, sounds with slightly different pitches are grouped together as one note. Suppose you play the thinnest string on a violin. You can press on the string near the top of the violin's neck. When you play, you hear a high-pitched sound. You can press a little away from this place on the same string. It plays a pitch that sounds almost, but not exactly, the same. But both pitches are called the F note since we call all sounds close to this pitch the F note. This is because we *digitize* music. To **digitize** means to group into sections that can be represented by letters or numbers.

Most instruments can make sounds with many different pitches. But 12 notes are used to represent all of these sounds. This is because we digitize music.

If you were on a dock, you could find the frequency by counting how many water waves pass one of the dock's posts in a minute. If only part of a wave passes the post at the end of a minute, you can round the number up. This is an example of digiziting.

⚙️ *Engineering Design*

3. Digitizing Waves and Measurements

You may not realize it, but many things are digitized all around you. But why are things digitized? Digitizing things makes communication easier.

Digitizing Waves

Breaking sounds into different notes is an example of digitizing sound waves. If music was not digitized, it would be very hard to read and write. For example, suppose you are a violinist and want to play a high-pitched sound. If music was not digitized, you would need a symbol for every sound that a violin can make. For many instruments, you would need hundreds of symbols! So, reading and writing music would be very hard. Digitizing all the pitches you can make into only 12 notes makes reading and writing music easier.

You can also digitize the properties of water waves. For example, think about finding the frequency of a water wave. If you are on a dock, you might count how many crests pass the edge of a post in one minute. But what if only part of a crest passes a post at the end of the minute? You can round the number up, which is digitizing a water wave. So, for example, if only part of the eighth crest passes a post at the end of the minute, you could still say that the water waves have a frequency of eight crests per minute.

You can also digitize the frequency of waves on a string. Think about playing jump rope. You jump while your friends swing a rope. When they swing the rope, they create a wave. You might measure a wave's frequency by counting how many times the rope goes under your feet in 30 seconds. But the rope might not be under your feet at the end of the 30 seconds. It might be 5 cm from your feet or 20 cm past your feet. But you could round the frequency to the nearest number.

Digitizing Other Measurements

Wave properties are not the only thing digitized. Other measurements are digitized, too. When someone measures your height, they might say that you are 120 cm. But you are probably not exactly this height. You might actually be 120 cm and 2 mm. But you round to the nearest whole centimeter and say you are 120 cm. Rounding your height is a form of digitizing.

Digitizing Makes Communication Easier

Digitizing makes communicating information easier. Grouping sounds with almost the same pitch together makes it easier to read and write music. Digitizing makes communicating the properties of waves easier. Digitizing also makes communicating measurements, such as height, easier.

You can also digitize the frequency of waves on a string. You can count how many times the wave goes under your feet to measure the frequency. If at the end of the time the wave is almost, but not exactly, under your feet, you can round to the nearest number.

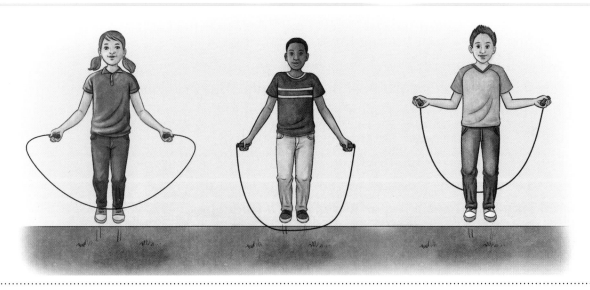

How Can Sound Waves Be Used to Send Messages?

1. Using Sound Waves to Send Information   Because sound waves travel, you can use them to send messages. Whenever you speak, you are using sound waves to send information. You can also communicate with other sounds. Some cultures use instruments, such as talking drums, to send information and communicate with each other.

2. Digitizing Sound Waves   You can make many sounds with different pitches when you play an instrument. Each sound that an instrument makes is called a note. But there are only 12 notes. This is because sounds that sound similar to each other are grouped together as one note. So, music is digitized, or broken into sections that can be represented by letters.

3. Digitizing Waves and Measurements   Digitizing sound waves makes it easier to read and write music. You can also digitize the properties of waves. You can digitize the frequency of water waves and waves on a string. Other measurements are also often digitized. Height is a measurement that is often digitized. We digitize measurements because it makes information easier to communicate.

The Loneliest Whale in the World

Like humans, whales use sound to "talk" to each other. However, scientists know of one whale that does not seem to speak the same "language" as other whales. How was this whale discovered, and how is its language different?

If you have ever gone to a place where the people do not speak your language, you know how hard it is to talk to people there. You try to ask for something, but no one seems to understand what you are saying! Now think about if you spoke a language that no else knew. You could not talk to anyone—ever. A whale in the Pacific Ocean has that exact problem. It makes sounds, but no other whales seem to understand it.

Whales make many different kinds of sounds. They click, whistle, squeal, and call. Whales sometimes even make sounds that many people describe as singing. Scientists are not sure what all the sounds are for. But they think that some of the sounds are used to get around and find food to eat. They also think that other sounds are used to "talk" to other whales. The whales don't have words like humans do, but they can use sounds to warn of danger or call out to other whales.

Whales make a lot of different sounds. Scientists think that some of these sounds are used to "talk" to other whales.

Whales use sound to communicate with other whales that may be very far away. Fortunately for whales, who live their whole lives in the ocean, sound waves travel easily and quickly through water. Sound waves can also travel long distances in water.

I Don't Understand You

Whales speak with very low voices. The sounds that whales make are even lower in pitch than the lowest key on a piano! The lowest key on a piano has a frequency of 27 hertz, or 27 crests in one second. The sound waves that whales make have frequencies of around 15–25 hertz. That is a very low-pitched sound!

A certain whale living in the Pacific Ocean has a much higher voice than other whales. The sounds that this whale makes have a frequency of around 52 hertz. That's a little higher than the lowest notes played by a tuba or a double bass. Those are low-pitch sounds, but they are high for a whale. The whale's unusually high voice has caused scientists to name it 52 Hertz. But poor 52 Hertz has also earned another name: The Loneliest Whale in the World.

As far as scientists can tell, the whale is living by itself. It often calls out with its high voice, but no other whales call back to it. It is as if the other whales do not know what 52 Hertz is saying. Or maybe they do not even know that 52 Hertz is another whale.

Scientists that study whales listen to the sounds that they make. This scientist hopes to hear whales as they pass by.

Who Are You?

Scientists do not know much about the whale they call 52 Hertz. The biggest mystery is that no one knows what kind of whale it is. No one knows because no one has ever seen it. But, if no one has ever seen it, how did scientists find out that this whale even exists?

The loneliest whale in the world was discovered by its voice. In 1989, a scientist was recording whale songs in the Pacific Ocean. The scientist was studying the different sounds that underwater animals could make. This scientist used underwater microphones to listen to whales. It was one of these microphones that first picked up 52 Hertz's calls. The scientist knew the sound was a whale call because it had similar patterns to other whale calls. But the sound was much higher than other whale calls.

Over the years, other scientists have continued to listen to 52 Hertz. They have different ideas on why 52 Hertz has such a different voice from other whales. One idea is that the whale is a cross between two different kinds of whales. Another idea is that 52 Hertz has a differently shaped blowhole. Yet another idea is that the whale simply has a strange accent.

These scientists are putting an underwater microphone into the ocean. Scientists have used microphones like this one to listen to 52 Hertz.

Where Did You Go?

So, is it good to be one of a kind? Maybe not for the whale, but scientists have found one good thing about 52 Hertz's voice. The unusual voice makes the whale easy to track as it moves around. Normally, scientists can track a single whale for only a few hours. All other whales sound alike, so scientists have a hard time separating the voice of one whale from the voices of others. But, the voice of 52 Hertz is easy to pick out. So, scientists have been able to make maps of where 52 Hertz goes. They have maps for almost every year since he was discovered. The maps show that the whale spends a lot of time in the North Pacific Ocean.

The scientists studying 52 Hertz are now hoping to follow the whale's voice to the actual whale. They want to see 52 Hertz. They want to find out what kind of whale it is and why its voice is so high. Scientists hope that finding 52 Hertz will answer some of these questions.

But, some people want to know just one thing. "Is the loneliest whale in the world really lonely?" Perhaps when scientists find the whale they will see that it is not really alone. Perhaps the whale travels with a group of friends and they think it just "talks funny."

Maybe someday scientists will be able to see 52 Hertz. They will know they have the right whale by just listening to its voice.

How Can Patterns Be Used to Send Messages?

Science Vocabulary

digital device

telegraph

Wave properties and other measurements can be digitized using 1s and 0s like you see in the image. Digitized information is used to send messages long distances. You can send words and pictures by using digitized patterns. In this lesson, you will learn about digitized words, pictures, and the electronic devices that use digitized messages.

NGSS | **4-PS4-3.** Generate and compare multiple solutions that use patterns to transfer information. | **PS4.C.** Digitized information can be transmitted over long distances without significant degradation. High-tech devices, such as computers or cell phones, can receive and decode information—convert it from digitized form to voice—and vice versa. **ETS1.C.** Different solutions need to be tested in order to determine which of them best solves the problem, given the criteria and the constraints. | **Patterns** Similarities and differences in patterns can be used to sort and classify designed products.

Constructing Explanations and Designing Solutions

Engineering Design

1. Sending Words with Morse Code

To communicate with someone far away, you might call or email them. But 150 years ago, sending messages long distances was much different.

Telegraphs like this one were used to send messages long distances.

One way to send messages quickly over long distances was to use a *telegraph*. A **telegraph** is a device that sends electric signals over wires. You do not talk into a telegraph. It can only send electric signals.

The first telegraph had 26 wires, one for each letter of the alphabet. In the 1830s, inventor Samuel Morse designed a telegraph that had only one wire. He created a digitized code, called *Morse code*, for this telegraph. It used a combination of dots and dashes to represent all 26 letters. Since his design had only one wire, it was easier to use than the first telegraph. When engineers compared the two designs, it was clear that Morse's was a better solution to the problem of sending messages long distances.

To send a message with a telegraph, a person translated a message into Morse code. Then they tapped the message into a telegraph. To make a dot, the person pressed the button for a short time. To make a dash, they pressed the button for a longer time. The telegraph receiving the signals would then write the dots and dashes on a piece of paper. Another person would then translate Morse code back into letters.

Although telegraphs are not used very much anymore, Morse code is still used today. Instead of telegraphs, Morse code today is transmitted over radios or through long and short flashes of light.

The Alphabet in Morse Code

A • —	B — • • •	C — • — •	D — • •
E •	F • • — •	G — — •	H • • • •
I • •	J • — — —	K — • —	L • — • •
M — —	N — •	O — — —	P • — — •
Q — — • —	R • — •	S • • •	T —
U • • —	V • • • —	W • — —	X — • • —
Y — • — —	Z — — • •		

2. Sending Pictures with a Telegraph

You just learned how to send messages with a telegraph. What if you wanted to send a picture far away? You cannot use Morse code, but you can use electrical pulses to send a picture.

One way you can send a black and white picture with a telegraph is to send it as dots and dashes. First, you need to draw a grid on the picture. The person at the other end of the telegraph needs a piece of paper with the same grid on it. Now look at the first square of the grid. If the square has more white, send a short pulse, or a dot, through the telegraph. If it has more black, send a long pulse, or a dash. The person reading the message then translates your dots and dashes. If the first pulse you send is a dot, they leave the first square on their grid white. If the first pulse is a dash, they fill in the square black. Repeat this method for each square. After, they should have a picture that is similar to yours.

Sending a picture this way is an example of digitizing because each square is represented by only one color. In other words, a square of the grid on the original picture might have mostly black but a little white. But you send a dash so that the square is translated as only black. You digitize the picture because it makes it easier to communicate over long distances.

You can communicate whether each square of the grid has more black or white using a dot or a dash. Then send the dots and dashes through a telegraph, so a person on the other side can recreate the image.

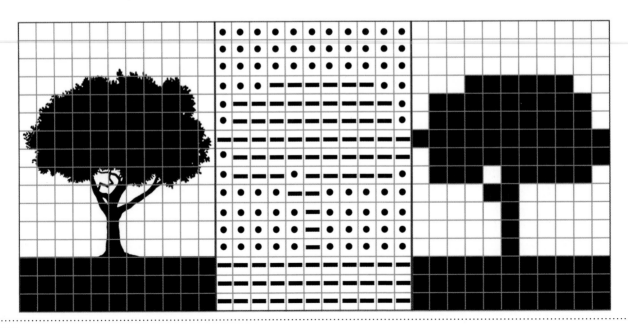

Letters	Morse Code	1s and 0s
Wave	•— — •— •••— •	011 01 0001 0
Tree	— •—• • •	1 010 0 0
Code	—•—• — — — —•• •	1010 111 100 0
Book	—••• — — — — — — —•—	1000 111 111 101
Phone	•— —• •••• — — — —•• •	0110 0000 111 10 0

3. Sending Messages as 1s and 0s

Think about the patterns used to send messages. You have learned about high- and low-pitched drums, long and short electric pulses, and dots and dashes. What do all of these patterns have in common?

All of these patterns are two parts. The drums are high and low pitched. The pulses are long and short, or dash and dot. There is another two-part code that is a pattern of 1s and 0s. It can communicate the same messages as the other patterns. Like the other patterns, sending messages with 1s and 0s is an example of digitizing.

You can translate Morse code into 1s and 0s to send words. The number 1 can represent a long pulse, or a dash. The number 0 can represent a short pulse, or a dot. Try to write the word "wave" with 1s and 0s. First, use the Morse code chart to translate each letter into Morse code. You should have found that "wave" translates into •— — •— •••— •. Then write each dash as a 1 and each dot as a 0. The word becomes 011 01 0001 0. Now you have written "wave" in 1s and 0s.

You can also draw pictures using a grid of 1s and 0s. Remember the picture you sent using a telegraph? You can use the same method to send pictures using 1s and 0s. If a square on the picture has more black, it is a 1. If the square has more white, it is a 0.

Morse code is a pattern that has two parts. You can translate words from letters into Morse code, then from Morse code into 1s and 0s. This table shows a few examples.

4. Digital Devices Use Digitized Messages

Many modern devices send and receive digitized messages. Cell phones and radios are digital devices. So are computers. Many cars even use digitized messages.

A device that uses digitized patterns to send and receive messages is called a **digital device**. Most digital devices use patterns of 1s and 0s that are electrical signals. When the signal is on, it is a 1. When the signal is off, it is a 0. Digital devices send information that is represented by 1s and 0s. For instance, each letter in the alphabet is represented by a combination of 1s and 0s.

Digital devices use 1s and 0s because they can be sent quickly and easily. Digital devices rarely mix up 1 and 0. They can send messages long distances that use many 1s and 0s without mixing up the numbers. This is why if you send a picture to a friend, it looks the same on your friend's device as it does on yours.

Cell phones are one example of a digital device that uses 1s and 0s. When you speak into a cell phone, the phone's microphone turns the sounds into a pattern of 1s and 0s. Then it sends this pattern through the air to another cell phone. Since the message is digitized, it is sent very quickly and without mistakes. When another cell phone receives the messages, it turns the digitized messages back into sounds.

Cell phones digitize sound into 1s and 0s. Then they send them through the air and change them back into sounds so that you can hear someone who is far away talk to you.

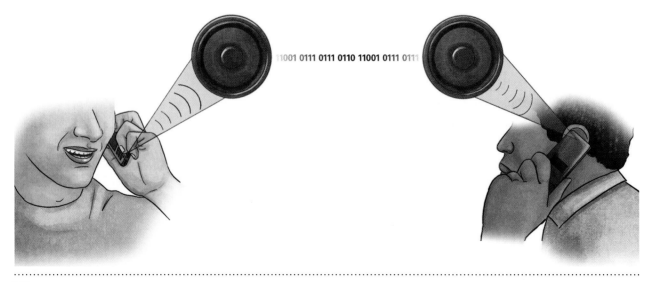

How Can Patterns Be Used to Send Messages?

1. Sending Words with Morse Code Before telephones and computers, people often sent messages with telegraphs. Samuel Morse was an inventor who improved the telegraph. The messages for his telegraph were written in a digitized code called Morse code. Morse code uses combinations of dots and dashes to represent the letters of the alphabet.

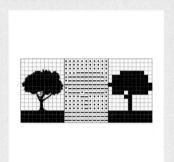

2. Sending Pictures with a Telegraph To send a black and white picture with a telegraph, you can use dots and dashes. First draw a grid on the picture. The person receiving the picture needs a piece of paper with the same grid. Then determine which color each square is and send a pulse with the telegraph. If a square is mostly white, send a dot. If a square is mostly black, send a dash.

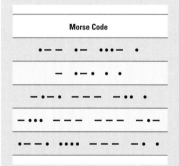

3. Sending Messages as 1s and 0s You can send messages with a code made up of 1s and 0s. This code is also a digitized pattern. To send a message with 1s and 0s, first write the message in Morse code. Then, turn this message into 1s and 0s. To do this, you can write dashes as 1s and dots as 0s.

4. Digital Devices Use Digitized Messages Many digital devices send messages with 1s and 0s. Digital devices can send 1s and 0s quickly without mixing them up. When you speak into a cell phone, the phone turns the sound into a pattern of 1s and 0s. This pattern is sent quickly to a phone receiving the message, which converts the 1s and 0s back into sound.

The Artist Behind Morse Code

"What hath God wrought!" Those were the first words sent in Morse code over a long-distance telegraph line. They traveled from Washington, D.C., to Baltimore in just a few seconds. What inspired Samuel Morse to invent the code that changed communication?

In 1825, Samuel Morse was in Washington, D.C., painting a portrait of a famous war hero, when a letter came for him by horse. It was from his father in Connecticut. The letter brought the terrible news that Morse's wife was dying. Morse rushed home to comfort his dying wife, but he was too late.

By the time Morse arrived home, his wife had already been buried. Morse was angry that he had missed seeing his wife during her final days. How had he not received the message that his wife was ill quickly enough? He blamed the slowness of the message. At that time, horseback was the fastest way to send messages over land. Still, the message had taken too long to reach him. If the message had arrived sooner, then he might have been able to see his wife before she passed away. Morse wondered if he could build a faster form of long distance communication. His wife would not die in vain.

Morse was angered by the fact that he did not see his wife before her death. Her death inspired him to improve long-distance communication. So, he tried to invent a faster way to send messages.

From Artist to Inventor

Samuel Morse was born on April 27, 1791, in Charleston, Massachusetts. In 1805, at the age of 14, Morse went to Yale College and studied art and science. As a student, he grew curious about electricity and took several classes on it. Even though he liked science, he spent more of his time painting.

After college, Morse worked as an artist. He painted portraits of some famous people, including President John Adams. He was working as a painter when his wife died in 1825. After that he started to wonder if it would be possible to build a faster form of long distance communication.

In 1832, Morse overheard a conversation on electromagnets. An electromagnet is a magnet that is made using electricity. Suddenly, it hit him. What if messages could be sent using electricity? Electricity can travel very quickly through wires. Morse worked on this idea for several years. The telegraph had already been invented, but Morse wanted to make it better. He built his first telegraph in 1835, and developed his code by 1838. In 1844, the first message written in the dots and dashes of Morse code was sent using a long-distance telegraph.

For many years, Morse worked as an artist. He painted many portraits and scenes, including some portraits of people like President John Adams. He was working on this portrait when his wife died.

Morse did not invent the first telegraph, but he helped improve it. His design was the first telegraph to use only one wire. People used his telegraph design for many years.

The Spread of the Telegraph

Morse was not the only person who worked on the telegraph. Many other people made improvements before he did. But Morse was the first to build a telegraph that used only one wire. Other telegraphs had more wires, some with as many as 26.

By 1854, just 10 years after Morse sent his first message, more than 37,000 km (23,000 mi) of telegraph wire was strung across the United States. In 1866, an underwater line connected Europe and the United States.

Many governments did not give credit to Morse for his invention. These countries, including the United States, refused to pay him. So he fought for the rights to his invention. His case made it all the way to the Supreme Court, which is the highest court in the United States. In the end, Morse won the rights to his invention. He earned what would be more than $2 million in today's money. His hard work paid off.

Morse spent the rest of his life with his grandchildren in New York. He donated a lot of the money he earned to charity. He donated to Yale and churches. He even helped found a college. Morse also gave money to artists like his younger self.

Morse's Legacy

Before his death in 1872, Morse was honored in New York City. Telegraph workers declared June 10, 1871, "Samuel Morse Day." They wanted to honor the man who made their jobs possible. The day of celebration included a parade and a ceremony. Thousands of people came to the event. They looked on as a bronze statue of Morse was revealed. The statue still stands in Central Park in New York City. In 1896, Morse, who loved drawing portraits of others, had his own portrait put on the back of two-dollar bills.

Before Morse code and the telegraph, messages were sent very slowly. But Morse set his mind to solving this problem. He overcame many obstacles to achieve his goal. He shows that hard work can have a lasting impact.

The telegraph that Morse designed is no longer used. It has been replaced by more modern methods of sending messages. Instead, you use phones and computers. These devices are faster than the telegraph. But Morse's invention still remains important. It is the foundation for modern methods of communication, such as the telephone.

There is a statue honoring Samuel Morse in Central Park in New York City. Morse worked very hard to improve long-distance communication.

Science and Engineering Resources

In Science and Engineering Resources, you will learn how to conduct safe investigations using the skills scientists and engineers use, called "practices." You will also learn how to use metric units and measurement tools.

So, what are science and engineering? *Science* is a way of understanding the natural world. Science involves asking questions and gathering evidence. It also involves constructing models and explanations. Science explanations depend on evidence. This evidence must be able to be observed or measured. But as scientists make new discoveries, scientific understandings can change.

Engineering is a way to solve real-world problems. Engineers use their understanding of science to do this. Engineering solutions include a new way of doing something, a new machine, or new structures. Engineering solutions are always changing as engineers test and improve their designs and apply new scientific ideas.

Science Safety

Science investigations are fun. Use these rules to keep yourself and your classmates safe before, during, and after an investigation.

Classroom Science Safety

✓ Wear safety goggles when needed to protect your eyes.

✓ Wear safety gloves when needed to protect your skin.

✓ Wear protective aprons when needed.

✓ Tie back long hair and loose clothing so that they do not touch investigation materials.

✓ Keep tables and desks cleared except for investigation materials.

✓ Carry and handle equipment safely to avoid accidents.

✓ Handle living things with care and respect to protect them and yourself.

✓ Do not eat, drink, or place anything in your mouth during science investigations.

✓ When you work in a team, make sure all members of the team follow safety rules.

✓ Tell your teacher right away if materials spill or break.

✓ Tell your teacher right away if someone gets injured.

✓ Place leftover materials and waste where your teacher tells you to.

✓ Clean up your work area when finished.

✓ Wash your hands with soap and water after cleaning up.

✓ Know your school's safety rules for classroom behavior and follow them.

Outdoor Science Safety

✓ Wear clothing that is good for walking on wet, rocky, or rough ground.

✓ Wear clothes and a hat to protect you from ticks, insects, sun, wind, and rain. It is best to wear shoes that cover the whole foot, have low-heels, and have non-skid soles.

✓ Wear sunscreen if your class plans to be outdoors for more than a few minutes.

✓ Check the weather and sky. Go indoors if lightning may be nearby.

✓ Do not touch plants or animals, alive or dead, without your teacher's permission. Know what plants and animals to be careful of in your area.

✓ Some things are poisonous when eaten. Never taste or eat anything you find outdoors without permission.

✓ Wash your hands with soap and water after any outdoor science activity.

✓ Make sure an adult brings along a first-aid kit.

Planning Investigations

✓ Choose materials that are safe to use.

✓ Plan how you will handle the materials safely.

✓ Include safety steps when writing your procedure.

✓ Always get your teacher's permission before carrying out your investigation plan.

Science and Engineering Practices in Action

Asking Questions and Defining Problems

Questions about the world drive science. A science investigation tries to answer a question. So, a scientist must be able to ask good questions. Questions can be based on observations. For example, "Why do some of my plants grow taller than others?" They can also be based on models, such as the question "Why do most habitats have more living things that make their own food than living things that eat food?" Scientists also ask really big questions like "What happened at the beginning of the universe?"

Asking Scientific Questions

There are many different kinds of questions. One kind is a scientific question. This is question with a definite answer that can be learned through investigation. A question like "Which color is the prettiest?" is not a scientific question. Each person can have their own opinion. So, all answers are correct. But "Which of these two glue recipes makes the strongest glue?" is a scientific question. This is because it has a definite answer.

These students are working to answer a scientific question. They want to know which glue recipe makes the strongest glue. So, they glued a plastic bag to a craft stick. Now they are adding washers to the bag to see how many it can hold.

Questions are also important to engineers. An engineer might ask, "Why did that bridge collapse in the earthquake?" or "Which material is best for a raincoat?"

The goal of engineering is to solve problems to make life better for people. They solve problems by building things or finding new ways to use things. But first they must define the problem they are trying to solve. Asking questions is important for defining problems. Then they can determine how good their solutions are.

Engineers might ask why a bridge collapsed during an earthquake.

Defining a Problem

Defining a problem has two parts. The first is defining the criteria for a successful solution. The *criteria* are the things the solution needs to do. Suppose you are designing a magnetic latch for a box. One of the criteria would be that the latch does not open unless you pull on it. Engineers might explain how much force you need to pull on it with.

The second part is defining the constraints. *Constraints* are the limits on the design. Constraints include limits on time, materials, or costs. A NASA engineer might design a shuttle to carry astronauts. But the shuttle needs to take less than one year to build. So, the time it takes to build is one constraint.

These students are observing that their box comes open when they shake it. So, they are defining a problem. Then they will design a solution using their knowledge of magnets.

Developing and Using Models

Models in science represent ideas in the real world. Diagrams and mathematical representations are examples of models. So are physical copies and computer simulations. Models are not perfect copies of the ideas they represent. They make some parts of the concept clearer. But they make some parts less clear.

A Spring Toy Model

One example of a model is a spring toy being pushed back and forth. It can represent a sound wave. This model makes the motion of the wave clear. It shows that matter compresses together in crests and spreads apart in troughs. But it does not show that sound waves traveling through air are moving through many particles. It also does not show that sound waves spread out in all directions. Still, the model helps show basic properties of sound waves like amplitude and wavelength.

These students are using a spring toy to model sound waves. They will use the properties they observe in this model to describe other kinds of waves.

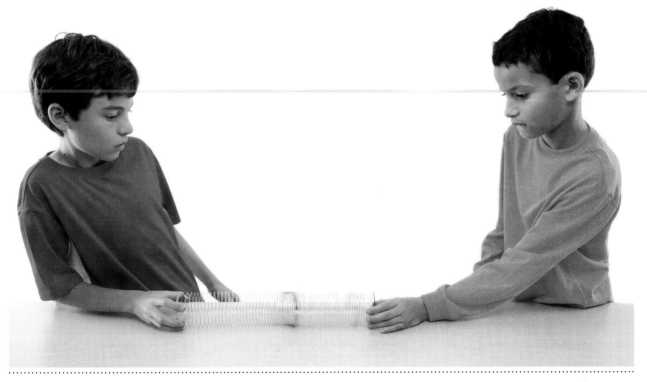

A Pinhole Camera Model

A pinhole camera is another example of a model. It can represent the human eye. It shows that light passes through the opening in the front of an eye and that the light is projected onto a screen in the back of the eye. It also shows that the image projected is upside down.

Many human eye functions can be investigated using a pinhole camera. However, a pinhole camera is unlike an eye in other ways. It is not made of the same materials as a human eye. It is also not filled with liquid. Instead of being round like an eye, it is a cylinder. And it does not have a lens in the front.

But the pinhole camera model is useful for understanding certain properties of the human eye. It shows how light enters the eye. It also shows how the light projects onto the back of the eye. But, as with all models, it is not a perfect representation. So, it is not useful for studying things like the specific structure of the eye.

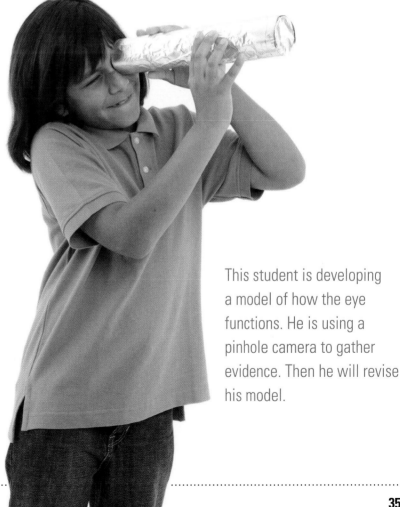

This student is developing a model of how the eye functions. He is using a pinhole camera to gather evidence. Then he will revise his model.

Planning and Carrying Out Investigations

Investigations are one of the main ways scientists and engineers gather evidence. This evidence supports their claims. Scientists use the evidence to construct and defend explanations and to answer questions. Engineers use evidence to identify problems or to decide between different solutions to the same problem. They also use it to determine how they can improve a solution.

Planning an Investigation

One of the key steps in successful investigation is planning. There are many different parts to plan. Here are a few important questions to ask while planning an investigation:

- What question am I trying to answer?
- What are my expected results?
- What data is the best evidence to answer my question?
- How will I collect and record my data?
- What errors are likely to occur during my investigation? And how can I prevent them?
- What safety issues do I need to think about?

These students are investigating how the height from which they drop a ball affects how high it bounces. They will use the data they gather to predict how high the ball will bounce in the future.

The Variables of an Investigation

The easiest way to do decide what data to collect in an investigation is to consider all the variables. A *variable* is a factor that can affect the outcome. Suppose you are testing a water filter. One variable affecting the test is the amount of water poured into the filter. Another is how quickly the water is poured.

Most investigations test the effect of one variable on the outcome. You might test how the rate of water being poured into the filter affects the effectiveness of the filter. In order to test just one variable, all the other variables must be the same in every test. So, you need to make sure you use the same amount of water and dirt in each test. But you need to change the rate that you pour water.

In most investigations, there are some variables that cannot be kept the same in every test. For example, the person holding the filter might shake a little bit. This makes the results change. So, scientists often repeat the same experiment many times. Each time is called a *trial*. They look at the average, or usual, results of the experiments. The more trials they do, the more confident they are that their results are correct.

These students are testing a design for a water filter. They consider variables to make sure their results are accurate.

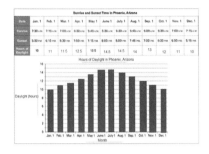

A bar graph can show patterns in data.

These students are analyzing measurements of the lengths of shadows during different times of the day. They will use their data to explain how the position of the sun affects the length of shadows.

Analyzing and Interpreting Data

Once you complete an investigation, you often have a data table full of numbers. But you might have pictures or words instead. How can you tell what all that *data*, or pieces of information, means?

Analyzing and interpreting data is the process of identifying patterns in data. It lets scientists turn their data into evidence. The evidence then supports their claim. Analyzing data might include graphing it to see a pattern. For example, you might make a bar graph that shows the length of shadows during different times of day. A graph will show the pattern of shadows better than a data table will. Analyzing data might also include identifying relationships between variables. Suppose you grow a bean plant. You might find that the plant grows 3 cm each week. Analyzing your data shows the relationship between height of the plant and time.

Scientists use many different methods to analyze data. They use many types of graphs. They also use mathematical formulas and tools. They compare data between trials and experiments. They even compare their data to data gathered by other scientists. They often use computers to help them find patterns in the data.

Finding Patterns with Graphs

Scientists use many different kinds of graphs and charts. These help them to find patterns. They use bar graphs to show how much of the data fits into a category. They might measure how much rain fell each month during a year. They could use a bar graph to show the amount of rain that fell in each month. The bar graph would show what parts of the year had more rain than other parts.

Line plots show a relationship between two variables. Line plots have two axes. There is one variable on each axis. They show how a change in one variable affects the other variable. A line plot might show how many hours of sunlight there are each day of the year.

These students are comparing the data each group gathered about rainfall in different years. They are looking for patterns in the rainfall during different seasons.

Using Mathematics and Computational Thinking

Mathematics plays a key role in science and engineering. Measurements and calculations provide evidence to support scientific explanations. The evidence can also disprove scientific explanations. Engineers use measurements to communicate their designs.

Using Measurements

One example of how measurements are useful in science is when you weigh things. You might measure the weight of cream before and after shaking it into butter. Without measurements, you may guess that the cream is about the same weight as the butter and buttermilk together. But by measuring, you can say with confidence that they are the same weight.

This student is measuring the weight of butter and buttermilk that she made by shaking cream. She also measured the weight of the cream. She will compare the weights before and after the change.

Graphing Data

Graphing is another example of how mathematics supports science. Often, scientists gather lots of data in tables. But it is difficult to see any patterns in the data. But when they graph it, they can see patterns more easily. These patterns suggest relationships between different factors. The data can then support explanations.

Graphing data also helps engineers. They use it to decide between different possible designs. They might test the amount of water several materials can absorb. Then they could decide which material will make the best sponge. By graphing the results of different designs using the same test, they can tell which design works best. Or they can see the strengths and weaknesses of each design.

This student learned that the weight of substances does not change. She is using this knowledge to predict how much an ice cube will weigh after it melts.

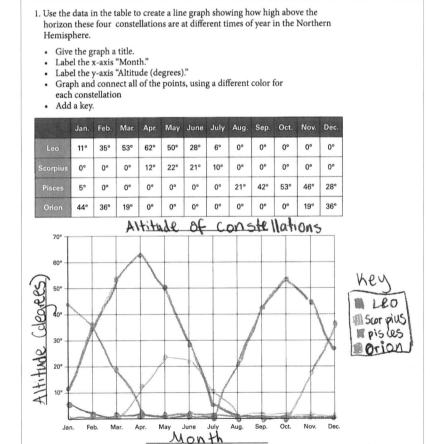

1. Use the data in the table to create a line graph showing how high above the horizon these four constellations are at different times of year in the Northern Hemisphere.

- Give the graph a title.
- Label the x-axis "Month."
- Label the y-axis "Altitude (degrees)."
- Graph and connect all of the points, using a different color for each constellation
- Add a key.

	Jan.	Feb.	Mar.	Apr.	May	June	July	Aug.	Sep.	Oct.	Nov.	Dec.
Leo	11°	35°	53°	62°	50°	28°	6°	0°	0°	0°	0°	0°
Scorpius	0°	0°	0°	12°	22°	21°	10°	0°	0°	0°	0°	0°
Pisces	5°	0°	0°	0°	0°	0°	0°	21°	42°	53°	46°	28°
Orion	44°	36°	19°	0°	0°	0°	0°	0°	0°	0°	19°	36°

Graphing data helps scientists and engineers see patterns in their data.

Constructing Explanations and Designing Solutions

The main goal of science is to construct explanations for things observed in the world. An explanation is almost always a claim about the world. It can be a claim about two variables. For example, a claim could be moths with camouflage patterns that match their background are more likely to survive than moths with camouflage patterns that do not match their background.

Scientists Construct Explanations

While constructing explanations, scientists often investigate to gather data. Then they analyze the data. Often they use mathematics to do this. They usually use models to help construct their explanation. They use evidence to argue that their explanation is correct.

After constructing an explanation, scientists may ask more questions to clarify the explanation. They may have to change their models. Scientists also often communicate their explanations to other scientists. They might do this by writing papers or giving presentations.

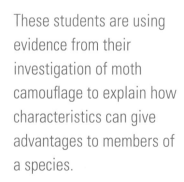

These students are using evidence from their investigation of moth camouflage to explain how characteristics can give advantages to members of a species.

One problem is converting energy stored in a battery into energy carried by light. So, these students design multiple solutions. They are using scientific ideas they learned about energy, electric current, and light to solve the problem.

Engineers Design Solutions

The main goal of engineering is to design solutions to problems. But the process has many of the same steps. Engineers still have to test their solutions. They also use evidence to show that their solution is the best one to solve the problem. After designing solutions, engineers often revise them. They ask questions about how they can improve the solution. Or they might ask what other related problems need to be solved. They communicate their solutions in similar ways as scientists.

The process of designing solutions has several steps. After defining the problem, engineers brainstorm many possible solutions. They compare the different possible solutions to decide which one is most likely to succeed. They may use models of the solution to compare them. After building the solution, engineers think about how the solution could be improved. They repeat this process several times to try to develop the best solution.

Engaging in Argument from Evidence

One process in scientific reasoning is engaging in argument from evidence. Arguments help scientists decide which explanation best fits the evidence. They help engineers decide which design solution best meets the criteria.

A Scientific Argument

There are three main pieces in a *scientific argument*. The first is a *claim*, which is the explanation that the argument supports. The argument claims that this explanation is correct. It is often a simple statement like "wolves eat meat."

The second piece is *evidence* that the claim is correct. This is the observations or data that support that claim. Evidence can be taken from investigations, research, or a model. For instance, one piece of evidence may be that "all wolves have sharp teeth."

The third piece is reasoning that connects the evidence to the claim. *Reasoning* explains why the evidence supports the claim. All evidence should have reasoning. Consider the example of wolves' teeth. The reasoning could be "animals that eat meat need sharp teeth for tearing the meat, but animals that eat plants need flat teeth for grinding plants."

This student is observing different kinds of animals' teeth. He will use his observations as evidence in an argument about how wolves and horses use their teeth to survive.

Obtaining, Evaluating, and Communicating Information

It is very rare for scientists and engineers to work alone. Almost all scientists work in teams, so they often communicate their investigations with each other. Many scientists are also often working on answering similar questions. This means that scientists share their results and information with each other.

How Scientists Obtain Information

Scientists make their results available in many ways so that others can learn from them. One way they do this is by writing up their results. Another is by presenting their research. In an investigation, you might present your research to your classmates.

While reading other people's research, scientists make sure that the information is reliable. They check to see if the data supports their explanations. They read about the methods used by the other scientists and look for possible errors. They also look to see whether the results of the experiment described match the results of similar experiments.

These students used a reliable source to find information about climates in different regions of the world. They are combining the information on one world map.

Using Science and Engineering Tools

The Metric System

The *metric system* is a system of measurement. It is used by scientists and engineers all over the world. Using the same system of measurement makes it easier to communicate scientific findings and engineering designs between different parts of the world.

Base Units

The metric system has several base units used for making different kinds of measurements. Here are a few of the most important ones:

Measurement	Base Unit	Symbol
Length	Meter	m
Volume	Liter	L
Mass or Weight	Gram	g
Time	Second	s
Temperature	Degree Celsius	°C

Prefixes

This chart shows you the prefixes of different units in the metric system. Each prefix makes a base unit larger or smaller.

The metric system also has prefixes that indicate different amounts of each unit. Adding a prefix to a base unit makes a new unit, which is made larger or smaller than the base unit by multiplying by a certain factor of 10. Each prefix represents a different factor of 10.

Prefix	Symbol	Word	Decimal	Factor of 10
kilo	k	Thousand	1,000	10^3
centi	c	Hundredth	0.01	1/100
milli	m	Thousandth	0.001	1/1,000

Using a Hand Lens

Hand lenses are tools for making observations. They make objects and living things viewed through them appear larger. This allows scientists to see parts of an object that they cannot see with just their eyes. It helps scientist see more details of an object.

To use a hand lens:

- hold the lens close to your face in between the object you want to magnify and yourself. The object should appear blurry.

- slowly move the hand lens away from your face. When the object is no longer blurry, it is said to be "in focus."

- find the position where the object is in focus, and hold the hand lens still while you observe the object.

This student is holding the hand lens the right distance from his face to keep the leaf in focus. It helps him see the structures that make up the leaf in more detail.

Measuring Length

Small lengths and distances are measured in centimeters. Larger lengths and distances are measured in meters or kilometers. There are other units to measure lengths and distances. Some are even smaller than centimeters or larger than kilometers.

To measure lengths and distances, you can use a ruler. Rulers have marks that show length on them. Each mark is the same distance from the mark before it. The marks are usually one centimeter or one inch apart. Many have centimeters on one side and inches on the other side.

To use a ruler:

- find the 0 cm mark on the ruler.
- line it up with one end of the length you are measuring.
- hold the ruler along the length.
- find the centimeter mark nearest to the other end of the length.
- the number on that mark is the length measurement you should record.

Remember to record what units you used!

To measure length, you lay a ruler next to the length you are measuring. Find the 0 mark and the other end, and then record the length and units. This drawer is 20 cm wide.

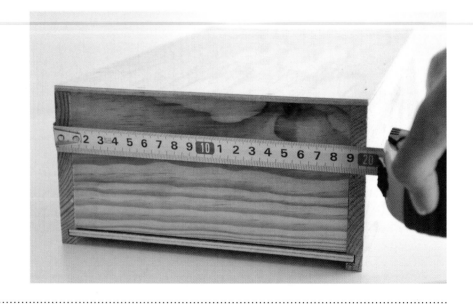

Measuring Temperature

Temperature is measured in degrees Celsius. You can measure temperature with a *thermometer*. Many thermometers are glass tubes with red liquid inside. As the temperature increases, the liquid expands and fills more of the tube. The thermometer has marks on it that show the temperature. Since these thermometers are made of glass, you have to be careful while using them to be sure not to break them.

Digital thermometers have a metal tip that you put in the substance you are measuring. They display the temperature on a screen.

To read a thermometer with a glass tube:

- hold it near the top where there is not liquid.
- hold it so the top of the liquid is level with your eye.
- find the mark that is closest to the top of the liquid.
- record the temperature indicated by the mark.

Remember to record the units your thermometer uses!

This ice water is 0° C. You can see that the top of the red liquid is exactly at the 0° C mark.

Measuring Liquid Volume

Liquid volumes are measured in liters. Smaller volumes might be measured in milliliters or fluid ounces. There are 1000 milliliters in 1 liter.

A *graduated cylinder* is a tool that accurately measures the volume of liquids. It is a thin cylinder with marks on the side. It shows the volume of liquid there is in the cylinder below the mark.

To accurately measure volume with a graduated cylinder:

- make sure the cylinder is completely empty and dry.

- fill it with the liquid you want to measure.

- set the cylinder down on a flat surface.

- make sure the liquid is not splashing back and forth.

- crouch down so your eye is level with the top of the liquid.

- the liquid should be curved slightly, so it is lower in the middle than at the sides.

- find which mark is closest to the bottom of the curve. That is the volume of the liquid in the graduated cylinder.

This graduated cylinder is full of liquid. Find the bottom of the curve in the top of the liquid. Which mark is it closest to? There are 96 mL of liquid in the graduated cylinder.

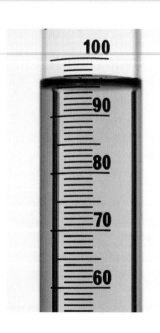

Remember to record the units you used to measure the volume!

Measuring Mass or Weight

Small amounts of mass or weight are measured in grams. Larger amounts of mass or weight are measured in kilograms. There are 1000 grams in a kilogram.

These weights can be used with a balance scale.

Using a Balance Scale With Two Pans

You can measure mass or weight using a *balance scale*. Some balance scales have two pans.

To use a balance scale:

- put the object you want to measure in one pan. That pan should sink down.

- put weights in the other pan. You should know the mass of each of the weights.

- add weights to the second side until the two sides are balanced. So, neither side sinks down.

- add up all the masses on the second side. Their total mass is equal to the mass of the object on the first side.

To measure the mass or weight of this orange, first you would put the orange on one pan of the balance scale. Then you would put weights in the other pan. You would add and take away weights until the pans are balanced.

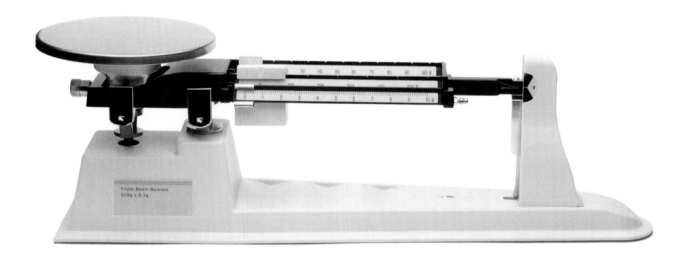

A triple beam balance scale uses one pan and three beams to measure the weight of objects. The beams measure hundreds, tens, and ones.

Using a Triple Beam Balance Scale

A triple beam balance scale is another kind of balance scale. It only has one pan, which is where you put the object you want to weigh. There are three sliders. One measures grams in hundreds, one measures them in tens, and one measures them in ones. There are also two lines, one on the beam with the weights and one on the frame. When the lines are lined up with each other, the scale is balanced.

An apple can weigh about 100 grams. But do all apples weigh 100 grams? Probably not. How heavy are different apples? To find out, you could carry out an investigation using a triple beam balance. You might collect some apples and measure their weights. You would place one apple on the pan of the balance at a time. Then you would find the weight and record it in a table. Finally, you would weigh some other apples and analyze your data.

To measure the weight of an object with a triple beam balance:

- place the object on the pan.
- slide the hundreds weight until the line on the beam falls below the line on the frame.
- slide the weight one notch back. The line on the beam should rise up above the line on the frame.
- slide the tens weight until the line falls down again.
- slide the weight one notch back. The line on the beam should rise up above the line on the frame.
- slide the ones weight until the beam is balanced, and the line on the beam is lined up with the line on the frame. Move the ones weight a little at a time to make sure your measurement is accurate.
- add up all of the weights to find the total weight of the object.

Remember to record the units you used!

Add up the weights to find the weight of the object. The scale reads 101.4 g.

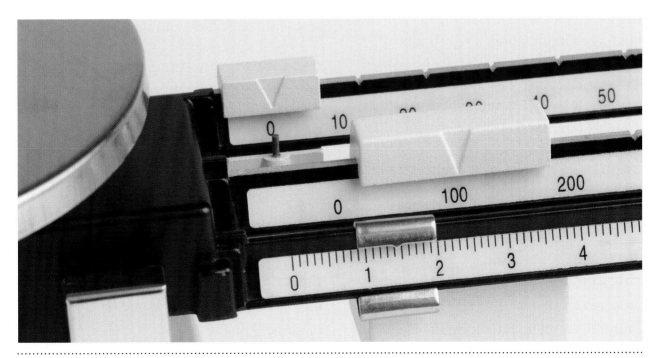

GLOSSARY

A

absorb   To take in. When light transfers energy to material, the material absorbs some of the energy.

amplitude   How large a wave is. The largest distance that matter in a wave moves from its rest position.

antenna   A long, stalk-shaped sense organ on the head of many invertebrates, like insects.

arteries   Blood vessels that carry blood away from the heart.

B

bark   The tough outer covering of the stems of most trees and many bushes.

behavior   The way an animal acts.

blood   A material consisting of solid parts floating in liquid plasma, which moves substances through an animal's body.

bone   A hard structure that is part of an animal's internal skeleton.

brain   An organ in the nervous system that is the control center of the body.

C

chlorophyll   A green substance found in leaves and some other structures that captures the energy in sunlight.

circulation   The process of moving blood and the materials it carries through an animal's body.

collide   To touch something while moving. A moving object hitting another object is called a collision.

cone   A type of plant reproductive structure that has scales but no petals, stamens, pistils, or ovary.

conserved   Having the same total amount before and after a change happens. Scientists say that energy is conserved since it cannot be created or destroyed.

crest   The highest point of a wave.

D

dam   A wall of material that blocks the flow of a stream or river. Dams are built by animals like beavers and humans.

dependent   Two things are dependent when they affect each other.

deposition   The settling of eroded material in a new place.

digestion   The process that breaks down food into smaller substances that the body can use.

digital device   A device that uses digitized patterns to send and receive messages.

digitize   To break into sections that can be represented by letters or numbers.

dust storm   A windy storm that blows dust from a dry region. Dust storms can blow huge amounts of dust thousands of kilometers away.

E

ear   A sense organ that contains receptors for detecting sound.

eardrum   A thin elastic membrane in the ear that vibrates and helps detect sounds.

earthquake   A shaking of the ground caused by the sudden movement of Earth's crust.

efficient   Being useful without making a lot of wasted energy.

egg   A female reproductive structure.

electric current   A flow of electric charge. An electric current carries energy to machines.

electricity   The interactions between moving electric charges.

elevation   The height of an area above sea level.

energy   The ability to make an object move or to cause a change.

erosion   The loosening and movement of weathered bits of rock or soil from one place to another.

exoskeleton   A type of skeleton on the outside of some animals' bodies. It is a hard cover. Many invertebrates, like insects, have exoskeletons.

eye   A sense organ in some animals that contains light receptors.

F

feather   A lightweight, flat structure that forms an outside covering of a bird's body.

fertilization   When a male structure and a female structure come together and combine for reproduction.

fin   A flattened structure on the body of a fish that that helps the fish move, steer, and balance.

fossil   A piece of evidence of an animal or plant that lived a long time ago.

fossil record   The history of how life on Earth has changed, as revealed by the fossils of plants and animals found all over the planet.

frequency   How often a wave passes a certain point in a certain amount of time. The number of waves that are made in a certain amount of time.

G

glacier   A slowly moving river of ice. Glaciers flow more slowly than you can see.

gravity   A force that pulls objects down.

H

heart   A pump made of muscle that moves blood through the body.

I

independent   Two things are independent when they do not affect each other.

instinct   A behavior that an animal is born knowing how to do.

J

joint   A place where two or more bones come together.

L

large intestine   A digestive structure that removes water from undigested food.

lava   Melted rock—which had been magma—once it reaches Earth's surface.

leaf   A plant structure where food is usually made.

lungs   Balloon-like structures in the bodies of some animals that take in air and release waste.

M

magma   Melted rock under Earth's surface.

matter   Anything that takes up space.

memory   Information stored in the brain that an animal remembers from its senses or by doing a learned behavior.

minerals   The chemicals that rock is made out of.

motor   A device that uses an electric current to produce motion.

muscle   A structure that contracts and relaxes to produce movement.

N

natural hazard   A danger caused by changes on Earth's surface or by weather.

natural resource   A material or type of energy found in nature that is useful to people.

nerve   A structure in the nervous system that carries messages from sense organs to the spinal cord and brain and from the brain and spinal cord to muscles.

nonrenewable resource A natural resource that cannot be replaced as quickly as it is used by people.

O

ovary The part of a pistil where seeds develop. When the ovary ripens, it becomes the fruit.

P

photosynthesis The process in which plants use energy from light to make food.

physical map A map that shows the physical features of an area, like its climate or elevation. Physical maps can also show plant cover or where mountains, bodies of water, and deserts are located.

pistil The female part of a flower.

pollen A powdery material made by stamens.

R

reflect To bounce off. All materials that you can see reflect light.

reflex A behavior that does not involve the brain.

renewable resource A natural resource that can be replaced as quickly as it is used by people.

reproduction Making more of the same kind of organism.

response What an organism does when it senses a stimulus in the environment.

rest position The position that matter is in before a wave travels through it.

root A plant structure that grows into the soil to support the plant and take in water and nutrients.

S

scale A flattened stiff plate that forms an outer covering on a fish or reptile.

sediment Any eroded material that is deposited in a new place. Weathered rock, sand, and soil are deposited as sediment.

sedimentary rock Rock that is formed from deposited sediment.

seed A plant structure that contains a tiny baby plant and its supply of food.

seismic hazard map A map that shows where earthquakes have occurred. These areas will likely have earthquakes again.

seismic wave   A wave that travels through Earth's crust and through Earth's layers.

sense receptor   A structure in the nervous system that detects stimuli.

skeleton   All of the bones or other structures that provide support to an animal's body.

small intestine   A digestive structure that mixes digestive juices with food and absorbs useful parts of the food.

solar cell   A tool made of thin layers of different materials that transfer energy carried by light to an electric current. The top layer lets light pass through and traps the light. A middle layer absorbs the light.

sperm   A male reproductive structure.

spinal cord   A long bundle of nerves that connects the brain to the rest of the body. The spinal cord lies inside the backbone, which protects it.

spine   A kind of leaf that is stiff, hard, thin, and very sharp.

spore   A tiny plant reproductive structure that grows into a new moss, fern, or some other plants.

stamen   The male structure of a flower. Stamens make pollen for reproduction.

stem   A plant structure that connects the leaves with the roots.

stimulus   Anything in the environment that makes an organism act in a certain way.

stomach   A digestive structure lined with muscles that stir the food and mix it with digestive juices.

T

taste bud   A structure on the tongue that has sense receptors that detect sweet, sour, salty, or bitter substances in food.

telegraph   A device that sends electric signals over wires. People used Morse Code to send information with a telegraph.

thorn   A sharp, pointy kind of branch or stem that is similar to a spine.

till   To break up or turn over the soil to prepare it for planting crops. Tilling the soil can increase erosion if it is done in the wrong places or with the wrong techniques.

transfer   To shift or move from one object to another. A moving object can transfer its energy to another object.

trough   The lowest point of a wave.

tsunami   A damaging type of fast-moving wave on a large body of water. They are often caused by underwater earthquakes or landslides.

V

vascular system   A system of tubes connecting the leaves, stems and roots. The vascular system carries food, water, and nutrients to all parts of a plant.

veins   Blood vessels that carry blood back toward the heart.

vibrate   To quickly move back and forth repeatedly.

volcano   A place where melted rock and other material erupts from deep inside Earth.

W

wave   A repeating pattern of moving matter. A wave has crests and troughs.

wavelength   How long a wave is. The distance between a crest and the next crest in a wave.

weathering   The natural process of breaking down rock. Water, wind, and living things can all cause weathering.

windbreak   A row of plants that is grown in an open area to help slow down the wind and reduce its harmful effects. Windbreaks can protect plants, people, and structures.

CREDITS

Cover and Title Page
iStockphoto

Front Matter
iii: iStockphoto **viii:** Image Source/Alamy **ix:** Steve Hix/Somos Images/Corbis **x:** Monty Rakusen/cultura/Corbis **xvi:** Darren Baker/Alamy **xviii:** Andresr/Shutterstock **xix:** Sascha Burkard/Alamy **xx:** Patrick Lane/Corbis **xxi:** iStockphoto

Unit 1, Unit Opener
xxii-1: Darren Baker/Alamy **3 L:** Thinkstock **3 TR:** Thinkstock **3 BR:** Thinkstock

Unit 1, Lesson 1
4: PelageyaKlubnikina/iStockphoto **5 L:** elina/Shutterstock **5 R:** Egon Zitter/Dreamstime **6 L:** Phil Degginger/Alamy **6R:** Thomas Biegalski/Dreamstime **7 T:** Connie Larsen/Dreamstime **7 B:** Synchronista/Dreamstime **8 B:** Valerianic/Dreamstime **8 T:** Tom Dowd/Dreamstime **10:** andersphoto/Shutterstock **11 (#1):** Egon Zitter/Dreamstime **11 (#2):** Phil Degginger/Alamy **11 (#3):** Connie Larsen/Dreamstime **11 (#5):** andersphoto/Shutterstock **12:** kkaplin/Shutterstock **13:** Thinkstock **14 L:** iStockphoto **14 R:** iStockphoto **15 B:** Linda Bair/Dreamstime **15 T:** Shutterstock

Unit 1, Lesson 2
16: Will Reece/Dreamstime **17:** Sarahgen/Dreamstime **18:** Patrick Allen/Dreamstime **19:** Sylvie Lebchek/Dreamstime **20:** Gardendreamer/Dreamstime **21 (#1):** Sarahgen/Dreamstime **21 (#2):** Patrick Allen/Dreamstime **21 (#3):** Sylvie Lebchek/Dreamstime **21 (#4):** Gardendreamer/Dreamstime **22:** Ingrid Curry/Shutterstock **23 L:** Thinkstock **23 R:** Thinkstock **24:** Thinkstock **25 T:** iStockphoto **25 B:** Thinkstock

Unit 1, Lesson 3
26: Subbotina/Dreamstime **27:** Jill Lang/Shutterstock **29 B:** Bogdan Wankowicz/Shutterstock **29 T:** Kratka/Dreamstime **30 B:** Brian Maudsley/Shutterstock **30 T:** arka38/Shutterstock **31:** Ryan Jorgensen/Dreamstime **32 T:** Karen Foley/Dreamstime **32 B:** Annestaub/Dreamstime **33 (#1):** Jill Lang/Shutterstock **33 (#3):** Brian Maudsley/Shutterstock **33 (#4):** Ryan Jorgensen/Dreamstime **33 (#5):** Annestaub/Dreamstime **34:** Mary Nguyen NG/Shutterstock **35:** FRANS LANTING, MINT IMAGES/Science Source **36:** Universal Images Group/SuperStock **37:** ASSOCIATED PRESS

Unit 1, Lesson 4
38: Tatjana Gupalo/Dreamstime **39:** Sebastian Czapnik/Dreamstime **40:** Bogdan Wańkowicz/Dreamstime **41 T:** MIMOHE/photos.com **41 B:** Thinkstock **42:** Steveheap/Dreamstime **43 (#1):** Sebastian Czapnik/Dreamstime **43 (#2):** Bogdan Wańkowicz/Dreamstime **43 (#3):** MIMOHE/photos.com **43 (#4):** Steveheap/Dreamstime **44:** Shutterstock **45:** Thinkstock **46:** Thinkstock **47:** Graham Holden/Dreamstime

Unit 1, Lesson 5
48: Milla74/Dreamstime **49:** Goce Risteski/Dreamstime **50:** Mariusz Blach/Dreamstime **51:** Creativenature1/Dreamstime **53:** Alexander Vasilyev/Dreamstime **55 (#1):** Goce Risteski/Dreamstime **55 (#2):** Mariusz Blach/Dreamstime **55 (#3):** Creativenature1/Dreamstime **55 (#4):** Alexander Vasilyev/Dreamstime **56:** Shutterstock **57:** iStockphoto **58 L:** Thinkstock **58 R:** Thinkstock **59:** Thinkstock

Unit 1, Lesson 6
60: Tony Campbell/Dreamstime **61 T:** Northernprairie/Dreamstime **61 B:** Arkadi Bojaršinov/Dreamstime **62 T:** Garytalton/Dreamstime **63:** Mularczyk/Dreamstime **64 T:** Michael Herman/Dreamstime **64 B:** Hudakore/Dreamstime **65 T:** Wildphotos/Dreamstime **65 B:** Arrxxx/Dreamstime **66 B:** Martin Maritz/Dreamstime **66 T:** Andamanse/Dreamstime **67 (#1):** Northernprairie/Dreamstime **67 (#2):** Garytalton/Dreamstime **67 (#3):** Mularczyk/Dreamstime **67 (#4):** Michael Herman/Dreamstime **67 (#5):** Wildphotos/Dreamstime **67 (#6):** Andamanse/Dreamstime **68:** ASSOCIATED PRESS **69 T:** NASA **69 B:** NASA **70 T:** NASA/SCIENCE PHOTO LIBRARY **70 B:** Robert Markowitz/NASA **71:** ASSOCIATED PRESS

Unit 1, Lesson 7
72: Gordon Miller/Dreamstime **73 B:** Menno67/Dreamstime **73 T:** Fireflyphoto/Dreamstime **74:** Deepwater/Dreamstime **75:** Artur Bogacki/Dreamstime **76 B:** Fiona Ayerst/Dreamstime **76 T:** Kjuurs/Dreamstime **77 (#1):** Menno67/Dreamstime **77 (#2):** Deepwater/Dreamstime **77 (#3):** Kjuurs/Dreamstime **78:** Thinkstock **79 B:** Thinkstock **79 T:** Thinkstock

Unit 1, Lesson 8
80: Olga Khoroshunova/Dreamstime **81 B:** Marilyn Gould/Dreamstime **81 T:** Amy Johansson/Shutterstock **82:** Orionmystery/Dreamstime **83:** Roughcollie/Dreamstime **84 T:** Alexey Kuznetsov/Dreamstime **84 B:** Michael Zysman/Dreamstime **85 T:** Kts/Dreamstime **85 B:** Victorpr/Dreamstime **86:** Riky66/Dreamstime **87 L:** Mirceax/Dreamstime **87 C:** Melissa Connors/Dreamstime **87 R:** Tomatito26/Dreamstime **88:** Stephan Breton/Dreamstime **89 (#1):** Marilyn Gould/Dreamstime **89 (#2):** Orionmystery/Dreamstime **89 (#3):** Roughcollie/Dreamstime **89 (#4):** Alexey Kuznetsov/Dreamstime **89 (#5):** Kts/Dreamstime **89 (#6):** Melissa Connors/Dreamstime **89 (#7):** Stephan Breton/Dreamstime **90 L:** Ted Kinsman/Science Source **90 R:** Ted Kinsman/Science Source **91:** iStockphoto **92:** Shutterstock **93 L:** Shutterstock **93 R:** iStockphoto

Unit 1, Lesson 9
94: Boleslaw Kubica/Dreamstime **95 T:** Chris Lorenz/Dreamstime **96 T:** Shubhangi Kene/Dreamstime **97 L:** Unclegene/Dreamstime **97 R:** Chatchai Somwat/Dreamstime **99:** Norma Cornes/Dreamstime **100:** Welshi23/Dreamstime **101 (#1):** Chris Lorenz/Dreamstime **101 (#2):** Shubhangi Kene/Dreamstime **101 (#3):** Unclegene/Dreamstime **101 (#5):** Norma Cornes/Dreamstime **101 (#6):** Welshi23/Dreamstime **102:** Goncaloferreira/Dreamstime **103:** Thinkstock **104 B:** Thinkstock **104 T:** Calv6304/Dreamstime **105:** Anke Van Wyk/Dreamstime

Unit 2, Unit Opener
106-107: Andresr/Shutterstock **109 T:** Thinkstock **109 BR:** Wavebreakmedia Ltd/ Dreamstime **109 BL:** Artranq/Dreamstime

Unit 2, Lesson 1
110: David Brimm/Alamy **111:** Thomas Mueller/Alamy **117 (#1):** Thomas Mueller/ Alamy **118:** Thinkstock **120:** Thinkstock **121:** iStockphoto

Unit 2, Lesson 2
122: isitsharp/iStockphoto **124:** lkpgfoto/ iStockphoto **126 T:** RBFried/iStockphoto **126 B:** iStockphoto **128:** all/Alamy **129 (#2):** lkpgfoto/iStockphoto **129 (#3):** RBFried/iStockphoto **129 (#4):** all/ Alamy **130:** TRL Ltd./Science Source **131:** Ninthsun9/Dreamstime **132:** iStockphoto **133:** James King-Holmes/First Technology Safety Systems/Photo Researchers, Inc.

Unit 2, Lesson 3
134: Inge Johnsson/Alamy **135 T:** Joshua David Treisner/Shutterstock **135 B:** Johan-JK/Alamy **136 B:** Cultura Creative (RF)/ Alamy **136 T:** music Alan King/Alamy **137:** GA161076/iStockphoto **138:** Cultura Creative (RF)/Alamy **139 B:** alexxx1981/ iStockphoto **139 T:** Sytnik/Alamy **140:** peepo/iStockphoto **141 (#1):** Joshua David Treisner/Shutterstock **141 (#2):** Cultura Creative (RF)/Alamy **141 (#3):** Cultura Creative (RF)/Alamy **141 (#4):** alexxx1981/ iStockphoto **141 (#5):** peepo/iStockphoto **142:** Antoniodiaz/Dreamstime **143 B:** Radius Images/Alamy **143 T:** iStockphoto **144:** Thinkstock **145:** Lenanet/Dreamstime

Unit 2, Lesson 4
146: nikonaft/iStockphoto **147:** Phil Degginger/Alamy **148:** iStockphoto **150 T:** imagedb.com/Shutterstock **152:** jaywarren79/iStockphoto **153:** Alan Falcony/ Shutterstock **154:** Nomadsoul1/Dreamstime **155 (#1):** Phil Degginger/Alamy **155 (#2):** iStockphoto **155 (#5):** jaywarren79/ iStockphoto **155 (#6):** Alan Falcony/Shutterstock **155 (#7):** Nomadsoul1/Dreamstime **156:** Thinkstock **157 T:** iStockphoto **157 B:** Wikimedia **158 B:** Stephen Mallon/ Corbis/AP Images **158 T:** Thinkstock **159 T:** Thinkstock **159 B:** Shutterstock

Unit 2, Lesson 5
160: Monkey Business Images/Dreamstime **161 L:** HAYKIRDI/iStockphoto **161 C:** Antikainen/Dreamstime **161 R:** Tomislav Pinter/Dreamstime **162:** XiXinXing/ Alamy **163:** Tom Wang/Dreamstime **164:** Lawrence Worcester/gettyimages **165:** Steve Hix/Somos Images/Corbis **166:** ZUMA Press, Inc./Alamy **161 L:** HAYKIRDI/iStockphoto **163:** Tom Wang/ Dreamstime **165:** Steve Hix/Somos Images/Corbis **166:** ZUMA Press, Inc./Alamy **167 (#1):** HAYKIRDI/iStockphoto **167 (#2):** Tom Wang/Dreamstime **167 (#3):** Steve Hix/Somos Images/Corbis **167 (#4):** ZUMA Press, Inc./Alamy **168:** Littleny/ Dreamstime **169:** Jannis Werner/Dreamstime **170:** iStockphoto **171:** iStockphoto

Unit 2, Lesson 6
172: Carlo Toffolo/Shutterstock **173:** Alexandros Aidonidis/Alamy **175:** Zbynek Burival/Alamy **176:** mironov/Shutterstock **177:** Speyeder/Dreamstime **178 T:** Dinodia Photos/Alamy **178 B:** Mikhail Tolstoy/ Alamy **179 (#1):** Alexandros Aidonidis/ Alamy **179 (#2):** Zbynek Burival/Alamy **179 (#3):** Speyeder/Dreamstime **179 (#4):** Dinodia Photos/Alamy **180:** Caro/Alamy **182:** Thinkstock **183:** Claus Lunau/Science Source

Unit 3, Unit Opener
184-185: Sascha Burkard/Alamy **187 B:** Thinkstock **187 C:** iStockphoto **187 T:** Thinkstock

Unit 3, Lesson 1
188: Shutterstock **189:** Thinkstock **190 L:** Thinkstock **190 R:** iStockphoto **191:** Shutterstock **192 L:** Shutterstock **192 R:** Shutterstock **193 (#1):** Thinkstock **193 (#2):** iStockphoto **193 (#3):** Shutterstock **193 (#4):** Shutterstock **194:** Thinkstock **195:** Ian Thraves/Alamy **196:** andy lane/Alamy **197:** Mike Charles/Shutterstock

Unit 3, Lesson 2
198: Shutterstock **199:** Thinkstock **200 T:** Thinkstock **200 B:** Thinkstock **201 B:** Thinkstock **201 T:** Thinkstock **202 T:** Thinkstock **203:** gary yim/Shutterstock **204 T:** Thinkstock **204 B:** iStockphoto **205 (#1):** Thinkstock **205 (#2):** Thinkstock **205 (#3):** Thinkstock **205 (#5):** gary yim/Shutterstock **205 (#6):** Thinkstock **206:** Thinkstock **207:** Shutterstock **208:** iStockphoto **209:** iStockphoto

Unit 3, Lesson 3
210: Nagel Photography/Shutterstock **211:** Jeannette Katzir Photog/Shutterstock **212 B:** Shutterstock **213:** Denis Burdin/ Shutterstock **214 B:** Ted Foxx/Alamy **214 T:** Thinkstock **215:** Corbis **216 L:** Eastcott Momatiuk/Getty Images **216 R:** Thinkstock **217 (#1):** Jeannette Katzir Photog/ Shutterstock **217 (#2):** Shutterstock **217 (#3):** Denis Burdin/Shutterstock **217 (#4):** Thinkstock **217 (#5):** Corbis **217 (#6):** Eastcott Momatiuk/Getty Images **218:** iStockphoto **219:** iStockphoto **220:** Minden Pictures SuperStock **221:** Shutterstock

Unit 3, Lesson 4
222: Thinkstock **223 L:** Shutterstock **223 R:** Shutterstock **224 B:** Yuriy Kulik / Shutterstock **224 T:** Thinkstock **225 T:** Anette Linnea Rasmussen/Dreamstime **226:** LOETSCHER CHLAUS/Alamy **227 T:** Mikelane45/Dreamstime **227 B:** Shutterstock **228:** Tran Van Thai/Shutterstock **229 (#1):** Shutterstock **229 (#2):** Thinkstock **229 (#3):** Anette Linnea Rasmussen/Dreamstime **229 (#4):** LOETSCHER CHLAUS/Alamy **229 (#5):** Shutterstock **229 (#6):** Tran Van Thai/Shutterstock **230:** iStockphoto **231:** iStockphoto **232:** NOAA George E. Marsh Album **233:** Thinkstock

Unit 3, Lesson 5
234: Konstantin Mikhailov/Global Look/ Corbis **235 B:** Kim Steel/Getty Images **235 T:** Thinkstock **236 T:** Photobank gallery/ Shutterstock **236 B:** Styve Reineck/Shutterstock **239 T:** Linda Bucklin/Shutterstock **239 B:** Chantal de Bruijne/Shutterstock **240 T:** Anthony Aneese Totah Jr/Dreamstime **240 B:** Patrick Poendl/Dreamstime **241 (#1):** Kim Steel/Getty Images **241 (#2):** Styve Reineck/Shutterstock **241 (#3):** Linda Bucklin/Shutterstock **241 (#4):** Patrick Poendl/Dreamstime **242:** iStockphoto **243:** Kostyantyn Ivanyshen/Shutterstock **244:** Shutterstock **245:** Thinkstock

Unit 3, Lesson 6
246: Thinkstock **249 T:** Fredy Thuerig/Shutterstock **250 T:** Malucs/Dreamstime **251 (#3):** Fredy Thuerig/Shutterstock **251 (#4):** Malucs/Dreamstime **252:** iStockphoto **253:** iStockphoto **254:** iStockphoto **255:** NASA/GSFC/MITI/ERSDAC/JAROS, and U.S./Japan ASTER Science Team

Unit 3, Lesson 7
256: ASSOCIATED PRESS **257:** Cholder/Dreamstime **258 L:** Thinkstock **258 R:** ASSOCIATED PRESS **260 B:** Thinkstock **260 T:** Siim Sepp/Alamy **261 R:** Thinkstock **261 L:** Thinkstock **262:** ASSOCIATED PRESS **263 B:** ASSOCIATED PRESS **263 T:** Thinkstock **264:** Shutterstock **265 (#1):** Cholder/Dreamstime **265 (#2):** Thinkstock **265 (#3):** Thinkstock **265 (#4):** ASSOCIATED PRESS **265 (#5):** Shutterstock **266:** iStockphoto **267:** National Geographic Image Collection/Alamy **268:** Jerome Minet/Kipa/Corbis **269:** Thinkstock

Unit 4, Unit Opener
270-271: Patrick Lane/Corbis **273 L:** Thinkstock **273 TR:** Thinkstock **273 BR:** Thinkstock

Unit 4, Lesson 1
274: Mangroove/Dreamstime **275 T:** Mark Ross/Dreamstime **283 (#1):** Mark Ross/Dreamstime **284:** Thinkstock **285:** Mikkel Juul Jensen/Science Source **286 L:** Captain Roger Wilson, Greenland, New Hampshire/NOAA **286 R:** Captain Roger Wilson, Greenland, New Hampshire/NOAA **287:** Thinkstock

Unit 4, Lesson 2
288: Kheng Guan Toh/Dreamstime **293:** Blend Images/Alamy **295 (#3):** Blend Images/Alamy **296:** salajean/Shutterstock **297 T:** ASSOCIATED PRESS **297 B:** Tim Clayton/TIM CLAYTON/Corbis **298:** andrejco/Shutterstock **299:** iStockphoto

Unit 4, Lesson 3
300: raisbeckfoto/iStockphoto **302:** Ron_Thomas/iStockphoto **303:** Centrill/Dreamstime **304 T:** DonSmith/Alamy **305:** philipdyer/iStockphoto **306:** Marc Wuchner/Corbis **307:** cristianl/iStockphoto **309 (#1):** Ron_Thomas/iStockphoto **309 (#2):** DonSmith/Alamy **309 (#3):** philipdyer/iStockphoto **310:** Ensign John Gay, USS Constellation, U.S. Navy **311 T:** iStockphoto **312 T:** iStockphoto **312 B:** NASA/Goddard/Anne Koslosky **313:** ASSOCIATED PRESS

Unit 4, Lesson 4
314: BluesandViews/iStockphoto **316 T:** Furchin/iStockphoto **321 T:** Tom Wang/Dreamstime **322:** Reuters/Corbis **323 (#5):** Reuters/Corbis **324:** Thinkstock **325:** ASSOCIATED PRESS **326:** Yoshinori Kuwahara/Getty Images **327 T:** ASSOCIATED PRESS **327 B:** Julie Dermansky/Corbis

Unit 4, Lesson 5
328: RapidEye/iStockphoto **329:** AFP/Getty Images **330 T:** Alenavlad/Dreamstime **330 B:** Andrew Gentry/Shutterstock **331:** ShaneKato/iStockphoto **333 (#1):** AFP/Getty Images **333 (#2):** Andrew Gentry/Shutterstock **334:** Thinkstock **335:** ASSOCIATED PRESS **336:** NOAA **337:** Shutterstock

Unit 4, Lesson 6
338: PicsNew/Alamy **339 T:** villorejo/Alamy **343 (#1):** villorejo/Alamy **344:** Smithsonian Photography Search **345:** ASSOCIATED PRESS **346:** Thinkstock **347:** Jim Henderson/Wikimedia Commons

Back Matter
349: Caro/Alamy **350:** Thinkstock **351:** Radius Images/Alamy **353 T:** weerayut ranmai/Shutterstock **367:** Cultura Creative Alamy **368:** Thinkstock **369:** Adam Hart-Davis/Science Source **370:** Thinkstock **371 T:** Asaf Eliason/Shutterstock **371 B:** JIANG HONGYAN/Shutterstock **371 B:** Thinkstock **372 T:** Martin Shields/Alamy **372 B:** Shutterstock **373:** Martin Shields/Alamy